A Pictorial History
of New Guinea

A Pictorial History of New Guinea

Noel Gash

Senior Lecturer in History
Kuring–gai College of Advanced Education

June Whittaker

Senior Lecturer in History and Government
International Training Institute

THE JACARANDA PRESS

First published 1975 by
THE JACARANDA PRESS
65 Park Road, Milton, Qld
9 Massey Street, Gladesville, N.S.W.
83 Palmerston Crescent, South Melbourne, Vic.
142 Colin Street, West Perth, W.A.
303 Wright Street, Adelaide, S.A.
4 Kirk Street, Grey Lynn, Auckland 2, N.Z.

Typesetting by Queensland Type Service Pty Ltd, Brisbane
Printed in Hong Kong
Reprinted in Hong Kong 1977, 1978, 1980

© N. Gash, J. Whittaker 1975

National Library of Australia
Cataloguing-in-Publication data

Gash, Noel
 Pictorial history of New Guinea/[by] Noel
Gash [and] June Whittaker. — Milton, Q.:
Jacaranda, 1975.

 Index.
 Bibliography.
 ISBN 0 7016 8218 3.

 1. Papua New Guinea — History — Pictorial
works.   I. Whittaker, June,
 joint author   II. Title.

995

Contents

Preface

In the course of research in the documentary sources of New Guinea history, we became aware of its richness in pictorial sources also. We were delighted when the opportunity came to undertake a serious research programme in this field. We have been struck by the variety and colour of the human story in its New Guinea setting and we have tried to convey it in this book.

Selection of the illustrations has been difficult. We have rejected material that could be included more suitably in an anthropological study. In our selection we have tried to show change as it affected the people of New Guinea in the face of European intrusion and occupation. At the same time we have emphasized the pictorial record of expatriate life in a colonial setting, for we feel that, like us, our European readers will learn something about their kind by seeing them at work and play in a situation not known in their homeland.

New Guinea, in many ways, has been a cultural warehouse. This is revealed in the pictorial record. Various European governments have come and gone, or are going. Wars have been fought on New Guinea soil. The word of God has been preached in different tongues and the social mores of European and Asian groups and classes have been visited on the indigenous people.

We have not written a comprehensive text. Whenever possible a map has been used to provide a setting for the topic. The captions of the pictures are intended to fill in some of the detail, but we do not profess to have told the complete story. We recommend this book to students, as an ancillary to a regular text. For others we recommend it for the same enjoyment we have experienced in compiling it.

Finally, we make a plea for the preservation of the pictorial material of New Guinea history. In our study we have used numerous private collections generously made available by their owners. No doubt many other collections exist whose owners have not realized their value to the student of New Guinea history. We would be happy to hear from such readers.

Sydney, N.S.W.   Noel Gash
1974   June Whittaker

Acknowledgments

The authors gratefully acknowledge the help given by the following: Dr J. Allen, University of Papua New Guinea; B. Backus, Esq., Mittagong, N.S.W.; Lady Bassett, Armadale, Victoria; Mrs C. B. Boughton, Sydney; Mrs S. Bulmer, University of Papua New Guinea; Dr Rolf Burmeister, Staats-und Universitätsbibliothek, Hamburg; J. D. O. Burns, Esq., Chairman, Burns, Philp and Company Ltd, Sydney; W. Campagnoni, Esq., Public Trustee Office, Sydney; W. R. Carpenter and Company Pty Ltd, Sydney; R. G. Clark, Esq., Sydney; Fr Coltré, Veifa'a, Papua New Guinea; Miss M. C. Dick, Sydney; Mrs M. Dick, Port Macquarie, N.S.W.; Charles Ebert, Esq., formerly of Department of Education, N.S.W.; Miss Thea Exley, Commonwealth Archives Office, Canberra, A.C.T.; A. P. Fleming, Esq., National Librarian, Canberra, A.C.T.; Edgar Ford, Esq., Sydney; C. Freeman, Esq., Librarian, New Guinea Collection, University of Papua New Guinea; Miss Louise R. Hussey, Librarian, Whaling Museum, Nantucket, Mass., U.S.A.; Mrs E. Jones, Castle Hill, N.S.W.; Miss P. I. Jones, Librarian, Mitchell Library, Sydney; Dr Ronald Klemig, Staatsbibliothek, Preussischer Kulturbesitz, Berlin; Rev. P. Koehne, Port Moresby; Nobru Kojima, Esq., Tokyo, Japan; W. R. Lancaster, Esq., Director, Australian War Memorial, Canberra, A.C.T.; M. J. Leahy, Esq., Zenag, Papua New Guinea; Rev. Bro. Lucien, Bomana, Papua New Guinea; K. G. MacDonald, Esq., Sydney; Dr Mackay, Curator, Papua New Guinea Museum and Art Gallery, Port Moresby; Hans Mannsfeld, Esq., Hamburg; S. Maris, Esq., Department of Territories, Canberra, A.C.T.; T. Matsumura, Esq., Attaché, Embassy of Japan, Canberra, A.C.T.; S. Matsunaga, Esq., Research Department, Mainichi Press, Tokyo, Japan; Mrs Z. Mattes, Sydney; Mrs S. M. Matthews, Port Moresby; Mrs M. Mennis, Madang, Papua New Guinea; Mrs D. Mercer, East Ballina, N.S.W.; Mrs E. Miller, Ballina, N.S.W.; Mrs P. Millward, Australian Joint Copying Project Officer, Australia House, London; W. F. J. Morzer Bruyns, Esq., Nederlandsch Historisch Scheepvaart Museum, Amsterdam; L. Newby, Esq., Director, Information and Extension Services, Administration of Papua New Guinea; Mr and Mrs A. V. Noall, Sydney; K. Penny, Esq., Chief Archivist, Commonwealth Archives Office, Canberra, A.C.T.; B. B. Perriman, Esq., Canberra, A.C.T.; Rev. Dr G. Pilhofer, Neuendettelsau, Bavaria; G. D. Richardson, Esq., Mitchell Librarian, Public Library of N.S.W.; Miss N. Rickard, Sydney; R. Robinson, Esq., Sydney; L. C. Roebuck, Esq., Port Macquarie, N.S.W.; A. E. Ross, Esq., Wollongong, N.S.W.; Prof. C. Rowley, University of Papua New Guinea; Mrs L. Rybak, Sydney; H. L. Schultze, Esq., Sydney; Professor H.-H. Schumacher, Tropeninstitut, Hamburg; The Secretary, Office of the Secretary of Defence, Washington, D.C.; Mrs G. Seidman, Sydney; E. A. Shepherd, Esq., Sydney; D. Smidt, Esq., Rijksmuseum voor Volkenkunde, Leiden; A. A. Speedie, Esq., Melbourne; R. Speedie, Esq., Sydney; Mrs S. Stephenson, Castle Hill, N.S.W.; J. L. Taylor, Esq., Goroka, Papua New Guinea; Miss L. K. N. Tjoa, Bibliotheek der Rijksuniversiteit Te Leiden; Mrs M. von Hein, Sydney; Mrs G. Wenzel, Weilheim, West Germany; Professor A. Westphal, Staats-und Universitätsbibliothek, Hamburg; Miss M. Westwood, Librarian, Hallstrom Pacific Library, Australian School of Pacific Administration; Dr J. Peter White, The Australian Museum, Sydney; T. D. Wilson, Esq., Third Secretary, Australian Embassy, Tokyo; Rev. Ralph M. Wiltgen, S.V.D., Rome; Colonel H. E. Woodman, Penrith, N.S.W.; Miss M. E. Woolnough, Sydney.

1 The First People

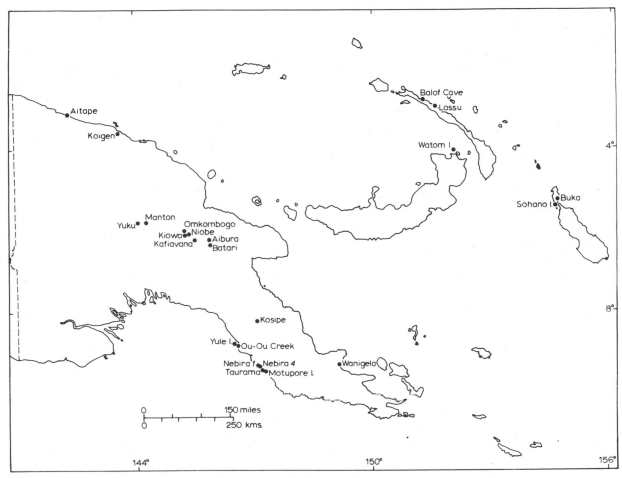

Plate 1

Plate 1. Archaeological sites in Papua New Guinea. Although research in many academic disciplines is being carried out, no complete picture of the prehistory of the country has yet emerged. Papua New Guinea has the least known, possibly the most complex, and therefore probably the most exciting culture in the world today. Systematic archaeological research there is but one decade old; at its present stage, considerable though incomplete evidence points to '. . . a very early settlement, perhaps 50 000 years ago, of a hunter people using simple but effective stone tools, colonizing the country from the direction of Indonesia, an ancestor of the earliest colonists of Australia. This hunting culture in New Guinea is at present best studied in the highlands. We suspect that it is there in the lowlands but it has not yet been found.

'At some subsequent stage, agriculture, food plants and animals were introduced into the country, possibly by the ancestors of Polynesians and Melanesians. After these food plants and animals were introduced they spread throughout the whole of the country and became the economic basis of all New Guinea society, although there were variations, which we can see today, depending on the nature of the landscape. Then at a relatively recent date we suspect the final plant, the sweet potato, was introduced into the highlands and caused a further growth of population and settlement by enabling people to exist in larger numbers at greater heights.' (Jack Golson, '50 000 Years of New Guinea History', typescript of a talk given at Port Moresby, 26 July 1966, p. 6.)

The most important archaeological projects that have been carried out are in the central New Guinea Highlands (for instance at Kiowa, Kafiavana, and the Manton site) and on Watom Island. The earliest carbon date for the Highlands has been registered at Kafiavana with a date of 10 730 ± 370 B.P. Susan Bulmer recorded a carbon date at Kiowa rock shelter of 10 350 ± 140 B.P. Carbon dates recorded at Kosipe of 26 870 ± 590 B.P., and 26 450 ± 880 B.P., make this the oldest site in New Guinea to date. On Watom Island two types of pottery have been excavated at a depth of 1·8 to 2·4 metres on a site near a coastal village. One type of pottery, well decorated, is similar to Lapita pottery found in Tonga, Fiji and New Caledonia. The Watom Island pottery has been dated at 500 B.C. The second type of pottery on this site has been dated at 600 B.C. and is similar in style to that recently excavated in the New Hebrides. This and other evidence suggest that New Guinea could have been a central area through which movements of peoples spread into the Pacific island world; and that these movements commenced about 1000 B.C., and concluded about A.D. 1000. The oldest date east of New Guinea is currently at Fiji, c. 1300 B.C. (Map courtesy of Dr J. Allen, U.P.N.G.)

Plate 2. A waisted axe-adze blade excavated at Chuave in the Highlands of New Guinea. The blade has a wide-flaked cutting edge. It was fashioned by striking a piece from a block of stone and then flaking off pieces to produce edges—some concave, some convex. This tool might have been hafted, not used in the hand. It could have been part of the tool kit of a pre-agricultural person, in which case it would have been used to fashion wooden spears and other weapons with which to hunt the cassowary, possum, wallaby, and other animals now extinct in New Guinea. The blade might have been used for agriculture; for example, to break ground for gardens. (Photograph courtesy of Dr J. Allen, U.P.N.G.)

Plate 2

Plates 3a, b, c. Prehistoric stone club heads from the Wahgi Valley. The greatest concentration of club heads found to date has been in this valley and in the Baiyer Valley. Nearly all are made of hard volcanic stones. A wide range of designs is present.

Plate 3a: Left, a 'pineapple' head; right, a flanged head. Plate 3b: A disc with sharp edges. Plate 3c: Top, 'sunflower' head; bottom, discs. (Papua New Guinea Museum and Art Gallery)

Plate 3a

Plate 3b

Plate 3c

Plate 4a

Plate 4b

Plate 5

Plates 4a, b. Two variations of stone mortars. Plate 4a: From the southern slopes of Mt Basavi, Western District of Papua. Plate 4b: From New Hanover—prehistoric. Mortars like these are found widely in New Guinea, but archaeologists are uncertain of their purposes. To date they have been found only in the places where no Melanesian–Polynesian language links exist; there appears to be therefore, a general correlation between mortars and pestles and non-Austronesian languages. There might be a link between these mortars and the waisted axe blades (see plate 2). Together they night indicate the first agriculture in New Guinea or a later agriculture independent of Melanesian–Polynesian speakers of the coast and of some of the New Guinea islands. (Papua New Guinea Musuem and Art Gallery)

Plate 5. A prehistoric black stone pestle from the Upper Korewari River area near the Western Highlands. The diversity in shape and size of pestles found in the Western Highlands suggests that their functions were diverse. They might have been used for the preparation of food-stuffs, poisons, pigments and medicines. This pestle has been fashioned in the shape of a bird. Figurine pestles of this type possibly had cult or ceremonial significance. They might have been used as exchange valuables in a trade network. (Papua New Guinea Museum and Art Gallery)

Plate 6. An unusual prehistoric stone carving from Amanab, West Sepik District. (Papua New Guinea Museum and Art Gallery)

Plates 7a, b. Bronze remains excavated by J. V. de Bruyn in August 1958 from a site on Jonokom island in Lake Sentani, Irian Djaya. The discovery poses the question of whether this region was a centre of prehistoric bronze culture. The style here suggests similarities with the South-east Asian Dongson cultural tradition. Whether these artefacts came by trade or were manufactured in New Guinea is not certain. Plate 7a: A bronze axe blade 17 centimetres high, possibly imported into New Guinea about 300 B.C. Plate 7b: A bronze axe blade from Asei (Lake Sentani) 16·5 centimetres high, possibly imported into New Guinea about 300 B.C. (Rijksmuseum voor Volkenkunde, Leiden)

Plate 8. Paintings on part of Kiowa rock shelter near Chuave. (Papua New Guinea Museum and Art Gallery)

Plate 6

Plate 8

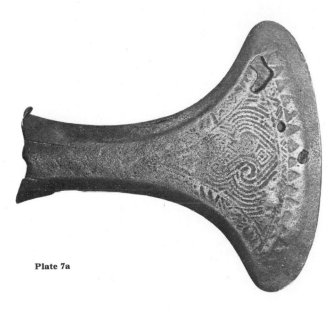

Plate 7a

Plate 7b

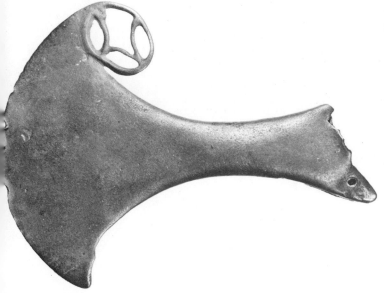

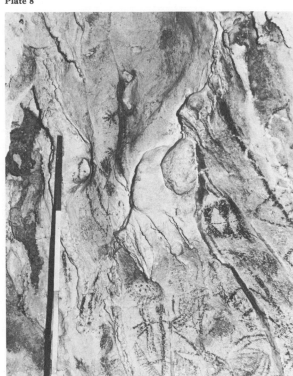

5

Plate 9. In the process of draining swamp land for tea cultivation, the cutting away of years of silt build-up has revealed to archaeologists some interesting wooden implements that are almost certainly agricultural. The walls of the ditches, like this one, indicate different levels of drainage ditches dug by agriculturalists at different times. Archaeologists are interested in pinpointing the various levels and the directions of the drainage ditches, as the former could help in the dating of agriculture for the area, and the latter could give the number of agricultural settlements in the area for that period. Botanists are interested in examining the ditches for samples that might contain pollen for analysis. (Photograph courtesy of Dr J. Allen, U.P.N.G.)

Plate 9

Plate 10. A Papuan bush pig. The pig has been an important element in the New Guinea economy. The pig, the dog and the fowl were in the Highlands of New Guinea at the time of first recorded European contacts. Pig bones have been excavated at a fairly early phase of Highlands development; bones at Kafiavana suggest around 6000 B.P. A build-up of pig bones excavated under rock shelters at Chuave, where simple hunting tools also have been found, suggests the beginning of a new economy at that stage. (Hallstrom Pacific Library)

Plate 10

2 The European Intruders

Plate 11

Plate 11. Part of the world map by Gerardus Mercator, 1569, redrawn by Richardo Gartho. Mercator's map shows New Guinea as a very large island, separated from Terra Australis by a strait, and bearing the inscription in Latin, 'New Guinea: which seems to have been called "Land of the Black People" by the Florentine Andrea Corsali, is perchance the island which Ptolemy named Labadius.' This was the first map depicting New Guinea. The existence of a great south land was advanced as a theory in the second century A.D. by Ptolemy and Pomponius Mela. The map is interesting in that the first recorded Western contact with New Guinea was in 1526 by a Portuguese, Jorge de Meneses. His contact, and the contacts of Saavedra in 1528, Grijalva in 1537, and de Retes in 1545, were limited to parts of the north coast of the mainland between the Kepulawan Schouten and Astrolabe Bay. It was not until 1606, thirty-seven years after Mercator published his map, that Luis Vaez de Torres's voyage established that New Guinea did not extend below ten degrees south latitude. (Mitchell Library)

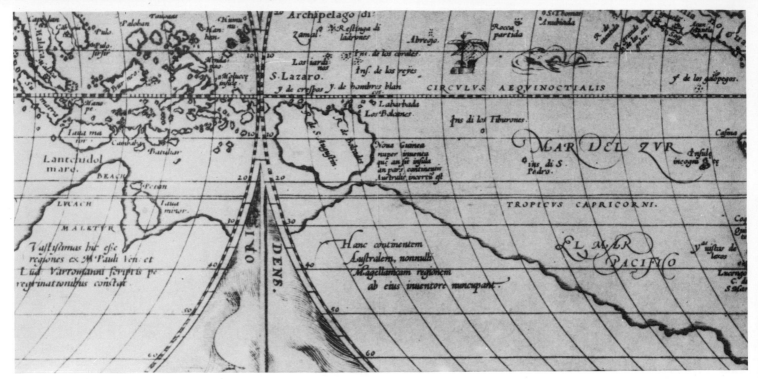

Plate 12

Plate 12. The Australian regions as shown by Ortelius in 1570. This map is probably based on Mercator's. It shows New Guinea as a large island and the Sepik River (R. de S. Augustin). The western area of the great south land from which New Guinea is separated is named 'Beach' above the Tropic of Capricorn and 'Lucach' below. The imagination of the European was gripped by the idea of 'Lucach' or 'Lochac', an island rich in gold which Marco Polo claimed existed in the seas south of Java. Sheba's land in the south ('Ophir'), Marco Polo's 'Lucach' and the 'great south land' of Ptolemy's theory were compounded in the European mind, and convinced

Westerners of the existence of a fabulously rich land in this region.

De Barros reports that from Malacca several voyages were made in search of islands of gold. The first to associate the land of gold with New Guinea was Antonio Pigafetta, who sailed with Magellan. He recorded, 'The King of these heathens, called Raja Papua, is exceedingly rich in gold, and lives in the interior of the island.' C. Kelly, 'Geographical Knowledge and Speculation in Regard to Spanish Pacific Voyages', *Hist. Studies Aust. & N. Z.* vol. 9 (1959–61), p. 12. (Mitchell Library)

Plate 13

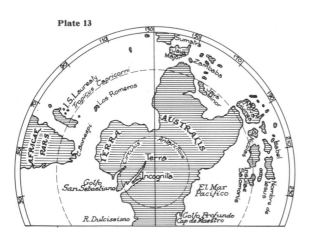

Plate 13. Wytfliet's map, published in 1596, showing New Guinea separated from Terra Australis by a narrow strait. It is thought that Luis Vaez de Torres was the first European to establish that New Guinea did not extend below ten degrees south latitude, when in 1606–07 he sailed west along the entire south coast of New Guinea (see plate 15). However, ten years before this voyage, the Dutch cartographer Cornelis Wytfliet published this map.

It is possible that Dutch cartographers such as Wytfliet and Mercator (see plate 11) were in possession of the Dieppe Maps, in which case the information they give is probably a rationalization of various second-hand reports. On the other hand, the information they contain could be the direct result of discoveries that were not publicized at the time. Torres might have had Wytfliet's map with him and therefore would have known of the existence of the strait. (Mitchell Library)

Plate 14

Plate 14. Luis Vaez de Torres, in the naval service of Spain. He was second-in-command on de Quiros's 1605 expedition in search of a great south land. At the New Hebrides, de Quiros's boat was separated from Torres's by strong winds. Torres sailed to twenty degrees south latitude and reached the east coast of New Guinea. Because he could not weather the east point he sailed west along the entire south coast of the mainland in 1606–07. In a letter to Philip III of Spain dated at Manila, 12 July 1607, Torres wrote: 'All this land of New Guinea is peopled with natives, not very white, and naked, except for their private parts, which are covered with a cloth made of the bark of trees, and much painted. They fight with darts, targets, and some stone clubs which are made fine with plumage.' Luis Vaez de Torres to His Majesty, 12 July 1607, in *The Voyages of Pedro Fernandez de Quiros, 1595–1606*, ed. C. Markham (London, 1904), Hakluyt Society, ser. 2, vol. 2, no. 15, p. 462. (Mitchell Library)

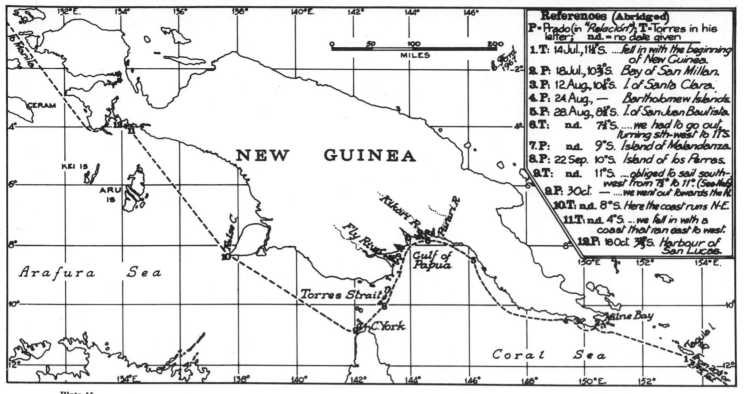

Plate 15

References (Abridged)
P=Prado (in "Relación"); T=Torres in his letter; n.d. = no date given

1. T: 14 Jul., 11½°S. ....fell in with the beginning of New Guinea.
2. P: 18 Jul., 10⅔°S. Bay of San Millan.
3. P: 12 Aug., 10⅓°S. I. of Santa Clara.
4. P: 24 Aug., — Bartholomew Islands.
5. P: 28 Aug., 8½°S. I. of San Juan Bautista.
6. T: n.d. 7½°S. ....we had to go out, turning sth-west to 11°S.
7. P: n.d. 9°S. Island of Malandanza.
8. P: 22 Sep. 10°S. Island of los Perras.
9. T: n.d. 11°S. ...obliged to sail south-west from 7½° to 11°. (See Nos)
9a. P: 30 Oct. — ....we went out towards the N.
10. T: n.d. 8°S. Here the coast runs N-E.
11. T: n.d. 4°S. ...we fell in with a coast that ran east to west.
12. P: 18 Oct. 3⅔°S. Harbour of San Lucas.

Plate 15. Map showing the course taken by Luis Vaez de Torres on his 1606–07 voyage along the south coast of New Guinea. Torres took possession of the country for the Spanish Crown at two separate places. In his journal, *Relación Sumaria*, Don Diego de Prado y Tovar, who accompanied Torres, describes white cockatoos, wallabies, a cassowary, birds of paradise, bananas, coconuts, breadfruit and custard apples. There is evidence to suggest that during the last days of August 1606 they reached a harbour that was probably Port Moresby. Prado recorded: 'On the 28th we set sail . . . steering to the west, and finding a mouth among the shoals we entered it, as the bottom was clear among the shoals and the land high, with from seven to eight fathoms of water, and even if there is a storm in the sea it does not come in here.' *Relación Sumaria of Captain Don Diego de Prado y Tovar, etc.*, ed. H. N. Stevens (London, 1930), Hakluyt Society, ser. 2, vol. 64, p. 157. (Map redrawn by Edgar Ford from original in Mitchell Library)

Plate 16. William Dampier, whose reputation as an English buccaneer has somewhat obscured his role of explorer. On his 1770 voyage in the *Roebuck* he planned to range along the coast of New Guinea to see if the land afforded spices. From the St Matthias group he voyaged along the east coast of New Ireland and the south coast of New Britain, but missed the strait separating the two islands and concluded that he had coasted one land, to which he gave the name New Britain. Towards the end of March, Dampier passed through the strait that bears his name. In his journal he wrote: 'As we stood over to the Islands we look'd out very well to the North, but could see no land that way; by which I was well assur'd that we were got through, and that this East-Land does not join to New-Guinea; therefore I named it Nova-Britannia. . . . It is generally high, mountainous land, mixt with large Valleys; which, as well as the Mountaines, appeared very fertile; and in most Places that we saw the Trees are very large, tall and thick. It is also very well inhabited with strong, well-limb'd Negroes, whom we found very daring and bold at several Places.' *Dampier's Voyages*, ed. J. Masefield (London, 1906), vol. 2, p. 254. (Hallstrom Pacific Library)

Plate 16

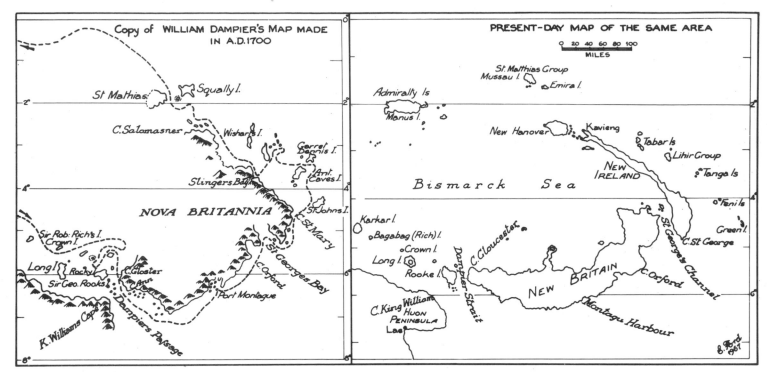

Copy of WILLIAM DAMPIER'S MAP MADE IN A.D. 1700

St Mathias — Squally I. — C. Salamasner — Wishart I. — Garret Dennis I. — Ant. Caves I. — Slingers Bay — St Johns I. — NOVA BRITANNIA — St Mary — St Georges Bay — Sir Rob. Rich's I. — Crown I. — Long I. — Rocky — C. Gloster — St Orford — Port Montague — Sir Geo. Rooks — Dampier's Passage — K. Williams Cap.

PRESENT-DAY MAP OF THE SAME AREA

0 20 40 60 80 100 MILES

St Matthias Group — Mussau I. — Emira I. — Admiralty Is — Manus I. — New Hanover — Kavieng — Tabar Is — Lihir Group — Tanga Is — NEW IRELAND — Bismarck Sea — Feni Is — Karkar I. — Bagabag (Rich) I. — Crown I. — C. Gloucester — Long I. — Rooke I. — Dampier Strait — St Georges Channel — Green I. — C. St George — NEW BRITAIN — C. Orford — C. King William — Huon Peninsula — Lae — Montagu Harbour

E. Ford 1967

Plate 17

Plate 17. William Dampier's chart of his voyage of 1700 compared with a modern map of the same area. The map shows his name, St Georges Bay, for the channel, and the names he gave to other features to honour his patrons: Cape Orford, Port Montague, King Williams Cape, Cape Gloster, Cape Ann, Sir Geo. Rook's Island, Sir Rob. Rich's Island. Dampier landed on New Britain to trade with the people for food and water. As they would part with nothing but coconuts, Dampier's men stole the things they wanted—hogs, wood, water and 'images'. Dampier was careful to repay the people for the things his men had brought in a canoe. 'In the Afternoon I sent the Canoe to the Place from whence she had been brought; and in her, 2 Axes, 2 Hatchets, 6 Knives, 6 Looking glasses, a large Bunch of Beads, and 4 Glass-bottles. . . .' (*Dampier's Voyages*, ed. J. Masefield [London, 1906], vol. 2, p. 540.)

Dampier's landing place has been identified by a district officer at Gasmata. 'The small river mentioned by Dampier is the Kabu and the village from which some fishing nets were taken is Ruakana, right at the cape now known as Cape Dampier. . . . I have no doubt at all that the *Roebuck* anchored in the bay into which the Kabu River flows; that Dampier landed on the left bank of the Kabu and inspected Ruakana village; and that it was the village of Awul (then, as now, a large place) that was bombarded, and from which the pigs were taken.' B. Calcutt to the Mitchell Library, dated Gasmata, New Britain, 21 April 1931. (Map drawn by Edgar Ford)

Plate 18

Plate 18. Louis Antoine de Bougainville, the French aristocrat who in 1768–69 navigated part of the east coast of New Guinea, the Louisiades and islands of the Solomon group. His ships, the frigate *La Boudeuse* and the storeship *L'Etoile*, reached New Britain; failing to find refreshment there, Bougainville put into English Cove on New Ireland, where ten months earlier the Englishman Philip Carteret had re-victualled. Of their contact with the inhabitants Bougainville wrote: 'We desired them to come on board, but our invitations, and even the gift of some pieces of stuff which we threw overboard, did not inspire them with confidence sufficient to make them venture alongside. They took up what was thrown into the water, and by way of thanks one of them with a sling flung a stone, which did not quite reach on board; we would not return them evil for evil, so they retired, striking all together on their canoes, and setting up loud shouts.' Louis de Bougainville, *A Voyage Round the World . . . 1766–69*, ed. J. R. Forster (Dublin, 1772), p. 344. (Hallstrom Pacific Library)

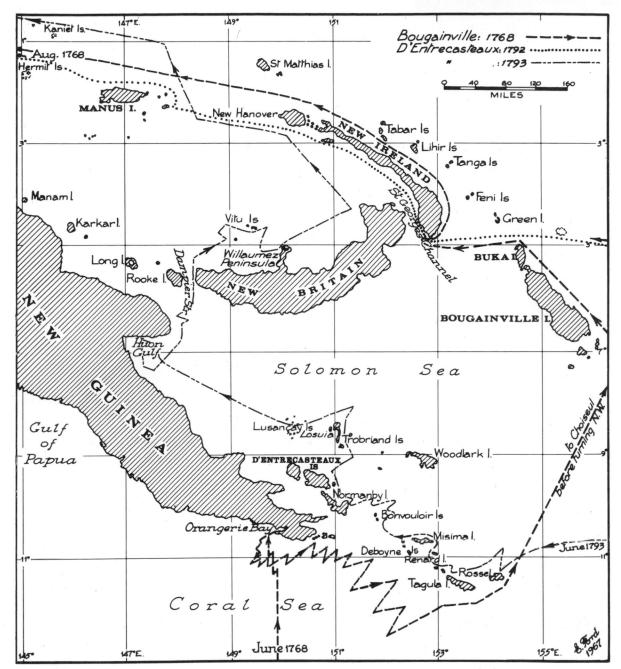

Plate 19

Plate 19. The routes taken by the Frenchmen Louis de Bougainville (1768) and Antoine d'Entrecasteaux (1792 and 1793) through the waters of east New Guinea. Bougainville was instructed to hand over his colony at the Falklands to the Spaniards in April 1767 and to explore the seas between the East Indies and the west coast of America. As his ships battled their way past the Louisiades they were in constant peril from storms, fogs and currents. Bougainville failed to recognize the islands of Choiseul, Buka and Bougainville as part of the Solomons group. In his charts he refers to them as part of the Louisiade Archipelago.

Antoine d'Entrecasteaux was commander of the French Indian Naval Station. He was appointed to command an expedition to search for La Pérouse, whose ships had not been seen since they sailed out of Botany Bay in February 1788. In June 1792 his two cumber-some storeships, the *Recherche* and the *Espérance*, reached the D'Entrecasteaux Reef. They rounded the Treasury Islands. Visibility was poor and d'Entrecasteaux was uncertain whether Bougainville and Buka were separate islands. On 15 July he sailed for New Ireland and anchored in Carteret Harbour. On the 24th he sailed through St George's Channel to New Hanover. The following year he made a second search. For three weeks the ships worked through the dangerous waters of the Louisiade Archipelago. Many of the islands were named after men of this expedition—Rossel, Lusançay, Trobriand. On 25 June the ships entered Huon Gulf. From here they approached the northern coast of New Britain and mistook Willaumez Peninsula for an island. D'Entrecasteaux died at sea, north of the Anchorite Islands. (Maps redrawn by Edgar Ford)

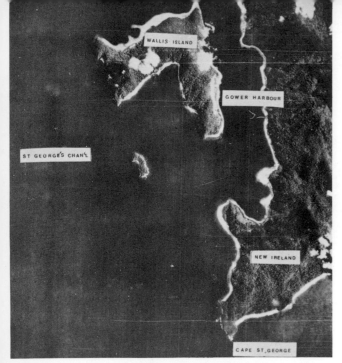

Plate 20. An aerial photograph of the southern tip of New Ireland, including Cape St George and Gower Harbour. On his 1766–69 voyage around the world, Philip Carteret in the *Swallow* sailed through the Solomon Islands group and in September 1767 found refuge and fresh food in St George's Bay, New Ireland. In navigating the 'Bay', Carteret found it to be a channel separating New Ireland from New Britain. '. . . We bore away to endeavour to find a passage to the westward by this bay, through what had been imagined to be land and called by Dampier, Nova Britannia. I was the more incoraged to attempt this from a strong current I had found constantly running into it and made me conjecture there must have been a passage through that part of the land to admit a discharge of so great a body of water. Accordingly I found it a very fine large Passage or Channell clear of all danger as far as I saw, so that instead of this being only one Island I found it to be two fine large Islands with several smaler ones about them, the Northermost I name Nova Hibernia and that which is the southermost and bigest one retains its Name Nova Britania. . . .' *Carteret's Voyage Round the World, 1766–1769*, ed. H. Wallis (Cambridge, 1965), p. 341. (Royal Australian Air Force)

Plate 20

Plate 21. Captain James Cook, who in 1770 sought provisions from inhabitants of the south coast of New Guinea. After navigating the east coast of Australia, Cook determined to clear up the question of whether New Guinea was a part of New Holland. On 22 August 1770 he established that New Guinea was separated from New Holland. His landing place on the coast of New Guinea has not been identified, but Dr Beaglehole is of the opinion that it was at a spot north of Frederik Hendrik Island. The natives were unwilling to trade; Cook would not force them to it, and prepared to leave. 'However,' he wrote, 'it was contrary to the inclination and opinion of some of the officers, who would have had me send a party of men ashore to cut down the Cocoa-nutt Trees for the sake of the Nutts; a thing that I think no man living could have justified . . . nothing but the utmost necessity would have obliged me to have taken this Method to come at refreshments.' *The Journals of Captain James Cook*, ed. J. C. Beaglehole (Cambridge, 1955), extra ser. no. 34, vol. 1, p. 410. (Mitchell Library)

Plate 21

Plate 22

Plate 22. Lieutenant John Shortland, R.N., whose voyage through the eastern waters of New Guinea assisted in the rediscovery and accurate charting of the Solomon Islands. Shortland was agent for transports with the First Fleet that reached Port Jackson in January 1788. He was ordered to return to England with three of the transports and three storeships at the instant the governor of New South Wales had no further occasion for them. Shortland left Port Jackson in the transport *Alexander* on 14 July 1788, with the *Friendship*, the *Prince of Wales* and the *Borrowdale*. Carteret Harbour, New Ireland, was appointed as the first place of rendezvous. Narratives and charts of Mendaña's discovery of the Solomons group in 1567 were inadequate for use by later navigators. Early cartographers located the islands of Mendaña's discovery (which did not include Buka and Bougainville) to the east of and at no great distance from New Guinea. Later cartographers located the islands too far to the east. Two hundred years after Mendaña, Carteret and Bougainville supplied the first clues to their correct locations and de Surville brought home conclusive proof. Lieutenant Shortland's voyage corroborated the discoveries of de Surville. He discovered and named Eddystone Rock and the Treasury Islands. He passed through Bougainville Strait, and, believing he was the discoverer, named the passage Shortland's Straits. 'To the whole of this land, consisting of the two principal islands on each side of the straits, and the Treasury Isles between them, Lieutenant Shortland gave the name New Georgia.' *The Voyage of Governor Phillip to Botany Bay* [The Journal of Lieutenant Shortland] (London, 1789), p. 201. (Etching from the *Illustrated Sydney News*, 1875, Mitchell Library)

Plate 23. John Hunter (1737–1821), after whom Port Hunter is named. Hunter was second captain, under Arthur Phillip, commanding the *Sirius* in the First Fleet to Botany Bay in 1788. He left Sydney in the Dutch transport *Waaksamheyd* in March 1791 to return to England to face an inquiry into the wreck of the *Sirius*. His course was by way of Lord Howe Island, New Britain, the Duke of York group, Batavia and the Cape of Good Hope. The company took on water at what is now Port Hunter, on Duke of York Island. After initial hostilities from the indigenes, lasting over four days, 'A number of the natives from the woods right above the watering place came down to the beach with green boughs in their hands, bringing with them cocoa-nuts, yams, plantains, accompanied by a song of friendship . . . a boat was sent on shore to meet them, with a green branch in the bow, and . . . when the boat landed the natives retired back a little, but not out of sight; having piled up upon the beach their peace-offering, which consisted of yams, cocoa-nuts, plantains, bananas, sugar-cane, and some other articles: on the top of this pile was laid a small living male and female dog, with their mouths and feet tied. . . .' (J. Hunter, *An Historical Journal of the Transactions at Port Jackson, etc.* [London, 1793], p. 230.) At this port, Hunter recorded seeing natives blow lime through bamboo pipes. The port was to become a well-known and oft-frequented watering place for ships voyaging through New Guinea waters. (Mitchell Library)

Plate 23

Plate 24. Jules Sébastien César Dumont d'Urville (1790–1842), French naval officer and navigator. In 1825 an expedition was arranged by the French Crown to explore the principal groups of islands in the Pacific and to augment the mass of scientific material acquired by Louis Duperrey on his 1822–25 voyage in the *Coquille*. Dumont d'Urville had sailed with Duperrey on this voyage. The *Coquille* was now renamed the *Astrolabe* and placed with the *Zelée* under Dumont d'Urville's command. The expedition visited New Britain and the mainland of West New Guinea. Dumont d'Urville was impressed by the sculptured models he saw at Manokwari, seeing in them 'a perfect resemblance to objects that have the same practical use and that are found every day in Egyptian tombs'. 'Voyage de Dumont d'Urville', *Voyages Autour du Monde*, ed. W. Smith (Paris, 1843[?]), vol. 6, p. 351. (Mitchell Library)

Plate 24

Plate 25. H.M.S. *Fly*, which in April 1845, under the command of Captain F. P. Blackwood, R.N., made a survey of 225 kilometres of the coast of New Guinea to the north and to the east of Torres Strait, including the mouth of the Fly River. The *Fly* had been accompanied in her survey work by H.M.S. *Bramble* (Lieutenant C. B. Yule). After the former's return to England at the end of 1845, the *Bramble* remained to join H.M.S. *Rattlesnake* (Captain Owen Stanley) in further survey work in New Guinea waters. (Mitchell Library)

Plate 25

Plate 26. Murray Islanders eager to barter with the men of H.M.S. *Fly* in 1843. Trade between Asia and the Australian colonies grew heavier in the nineteenth century as the colonies became firmly established, and the need for accurate and detailed information on New Guinea waters became apparent. In 1842 the British navy conducted the first of a series of important surveys. Captain F. P. Blackwood in H.M.S. *Fly* led an expedition to survey Torres Strait, the Gulf of Papua, and the south coast of New Guinea from 1842 to 1846. This engraving shows Captain Blackwood, J. Beete Jukes and the artist, Mr Melville, in one boat and a guard of marines in the other. Blackwood was instructed by the Admiralty Commissioners: 'You will endeavour to preserve an amicable intercourse with them at all times. You should appear to forget their former crimes, and to caution your people against giving them any offence. When purchases are made an officer should be present to prevent any misunderstanting.' J. Beete Jukes, *Narrative of the Surveying Voyage of H.M.S. Fly Commanded by Captain F. P. Blackwood R.N. in Torres Strait, New Guinea, and Other Islands of the Eastern Archipelago, During the Years 1842–1846* (London, 1847), appendix I, p. 260. (Hallstrom Pacific Library)

Plate 26

Plate 27

Plate 28

Plate 29

Plate 27. Detail from a watercolour by Captain Owen Stanley. On 15 June 1849, H.M.S. *Rattlesnake* entered Coral Haven, an anchorage in the Louisiade Archipelago formed by Piron, Joannet and Sudest Islands. The ship stayed in this anchorage until 26 June. John Macgillivray (naturalist) recorded for 24 June: '. . . In the course of the day no less than seven canoes with natives, including several women and children, came off to the ship boldly and without hesitation. . . . At one time we had five canoes alongside with a brisk and noisy traffic going on.' (Mitchell Library)

Plate 28. An incident near Cape Possession on 16 April 1846, as portrayed in the *Illustrated London News*, 5 August 1848. Lieutenant C. B. Yule of the survey ship *Bramble* had gone ashore to make astronomical observations. The expedition's journal tells the story: 'Having made the necessary observations Lieutenant Yule next proceeded to hoist the union jack and take possession of the country (in the name of H.M. Queen Victoria) . . . the party then prepared to re-embark; but in the attempt the second gig was swamped and everything in her including the arms lost . . . the natives now seeing our numbers decrease, laid hands on us in the most violent manner. My quintet was first wrested from my coxswain, who in a tone of grief made known the circumstance. I immediately turned round and exclaimed, "Oh, don't part with that!" but it was too late. . . . I then endeavoured to struggle out of their clutches and escape with the pocket chronometer and notebook; but these, as well as every article of clothing I had about my body, were stripped off.' (Mitchell Library)

Plate 29. Bartering between Europeans and men of the Louisiades. On 16 June 1849, T. H. Huxley, naturalist, Lieutenant Simpson, R.N., John Macgillivray, naturalist, and Oswald Brierly, marine artist, of H.M.S. *Rattlesnake*, landed on Pig Island in Coral Haven. Macgillivray recorded: 'Meanwhile Lieutenant Simpson and I remained behind watching the natives who quickly surrounded the two others, offering tortoise-shell, green plantains and other things for barter . . . at length a live pig was brought down from the village, slung on a pole and was purchased for a knife and a handkerchief.' (Mitchell Library)

Plate 30. An incident at Brumer Island during the cruise of H.M.S. *Rattlesnake* to the Louisiade Archipelago from May to August, 1849. T. H. Huxley recorded for 28 August: 'Yesterday afternoon catamarans and some canoes from the island came alongside. The natives brought four or five of their women with them and these were, without difficulty, persuaded to come up. We did the honours and dressed the ladies up to their infinite satisfaction. Afterwards two of the men got their own native drums (wh. we had on board) and performed a dance for our amusement!' (Mitchell Library)

Plate 30

Plate 31. H.M.S. *Blanche* at anchor in Port Jackson. In 1872, under the command of Captain Cortland H. Simpson, the *Blanche* voyaged through the Bismarck Archipelago and made the first official entry into Blanche Bay and Simpson Harbour. Simpson reported, 'The following morning [18 July 1872] I weighed and stood in with the ship; the distance to the mainland across the entrance of the bay at Praed Point is about 4 miles . . . this bay I have called Blanche Bay.' (From a watercolour in the Mitchell Library)

Plate 31

Plate 32. A photograph taken about 1880 of the larger of the Beehive Rocks at the entrance to Simpson Harbour. On 1 July 1872, Captain Simpson in H.M.S. *Blanche* entered Simpson Harbour and reported later, '. . . about a mile south from Point Bridges are two remarkable sandstone rocks . . . clustered on a narrow ledge which surrounds them, and which is partly under water, is a village containing, I suppose, 200 inhabitants. . . . These rocks I have called the Beehives.' (Mitchell Library)

Plate 32

Plate 33. Officers of H.M.S. *Challenger* bartering with Admiralty Islanders, March 1875. *Challenger*, under the command of Captain G. Nares, visited the Admiralty Islands in the course of a world hydrographic cruise, 1872–76. W. J. Spry, R.N., who was aboard *Challenger*, wrote of the visit: 'Having reached a convenient anchorage (which was afterwards named Nares Harbour) the beautiful view before us, and the smoke rising from the native huts between the trees completed a perfect landscape . . . almost immediately a landing was effected, all being armed so as to be on guard against any treachery. . . . Of there being cannibals there can be no doubt; so at our first intercourse great caution was certainly necessary. After a while, however, when we had got somewhat familiar, and numerous presents had been given to the chiefs, there was no obstacle in the way, and we were free to wander through the village, and even enter their houses and see their women and children.' W. J. Spry, *The Cruise of Her Majesty's Ship 'Challenger'* (London, 1877), pp. 268–9. (Mitchell Library)

Plate 33

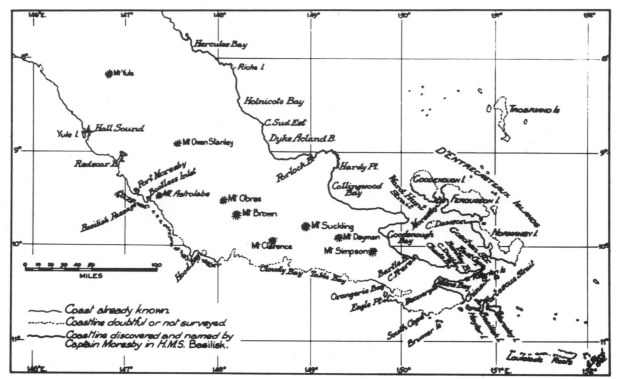

Plate 34

Plate 34. Map showing the 450 kilometres of the New Guinea coastline surveyed by Captain John Moresby in H.M.S. *Basilisk* in 1873. The charting of this part of the coastline had been long neglected because of the dangerous shoals, currents, reefs and strong south-east winds, which made the eastern extremity of the island difficult to negotiate. Moresby hoped to find a passage through the Louisiades which would shorten the trade route between Australia and China. Moresby was acclaimed for his accurate surveying of these waters and for his tact in dealing with the peoples he encountered. (Map redrawn by Edgar Ford from Moresby's original chart)

Plate 35. H.M.S. *Basilisk* which, under the command of Captain John Moresby, made important surveys in New Guinea waters in 1873. The *Basilisk* was a paddlewheel steamer of 1074 tons and 100 horsepower. It carried a complement of 178 officers and men. This engraving was published in the *Illustrated Australian News*, 10 July 1871. (National Library of Australia)

Plate 35

Plate 36

Plate 36. The *Basilisk* at anchor in Discovery Bay. On 27 April 1873, H.M.S. *Basilisk* entered Milne Bay, which was named by Moresby after the senior naval lord of the Admiralty, and anchored in Discovery Bay, a small inlet on the south shore about 32 kilometres from the China Straits. Moresby recorded, 'The cove we had entered was semi-circular and fringed all round with graceful cocoa-nut palms, the blue water rippling up to their roots. Pretty native houses were scattered amongst the trees, every one of which seemed to have sent forth its inmates to gaze at us.' (Mitchell Library)

Plate 37. An affray at Traitors' Bay. On 9 May 1873, H.M.S. *Basilisk* was taking on wood at Traitors' Bay (Mambare Bay near Cape Ward Hunt) when a party of the local inhabitants threatened three of the ship's officers who were walking on shore. Captain Moresby, who had come ashore to warn his officers of their danger, fired a shot at the leading man which pierced his shield but did not wound him. 'There was no need to fire again and take life,' reported Moresby, 'for the whole body of warriors turned instantly, in consternation, and ran for the canoes, and we followed till we drove them on board.' (Mitchell Library)

Plate 37

19

3 First Settlement: Sailors, Whalers, Adventurers

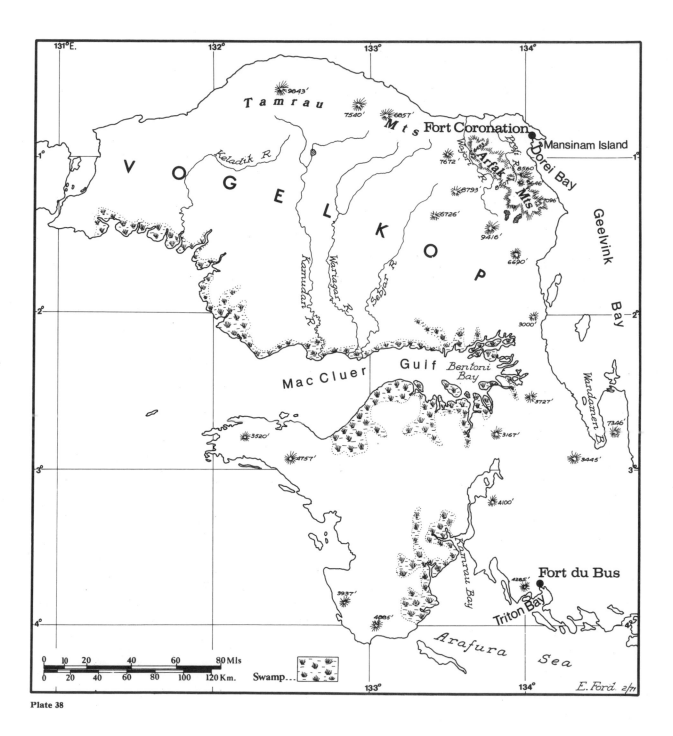

Plate 38

Plate 38. The Vogelkop, or western tip of the mainland of New Guinea. It was along this coastline that the first sustained contacts were made by Indonesians, Chinese and Europeans; regular trading trips were made by people from Ceram and Aru (see plate 40). The Dutchmen Pool (1636) and Keyts (1678) sought to regularize trade on behalf of the Dutch East India Company, but without success. Dorei Bay saw the earliest sustained contact by Europeans. Thomas Forrest of the British East India Company was received there in a friendly manner in 1775, and in 1793 Lieutenant John Hayes tried to form a British settlement, renaming the bay Restoration Bay and building a fort for the settlement, Fort Coronation. The settlement lasted only a year—John McCluer arrived there late in 1794 to find all the survivors ill. Some had died from fever and some had been captured by the inhabitants. Two years before, McCluer had proceeded on orders of the British East India Company to make an extensive survey of this coastline. The British naturalist Alfred Wallace spent nearly six months at Dorei Bay in 1858. On Mansinam Island at this time were two German missionaries, C. W. Ottow and J. G. Geissler. In 1873 the Italian naturalists Odoardo Beccari and Luigi d'Albertis studied there and explored the Arfak Mountains. A French naturalist, Raffray, spent a short time in the same area in 1876, and in 1883 Dr Guillemard led a natural science expedition to this part. The first Dutch attempt at settlement was made at Fort du Bus, Triton Bay, in 1828 but it was abandoned in 1836—see plate 39. (Map drawn by Edgar Ford)

Plate 39

Plate 39. Fort du Bus, the first Dutch settlement in New Guinea, 1828–36. Fear of British intentions in New Guinea persuaded the governor of the Moluccas, Pieter Merkus, to make a formal claim over west New Guinea by establishing a settlement. A. J. van Delden set forth with a small military garrison in the corvette *Triton* and the schooner *Iris* on 21 April 1828. The garrison consisted of a lieutenant, a doctor, eleven European and twenty Indonesian soldiers with their families, and ten Javanese convict labourers. Towards the western extremity of Onin a bay in the region, known locally as 'Lobo', was chosen for the settlement. The bay was renamed Triton Bay and the region was renamed Merkusoord in honour of the governor. Construction of the fort took seven weeks. The settlement was described by Jan Modera:

'The Fort du Bus has two palisades and is square. . . . At the four corners canon have been placed and on the sides one three-pound and one six-pound gun have been placed on mountings. . . . On the right side of the Fort are the officers' homes with two rooms and an outside balcony and at the back of that there is a store for provisions, clothing, etc., and at the back of that there is the powder-box under a roof. On the left side of the Fort is a sentry box and cookhouse with the barracks behind, consisting of bunks and an outside balcony.' J. Modera, *Verhaal van eene Reize naar en langs de Zuid-Westkust van Nieuw-Guinea Gedaan in 1828, door Z. M. Corvet Triton, en Z. M. Coloniale Schoener de Iris* (Haarlem, 1830), p. 142. (Mitchell Library)

22

Plate 40. Ceramese traders on the Dodinga River, west New Guinea. The Ceramese and Aru islanders were accustomed to making regular trading trips to the coast of New Guinea to procure massoi bark, nutmegs, trepang, tortoiseshell, birds of paradise and slaves. The Dutch historian and botanist, Rumphius, reported the trade practice: 'The natives [of New Guinea] place the massoi on the beach, the bundles placed on top of each other. The most courageous appear on the scene and with signs explain what they like to have in return for their massoi. The articles given in return for their goods consist of swords, hatchets to peel the massoi, poor quality rugs, sago bread, rice and black sugar.' P. A. Leupe, *De Reizen der Nederlanders naar Nieuw-Guinea en de Papoesche Eilanden in de 17 de en de 18 de eeuw* (S'Gravenhage, 1875). (Hallstrom Pacific Library)

Plate 40

Plate 41

Plate 41. Mansinam village, Dorei Bay (Manokwari), with the Arfak Range in the distance, 1884. It was at this site that the first protracted contacts were made between Europeans and New Guineans. Two German Protestant missionaries, Johann Geissler and C. W. Ottow of the Christian Workman Mission Society, landed at Mansinam in 1855. As more missionaries arrived, four stations were established on the mainland. From March to July 1858 the naturalist Alfred Wallace lived on the shores of the bay. The German explorer Dr Adolf Meyer landed here with thirty-five Indonesians and claimed to be the first European to cross New Guinea at the isthmus below the Vogelkop to MacCluer Gulf. His claim was later found to be false. Another German, Dr Bernstein, spent some time here about 1864, and in 1869 a Dutch colonial officer, Count von Rosenberg, spent some time at Andai, just south of the bay. The Italian naturalists Luigi d'Albertis (see plate 59) and Odoardo Beccari spent some of 1873 in the area. (Hallstrom Pacific Library)

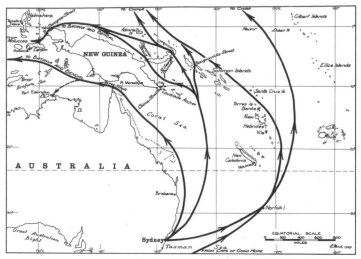

Plate 42

Plate 42. Shipping routes through New Guinea waters in the late eighteenth century and in the first half of the nineteenth century. Following the founding of Sydney in 1788, shipping routes were laid down between that port and Bengal, Batavia and Canton. Some of these routes passed through or near New Guinea waters and used the knowledge of these waters discovered by the navigators Dampier, Carteret, Bougainville, Cook, Shortland, Hunter and others (see plates 16–23). The most easterly route to Canton skirted the Solomon Islands and ran parallel to the east coast of New Ireland. A shorter route passed through Bougainville Strait and then followed the east coast of New Ireland. Sailing directions for ships requiring water, fuel and fresh food recommended the use of the shipping route through St George's Channel (see plate 43). This route, if used on the passage to Bengal, was parallel to the north coast of New Guinea. The route through Dampier Strait between New Guinea and Rooke (Umboi) Island was recommended—with the warning of difficult navigational conditions. The Torres Strait route had the advantage of being the shortest route between Sydney and Bengal, but it involved formidable navigation difficulties. However, the attempts by the Admiralty to determine a safe route through Torres Strait led to important surveys in Papuan coastal waters in the 1830s and 1840s. The use of these routes through New Guinea waters was important in the history of contact between European ships and the people of the islands and coastline of New Guinea. (Map drawn by Edgar Ford)

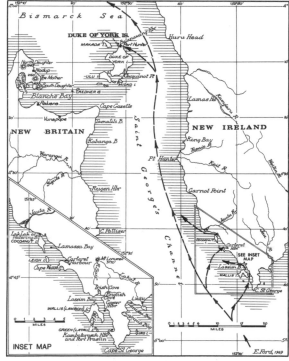

Plate 43

Plate 44

Plate 43. The shipping route through St George's Channel used by ships on the Sydney to Canton and Sydney to Bengal run. This route had the advantage of offering several easily accessible anchorages for ships' refreshment. Those recommended in the published sailing directions were: English Cove on Gower Harbour just within Cape St George on the southern tip of New Ireland; Carteret Harbour about three kilometres to the north of Gower Harbour; Port Hunter on the north-east corner of Duke of York Island. These places were used by ships in the late eighteenth century and throughout the first half of the nineteenth century. (Map drawn by Edgar Ford)

Plate 44. An engraving published in Paris in 1837 of European sailors watering ship in Carteret Harbour on St George's Channel. In Horsburgh's *Sailing Directions* of 1811 it was recommended that 'if a supply of wood or water is wanted, it may be got at Gower's Harbour, Carteret's Harbour or at Port Hunter. . . . *Carteret's Harbour*, situated about 2 leagues to the N. Westward of Wallis Island . . . a ship may anchor in 25 or 30 fathoms soft mud, close under the North side of Cocoanut Island, and be well sheltered. Wood is got on this island, and very good water conveniently, on the coast of New Ireland, to the northward of the anchorage; but this harbour affords no other refreshments.' (Mitchell Library)

Plate 45. The cascade at Port Praslin in southern New Ireland, as depicted in Paris in 1837. First described by Bougainville during his stay there, this feature was reproduced in illustration throughout the nineteenth century. Port Praslin (French placename) or Gower Harbour (English placename) was highly recommended in sailing directions as a refreshment point for ships using the St George's Channel sea route, lying as it did just within Cape St George on the west coast of southern New Ireland. Dr D. Parker Wilson, surgeon of the London whaler *Gypsy*, recorded in his journal on 6 December 1840: 'Captain Brown informed us that the *Caroline* and one other Sydney craft had been at anchor in Gower's Harbour close to Cape St George, the East point of New Ireland, to procure wood and water, and there 14 of the crew of the *Caroline* deserted her and with 4 other men from another ship, probably runaway convicts afraid to return, they have formed a *Settlement* near the Harbour.' (Mitchell Library)

Plate 46. Mioko Harbour in the Duke of York Islands group. In the second half of the nineteenth century this harbour was an important refreshment point for ships using the St George's Channel shipping route. Thomas Farrell and Emma Forsayth ('Queen' Emma) established a trading station and a ship's supply depot on Mioko Island in 1880 and this was later sold to the German firm, Deutsche Handels-und Plantagen Gesellschaft. In April 1881 the famous 'Mioko Massacre' took place on Utuan Island shown here. This followed the killing by the Utuans of the German naturalist Kleinschmidt. The Europeans in the area, organized by Farrell, mounted a punitive expedition that took a heavy toll of life. In 1884 the German protectorate over the Bismarck Archipelago was proclaimed at the station of Deutsche Handels-und Plantagen Gesellschaft on Mioko Harbour. (Royal Australian Air Force)

Plate 45

Plate 46

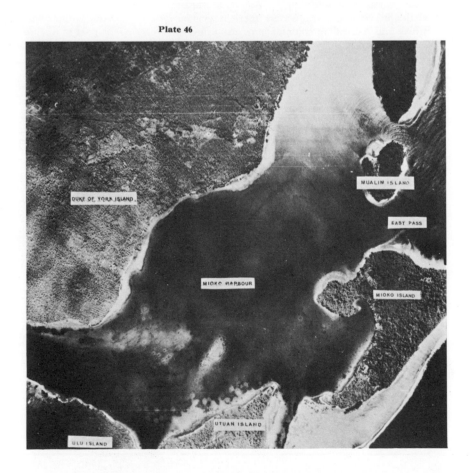

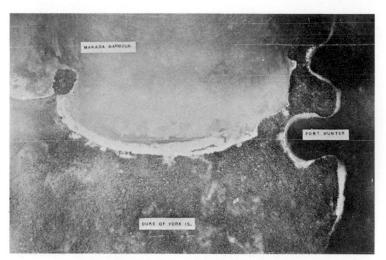

Plate 47

Plate 47. Port Hunter on the north-east corner of Duke of York Island. Discovered by Captain John Hunter in 1791 (see plate 23) it became a recommended refreshment point for ships on the Sydney to China run via St George's Channel. In 1875 it was the site of the founding of the first mission station of the Australasian Wesleyan Methodist Missionary Society under the leadership of the Reverend George Brown. (Royal Australian Air Force)

Plate 48. Nineteenth-century whaling grounds in New Guinea waters. In 1935 an American zoologist, Charles H. Townsend, published an article, 'The Distribution of Certain Whales as Shown by Logbook Records of American Whaleships' (*Zoologica*, vol. 19, no. 1, pp. 3–17), which was illustrated by maps showing where American whalers took sperm whales in the nineteenth century. Townsend obtained his information from large numbers of logbooks in the whaling museums and libraries of the nineteenth-century whaling ports of the Atlantic coast of the United States. Townsend's maps show that New Guinea waters were important in the American whaling industry, and the map here, adapted by Edgar Ford, illustrates the position of the grounds in these waters. In addition to American ships taking whales in New Guinea waters there is evidence that British and Australian colonial ships also fished the New Guinea whaling grounds. In the history of contact between Europeans and the people of the coast and islands of New Guinea in the nineteenth century, the proximity of the whaling grounds was an important factor. There is evidence that the people of Bougainville and Buka Island and the people on the eastern coast of New Ireland traded with the crews of whaling ships, providing fresh food in return for metal (hoop iron) and manufactured articles. On at least one occasion, for a short period in 1839, a group of deserters from whaling ships formed a temporary settlement on the shores of Gower Harbour (Port Praslin), within Cape St George on the southern tip of New Ireland at the entrance to St George's Channel. The New Guinea whaling grounds were an important part of the pattern of Pacific whaling grounds, used in conjunction with the very large grounds further to the north in the central Pacific (the 'On the Line' Ground) and the Coast of Japan Ground. The New Guinea whaling grounds were used by the whalers as part of a seasonal programme of killing, as shown in the months of operation noted beside each ground on the map.

Plate 48

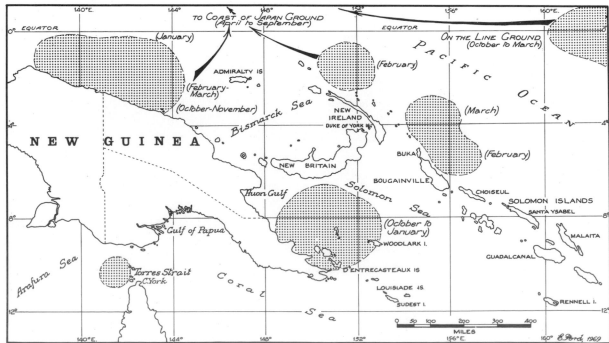

Plate 49. South Sea whalers, from a watercolour by O. W. Brierly, marine artist who sailed in the *Rattlesnake* on a New Guinea voyage (see plate 29). The operation depicted here was described in the *Illustrated London News*, July 1876, when the painting was exhibited in London. 'In the South Sea ships which capture both sperm and "right" whale, the whales are brought alongside where the blubber is first stripped off in great masses, called "blanket pieces", which are then cut up into more manageable sizes and finally boiled down in try-pots, large boilers fixed into brickwork on the forepart of the ship, the fuel being supplied from the scraps from which the oil has been extracted. A whaler so employed at night, with a mass of smoke rising high above the sails, which are lighted up by the red glare as the fires are stirred up, has much the appearance of a ship on fire.' Dr D. Parker Wilson recorded such operations off Buka Island (see plate 52). Of the seventy-one whales caught during the voyage of the *Gypsy*, from May 1840 to December 1842, approximately thirty-nine appear to have been taken in New Guinea waters. The scene shown in Brierly's painting must have become a familiar one for people living adjacent to New Guinea whaling grounds. (Mitchell Library)

Plate 49

Plate 50

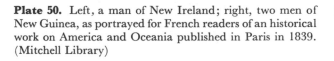

Plate 50. Left, a man of New Ireland; right, two men of New Guinea, as portrayed for French readers of an historical work on America and Oceania published in Paris in 1839. (Mitchell Library)

Plate 51

Plate 51. The *Carl*, blackbirding off Buka and Bougainville Islands in July 1871. This engraving was published in Melbourne in December 1872 when two men were on trial for their part in the incident. The men were found guilty on evidence such as the following: 'There were a great many canoes came alongside. They were smashed just as usual and the boats lowered. We were that busy that I can't tell how many canoes or natives were got. As fast as we smashed one canoe another would come up before we could look round. The natives were very bruised when they came on board, and the bilge water of the two boats was mixed with blood. The natives had swum away, and the boats went after them, so I did not see them caught . . . we took about 400 that day . . . we got about 80 or 82 natives together at Bougainville in 3 days.' 'Deviscove's Evidence' in G. S. Searle, *Mount and Morris Exonerated: A Narrative of the Voyage of the Brig 'Carl' in 1871* (Melbourne, 1875), p. 14. (National Library of Australia)

Plate 52

Plate 52. Buka Islanders visiting a whaling ship, *c.* 1840, from a sketch in the log and private journal of Dr D. Parker Wilson, ship's surgeon of the South Sea whaler *Gypsy* of London. Wilson recorded on his first visit to Buka Bay (formed by Buka Island and Bougainville Island on the east) in December 1840: 'The natives of *Bougainville* seldom or ever come off to the ships, afraid to venture near vessels the like of which have vomited forth lightning and death! The natives of *Bouka* [*sic*] it is, who come off; and by treating them fairly a pretty contant supply of refreshments can be depended on while cruising there, a desideratum in a long cruise in rainy wet weather and a hot exhausting climate.' (Royal Geographical Society)

Plate 53

Plate 53. The *Illustrated Monthly Herald* (Melbourne) published this engraving with explanation at the time of the Melbourne trial of two members of the crew of the *Carl*: '[A witness] testified that the night after the schooner sailed from Bougainville where the natives had been captured there arose a noise among them. They had been crammed anyhow into the hold and possibly did not like it so they began first fighting amongst themselves and then tried to get out . . . all hands then commenced firing down the hatchway. Everyone fired at first. The prisoner Mount had his own revolver. I saw him fire down the main hatchway. The prisoner Morris was in the cabin loading the muskets which were passed down to him . . . this firing continued on and off from half past ten till daylight.' (Library of New South Wales)

Plate 54. This engraving, based also on the evidence at the Melbourne trial of Mount and Morris, had the explanatory text: 'All night long that fire had lasted and the next morning, when a slight stirring was heard, the master fiend [Dr Murray, the leader of the expedition] ordered holes to be bored in the bulkhead and commenced firing on the defenceless heap till some of the less hardened of his comrades cried shame . . . the hatchways were opened . . . one by one the miserable wounded wretches were dragged on deck—some by means of ropes tied round their necks—and then they were one by one flung overboard to struggle out their dying agonies in the water.' (Library of New South Wales)

Plate 54

Plate 55. Nicolais Miklouho-Maclay (1846–1888), Russian scientist who lived near Garagassi Point on Astrolabe Bay from September 1871 until December 1872 and from June to December 1876. The portrait of Miklouho-Maclay shown here was made in St Petersburg shortly before his death. Miklouho-Maclay, besides carrying out important scientific work, appears to have built up a remarkable rapport with the local people. In June 1881, H. H. Romilly visited the Maclay Coast and recorded, 'We saw a few canoes coming off to us, but they seemed rather shy at first, till I shouted out the magical name of Maclay; then they came up, as fast as they could. . . . I was able to inform them that he would come back to them soon; that I was his brother (in the native sense); and that I wanted to see their towns. They at once became extremely friendly, and kept telling each other that I was Maclay's brother.' H. H. Romilly, *The Western Pacific and New Guinea* (London, 1886), p. 221. (Mitchell Library)

Plate 55

Plate 56. Tui of Gurendu village on Astrolabe Bay; a sketch by Miklouho-Maclay of a close acquaintance during his stay, 1871–72. On 30 September 1871, Maclay recorded, 'When Tui came I asked him to be my teacher in the native language. After the first lesson, I gave Tui a box of cigars and Olsen gave him one of his old hats. Tui was enthusiastic and went quickly to his village, as if afraid that to remain longer would lose him his presents; perhaps also he wanted to show off to his fellow men.' (Mitchell Library)

Plate 57

Plate 56

Plate 57. Miklouho-Maclay's hut at Garagassi on Astrolabe Bay. An entry in his journal for 21 September 1871 reads, '. . . at 3 P.M. a crew went with me to make a start in erecting the hut . . . [later, 26 September] . . . I showed the Captain and others a place where I would hide my diary or other reports just in case of sickness or attack by natives. About 3 in the afternoon Constantine Bay (as the little bay was named on which my house was situated) looked like the busiest harbour in the world. Boats rushed to and from the ship to get all my possessions ashore, provisions, the last hands were laid on the house to put the finishing touches to it.' (Mitchell Library)

Plate 58. The interior of Miklouho-Maclay's hut. On 30 October 1872, Maclay recorded, 'Rain, rain, rain again. The roof of the house is leaking badly and drips of rain are on the table, bed and worst of all on my books. All my provisions have gone and quinine is running low. I have about 100 shots left for hunting and supplementing my food. Fever is taking all my strength. The house is in a pityful state of repair.' (Mitchell Library)

Plate 58

Plate 59

Plate 59. Italian naturalist Luigi Maria d'Albertis (1841–1901), who reached New Guinea in 1872 with a companion, Beccari, and spent two years living and working in the Arfak Mountains behind Dorei (Manokwari). D'Albertis then shifted to Yule Island, from where he undertook the first navigation of the Fly River in 1875. A second expedition was mounted in 1876 and a third in 1877. D'Albertis was an intensely patriotic man and would have liked New Guinea to be added to the empire of the House of Savoy. (Information and Extension Services, Administration of Papua New Guinea)

30

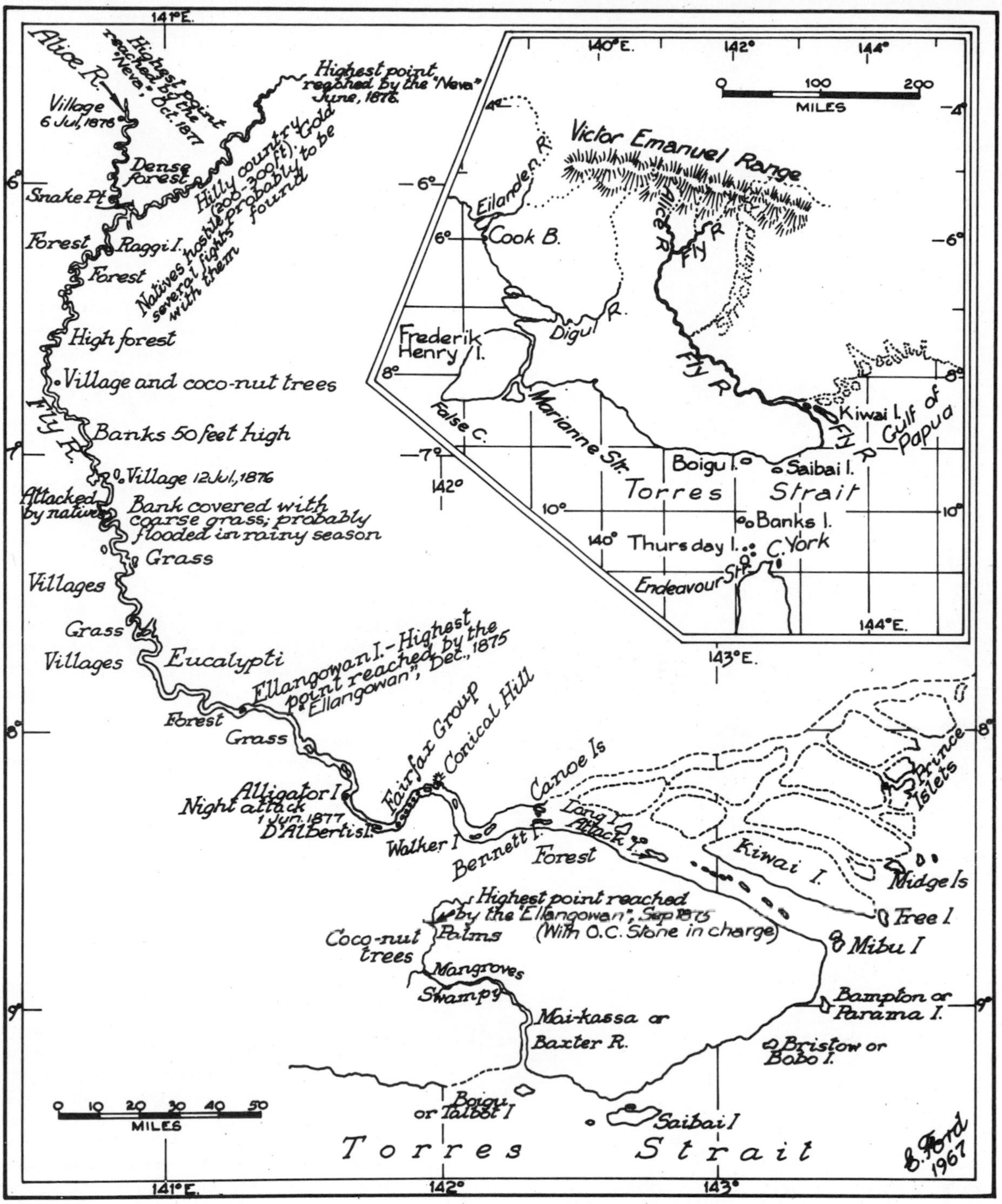
141°E.
Alice R.
Highest point reached by the "Neva", Oct. 1877
Highest point reached by the "Neva" June, 1876.
Village 6 Jul, 1876
Dense forest
Hilly country (200-300 ft.) Gold probably to be found
Natives hostile, several fights with them
Snake Pt.
Forest
Raggi I.
Forest
High forest
Village and coco-nut trees
Fly R.
Banks 50 feet high
Village 12 Jul, 1876
Attacked by natives
Bank covered with coarse grass; probably flooded in rainy season
Grass
Villages
Grass
Villages
Eucalypti
Ellangowan I.-Highest point reached by the "Ellangowan", Dec., 1875
Forest
Grass
Fairfax Group
Conical Hill
Alligator I.
Night attack 1 Jun. 1877
D'Albertis I.
Walker I.
Canoe Is
Long I.
Attack I.
Bennett I.
Forest
Kiwai I.
Prince Islets
Midge Is
Tree I.
Highest point reached by the "Ellangowan", Sep 1875 (With O.C. Stone in charge)
Coco-nut trees
Palms
Mangroves
Swampy
Mai-kassa or Baxter R.
Mibu I.
Bampton or Parama I.
Bristow or Bobo I.
Boigu or Talbot I.
Saibai I.
Torres Strait
MILES
0 10 20 30 40 50
141°E.
142°
143°
E. Ford 1967
140°E.
142°
144°
0 100 200
MILES
Victor Emanuel Range
Eilanden R.
Cook B.
Alice R.
Fly R.
Digul R.
Frederik Henry I.
False C.
Marianne Str.
Fly R.
Kiwai I.
Gulf of Papua
Boigu I.
Saibai I.
Torres Strait
Banks I.
Thursday I.
C. York
Endeavour Str.
144°E.
143°E.

Plate 60

Plate 60. Chart of the Fly River, drawn by Lawrence Hargrave, a young engineer who accompanied Luigi d'Albertis on his second (1876) expedition up the Fly River. Hargrave was one of the organizers of the ill-fated *Maria* gold prospecting expedition in 1872. In 1875 he joined William Macleay's natural science expedition as an articled engineer, then he accompanied Octavius Stone on a trip to Port Moresby. From there he made three trips to the Laroka River, to the Astrolabe Range and to the Owen Stanley Range. He was the first European to enter some of the villages in the Owen Stanleys. Upon returning to Katau after the expedition with d'Albertis, he wrote to his father: 'How truly Robertson spoke when he said I should get nothing by going but hard work; after my taking the *Neva* about 1500 miles and doing the engineering, navigating, and almost everything but steering, collecting specimens and cutting fire-wood, D'Albertis turns round and says I am not even his companion, and have done nothing but make the fire. However, when I am once clear at Cape York, I will have nothing more to do with such an ungrateful fellow.' Lawrence Hargrave to his father, dated Kat-tow, 25 September 1876. Papers of Lawrence Hargrave, Microfilm FM4/1060, Mitchell Library. (Chart redrawn by Edgar Ford)

Plate 61

Plate 61. The steam-launch *Neva*, which Luigi d'Albertis acquired from Sir John Robertson, premier of New South Wales, for his second expedition up the Fly River in 1876. The *Neva* measured about sixteen metres by two metres and had neither deck nor cabin but a zinc canopy covering two-thirds of her length. The crew under d'Albertis's command were: Lawrence Hargrave, engineer; Clarence Wilcox, seventeen-year-old assistant collector; two West Indian Negroes; a Filippino; a Chinese cook; a New Caledonian and a man from the Sandwich Islands. On this expedition the party reached the foothills of the Victor Emmanuel Range, so named by d'Albertis. On 17 July 1876, d'Albertis wrote in his journal: 'At last I have seen the lofty mountains of the interior of New Guinea! I have seen them, like giants of different height, towering one above the other, and extending from the principal chain down to the river. But we are still far from these Papuan Alps—forty or fifty miles, or even more. My mind is on the rack. I feel like Moses, in sight of the Promised Land, destined never to enter it!' L. M. d'Albertis, *New Guinea: What I Did and What I Saw* (London, 1880), vol. 2, p. 91. (Hallstrom Pacific Library)

Plate 62

Plate 62. An engraving from the *Australasian Sketcher*, 12 June 1875, showing members of the first Australian natural science expedition to New Guinea and their barque, *Chevert*. Top left, William Macleay, leader of the party; right, Captain Edwards, master of the vessel; bottom left, G. Masters, an expert on plants and insects; right, John Brazier, an expert on birds and shells, who three years earlier had accompanied Captain Simpson in H.M.S. *Blanche* on a voyage to the Bismarck Sea. Others in the scientific party were: Onslow, second in command and nautical adviser; James Pettard, a young Tasmanian naturalist; Dr James, an American surgeon; Lawrence Hargrave; Spalding, an authority on bird life; and two skilled gardeners from Sir William Macarthur's Camden estate. Macleay was excited by J. Beete Jukes's speculation on the existence of a great river on the south coast of the New Guinea mainland, almost opposite Cape York—a river that could prove to be a waterway into the interior of New Guinea. The *Chevert* left Port Jackson in May 1875. At Darnley Island bad weather and dangerous shoals made Captain Edwards decline to run the risks seen in the entrance to the Fly River, and to enter instead the eastern side of the gulf. They anchored off the village of Mawatta on the Katau River. 'The people themselves,' wrote Macleay, 'are lively, particularly the young men, but wonderfully unlike Australians: they are strong, middle-sized, black, woolly haired and small in the lower extremities, but instead of the large head and flat nose of our aborigine, they have well-shaped heads and noses of a very marked Jewish character.' ('Journal of William Macleay: The New Guinea Expedition', MS., Linnean Society, Sydney.) The trip proved rewarding for the collection of natural specimens, but disappointing in that they had missed the Fly, and the Katau did not prove to be a great waterway. (National Library of Australia)

Plate 63. Brigadier-General H. R. H. MacIver. In 1883, MacIver proposed a European colonization scheme for New Guinea. He intended to lead an armed expedition to New Guinea to acquire land on an extensive scale and to trade. MacIver enjoyed a varied career as a mercenary, fighting in wars in America, Brazil, the Balkans, Italy and France. When the Colonial Office refused his scheme for New Guinea he conducted a campaign in Australia in an attempt to influence the British government to open New Guinea to European land settlement schemes. (Mitchell Library)

Plate 64. George E. Morrison, who at the age of twenty-one began an exploring trip in New Guinea and wrote of it for the Melbourne *Age*. Morrison was with Professor Denton (see plate 65) until Cooktown, where he recruited his own party, which included Ned Snow and a prospector, John Wheeler Lyons. At Port Moresby he employed two Papuans, Dick and Bosen, and on 21 July 1883 he set out for the Goldie River, a tributary of the Laloki. Morrison had plenty of courage but little understanding of the people. He shot a man who stole some of his supplies, and was consequently attacked. He received two spear wounds and was fortunate to survive the return trip of thirteen days to Port Moresby. The missionary Chalmers wrote in his journal, 'The immediate cause of the attack was the shooting of a young man for stealing a knife. It was at first reported that he was dead, but they afterwards found that he was alive, but still suffering. He is the son of a chief who has always been friendly with the white man. He himself warned Morrison back by putting a shield and spear in his path before him.' (W. G. Lawes, 'Journal 1876–84', MS., Mitchell Library.) George Morrison later became famous for his exploits in China. (State Library of Victoria)

Plate 63

Plate 64

33

Plate 65

Plate 65. An artist's impression in the *Australasian Sketcher*, 21 November 1884, of the death of Professor Denton from malaria in New Guinea. W. E. Armit, leader of the *Argus* exploring party, reported the death in a telegram to the *Argus* on 24 October 1884: '. . . Professor Denton was completely exhausted, having refused all nourishment and medicine since becoming ill. . . . On the 24th Belford was prostrated with fever, Professor Denton getting weaker, yet obstinate even regarding food as well as physic. On the 26th we started for Moroka, Professor Denton and Belford on stretchers. The fever attacked me before breakfast and I had a terrible day. We reached Berigabadi at 2 p.m. . . . Mr Hunter who was the only sound man of the party made our beds. At half-past 8 p.m. Professor Denton had very slight convulsive fits; five minutes afterwards he was dead.' W. E. Armit's telegram reported in the *Argus*, 24 October 1884, in *Journ. & Proc. R.G.S.*, 1884, p. 37. (National Library of Australia)

Plate 66. H. C. Everill, master of the *Bonito*, a steamship which left Sydney on 10 June 1885 with the intention of navigating the Fly River to the mountain foothills, to allow the party of scientists on board to collect natural specimens. About 240 kilometres up the river they saw a broad stream entering the Fly from the east (Strickland River) and entered it, assuming that a river trending thus would lead them sooner into the mountains. The people they met were frightened and aggressive. W. Bauerlen, a botanist in the party, described their attempt to make friendly contact: 'Captain Everill very bravely ventured to land and go amongst them, taking a lot of presents with him. They did not oppose his landing, but, for all that, they were in no way friendly disposed. The presents they scarcely took notice of, some they left lying on the ground, and the brightest coloured handkerchiefs they dragged along the mud.' (W. Bauerlen, *The Voyage of the 'Bonito': An Account of the Fly River Expedition to New Guinea* [Sydney, 1886], p. 15.) The party failed to reach their mountain destination. (Information and Extension Services, Administration of Papua New Guinea)

Plate 66

Plate 67

Plate 67. Dr F. H. Otto Finsch (1839–1917), German zoologist, anthropologist and explorer. Finsch was commissioned by the German Neuguinea-Kompagnie to survey the east and north-east coasts of New Guinea to find suitable places for German colonization. He left Sydney in September 1884 in the steamship *Samoa* (Captain Dallmann) bound for Mioko, Duke of York Islands. From his base at Mioko, Finsch made five voyages to the New Guinea mainland in the region stretching from the Huon Gulf to Humboldt Bay. This area he named Kaiser-Wilhelmsland. The Bismarck Range was also named by him after the German chancellor. Finsch penetrated the mouth of the Sepik River in May 1885 and called it Kaiserin Augusta River after the German kaiserin. Of the inhabitants he contacted at Venus Huk, east of the Sepik River, Finsch wrote: 'These people were real Papuans, their colouring a little lighter than that of the New Britain people. They looked stronger than the people on the east coast. . . . They were easy to barter with although they were noisy and fought among themselves. They did not have any European things such as glass, beads, tobacco or knives, but they were happy to see hoop-iron.' Otto Finsch, *Samoafahrten: Reisen in Kaiser Wilhelmsland und Englisch-Neu-Guinea in den Jahren 1884, 1885, an Bord des Deutschen Dampfers, 'Samoa'* (Leipzig, 1888), p. 298. (Hallstrom Pacific Library)

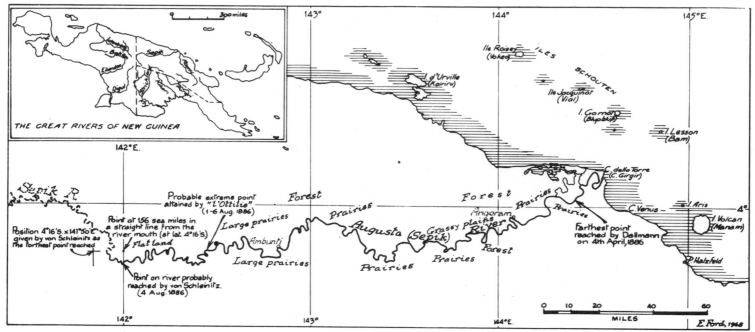

The Great Rivers of New Guinea

Plate 68

Plate 68. Map showing the stages of navigation of the Sepik River. In May 1885, Dr Otto Finsch (see plate 67) recognized in the changes in colour of the water, and in floating branches, the outflow of a great river and named it Kaiserin Augusta River. These signs had previously been noted by the Dutchmen Le Maire and Schouten in 1616, by Abel Tasman in 1643, and by the Frenchman Dumont d'Urville in 1827 (see plate 24). It took Finsch one and a half hours to navigate three kilometres into the mouth of the river. In April 1886 a small expedition under the command of Captain Dallmann in the *Samoa* was organized for its further navigation. The *Samoa* negotiated fifty-five kilometres of the river. On 24 July of the same year a third expedition was mounted by G. E. G. von Schleinitz, the high commissioner for German New Guinea. He left Finschhafen in the *Ottilie*, accompanied by Dr Knapp, the vice-consul of Apia; Carl Hunstein, an albino prospector who had at one time managed Andrew Goldie's store at Port Moresby; and members of a scientific expedition, Dr Schrader and Dr Hollrung. It was the dry season and the river became shallow. Von Schleinitz used a whaleboat to reach a point above Ambunti. Dr Schrader thought this area would lend itself to agricultural settlement: 'It is in this region that it would be best to make the centre for future agricultural development, as well as one can judge from the knowledge we have of the country. The river flats in the lower river reaches which have an area of several hundred square kilometres constitute an area suitable for raising cattle. Rice and sugar-cane cultivation would give the best results.' (Prince Roland Bonaparte, *La Nouvelle-Guinée*, book 3, *Le Fleuve Augusta* [Paris, 1887], p. 14.) In 1887 the Neuguinea-Kompagnie sent another expedition under Dr Schrader, accompanied by Schneider, Hollrung and Hunstein. This time the river was ascended for 600 kilometres. (Map reconstructed by Edgar Ford)

4 The Pioneer Traders and Planters: Bismarck Archipelago

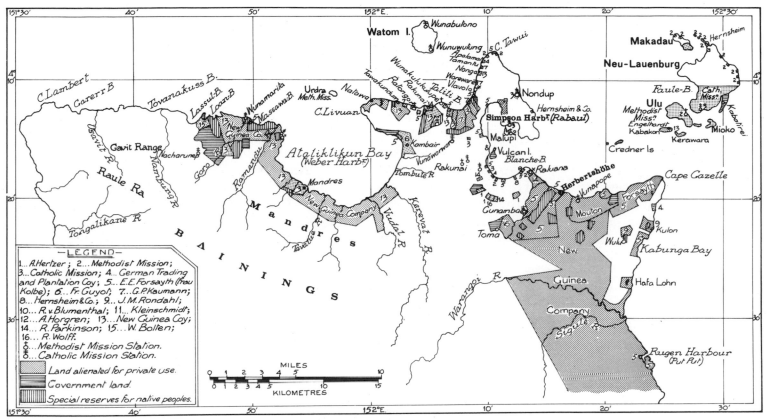

Plate 69

Plate 69. European plantations on the Gazelle Peninsula and the Duke of York Islands, *c.* 1906. In the whole of the Bismarck Archipelago, 70 135 hectares had been acquired by Europeans at this date. Of this about 11 100 hectares had been planted and 1983 hectares were in production, 1846 hectares of this being under coconuts. The labour force for these plantations was made up of 63 Europeans and 5334 coloured labourers (German New Guinea Report for 1906). Land purchase by Europeans in the Blanche Bay area began with Thomas Farrell and Emma Forsayth. In February 1908, Emma (Forsayth) Kolbe described her Blanche Bay holdings (shown on the map) thus:

'*Ralum*: has at present 500 acres full bearing in cocoanuts and producing an average annual crop of from 125 to 145 tons of copra.

'*Tokuka*: adjoins the above and has 625 acres planted with cocoanuts, $\frac{3}{4}$ bearing and produces from 75 to 95 tons of copra per annum.

'*Ravalien:* also adjoining consists of 1000 acres of cocoanuts (half bearing) and Ficus elastica. The former returning an annual crop of from 100 to 130 tons of copra. The Ficus elastica plants range from 5 tears to two years and 12 and 6 months old.

'*Matanata*: is 750 acres or more in extent, 470 acres being planted with cocoanuts and 280 acres with Ficus elastica with plantings of Cocoa, Nutmegs and Vanilla . . . planted in between the Cocoanuts are some 50 acres of sisal hemp.

'*Girgire*: has some 500 acres planted with cocoanuts and Ficus elastica but not yet producing . . . .

'The above plantations are known as Ralum Plantations and are contained inside a Block, the area of which is 12,000 acres with a frontage of 2½ miles along the sea shore.' (E. E. Kolbe to Col. Burns, dated Neutral Bay, 21 February 1908, company records, Burns, Philp and Co.)

Before the Neuguinea-Kompagnie's regulation of land sales around Blanche Bay commencing in 1884, the purchasers negotiated directly with the local people. Thus Thomas Farrell and Emma Forsayth bought their first land in 1880, as did also the father of J. B. O. Mouton at Kiningunan (Kokopo), the Australasian Wesleyan Methodist Missionary Society at Raluana, and the Sacred Heart Mission at Kiningunan. Typical of these early purchases was the buying of land by the leader of the Sacred Heart Mission, Rev. L. A. Navarre, in 1882. Father Navarre wrote: 'I purchased a new site which is situated towards the centre of the beach, not far from the village of Kiningunan . . . . We bought six acres on which there are bread-trees, cocoa trees etc. etc. . . . The whole property far from costing 1200 francs was given to us for an old gun and ten *brasses* of *diwara*. *Diwara* is the currency of the country and consists of small bleached shells, circular pieces of coral and mother-of-pearl strung with bird-seed. A *brasse* is equivalent to one franc or thereabouts. The Kanakas do not prize gold or silver, being totally ignorant of the value of either one.' L. A. Navarre to Rev. Jules Chevalier, dated Beridni, New Britain, 12 November 1882, in *The Australian Annals of Our Lady of the Sacred Heart* (Randwick, N.S.W.), vol. 2, no. 6 (1 May 1891), p. 131. (Map adapted by Edgar Ford from one in Hans Meyer, *Das Deutsche Kolonialreich* [Leipzig, 1910])

Plate 70. The trading station and ship supply depot of Thomas Farrell and Emma Forsayth on Mioko Harbour (see plate 46), Duke of York Islands, in 1881. Dr A. Badouin of the French colony visited here in 1881 and recorded, 'At last the attractive anchorage of Meoko with its charming fringe of cocoanut islands was stretched out before us. On our left was a schooner at its mooring. We passed by it and saw Mr Farrell's colony in front of which were stationed two other ships and a countless number of large sailing canoes set aside for the long journeys which his trade involved. To the right and left were large gardens. On the actual spit of the island were three shops most likely containing imported goods. From this spot Mr Farrell could see St George's Channel and all the other passages of water between the nearby islands. He had a charming house with a verandah which was surrounded by splendid palm trees.' (Mitchell Library)

Plate 70

Plate 71. The European graveyard at Mioko, Duke of York Islands, 1898. This island was a copra and recruiting station for the firm of Godeffroy und Sohn of Hamburg. Here lie buried Dr Kleinschmidt and his two assistants, Herren Schultze and Becker, who were murdered by islanders of Utuan, another of the Duke of York group. These graves, as well as others whose names, even at that time, had been erased by weather, were all of Europeans killed in this island group. (Hallstrom Pacific Library)

Plate 71

Plate 72

Plate 72. 'Queen 'Emma (1850–1913) and her husband, August Karl Paul Kolbe, in 1892. Emma Kolbe was the daughter of Jonas Coe, U.S. commercial agent and later U.S. official representative at Apia, and Le'utu, daughter of a Samoan chief. In 1869 Emma married James Forsayth, a trader, but after the birth of Emma's son in 1872 Forsayth faded out of her life. In 1877 she began an association with Thomas Farrell, an Australian saloon keeper and trader in Apia, and they traded as Thomas Farrell and Company. The following year they sold their interests in Apia and established a business on Mioko, Duke of York Islands, trading, and recruiting labour for Samoan plantations. In 1881 they began to buy land around Blanche Bay and some of the islands and archipelagoes, including the Witu group, which were bought for fifty pounds. They were soon joined by some of Emma's family, including her sister Phoebe and her brother-in-law Richard Parkinson. With Parkinson's help, Emma selected Ralum as headquarters for the Farrell-Forsayth-Parkinson coconut planting enterprise.

After Farrell's death, Emma began a new association with Captain Agostino Stalio, the Italian master of her largest vessel. A trading station was built at Ralum. Parkinson established the huge plantation, Melapau, behind Ralum and then the bungalow Gunantambu was built just south of Ralum. Stalio was shot dead in 1892 on a punitive raid. The following year Emma married Captain Kolbe, a German who, she thought, would secure her position in the German colony. In the tense political situation that preceded the outbreak of World War I, 'Queen' Emma became disturbed that on her death her wealth would pass to Kolbe and his German relatives, rather than to her own family. She therefore sold all her property, except a small part that was reserved for her son, to Hamburgische Südsee Aktien-Gesellschaft (Hasag) for close to a million U.S. dollars, and retired to Mosman, N.S.W. Kolbe fell ill while in Monte Carlo, and Emma joined him there. He died on 19 July 1913, and Emma died two days later. (H. L. Schultze Collection)

Plate 73. The offices of the E. E. Forsayth & Co. enterprises at the port of Ralum. 'Queen' Emma drove in her carriage almost every day from Gunantambu to this office and store from which she ruled her business empire. (S. Stephenson Collection)

Plate 74. Gunantambu, the home of 'Queen' Emma Forsayth. When this photograph was taken in 1914 it was the home of H. R. Wahlen, who is seen in the car with his wife. Wahlen was director of the company that bought the Forsayth properties (see plate 72), and acted as consul for Sweden—hence the flag. The caption of the photograph, published in the *Sydney Mail* in September 1914, was 'Captured by Australians for the Empire'. Lilian Overell visited Gunantambu with Emma's sister, Phoebe Parkinson, in 1920 and recorded, 'The bungalow was on the levelled top of the hill. It covered a large extent of ground with its six spacious rooms and the widest verandas I have ever seen. A little distance away were the guest-houses and the kitchen quarters. There were very gay doings here in Queen Emma's day, for she kept open house and everyone was welcome: the officers from the German warboats, stray travellers and explorers, sisters from the mission, planters from far and near—all shared her lavish hospitality. . . . We sat on the veranda and tea was brought by a dignified old man, with the air of the last faithful retainer of a noble family. He had been Queen Emma's butler and he wore the livery of her house servants. It was very quaint, a long white linen coat, with numerous buttons.' Lilian Overell, *A Woman's Impressions of German New Guinea* (London, 1923), p. 149. (Mitchell Library)

Plate 73

Plate 74

Plate 75

Plate 75. A section of the large living room at Gunantambu, home of 'Queen' Emma Forsayth. Note the punkah cooling device suspended from ceiling at top left. The heavy sideboard, centre, and some of the other furniture, had belonged previously to the writer Robert Louis Stevenson. Stevenson, while living in Samoa, was befriended by Emma's father, Jonas Coe, American consul at Apia, and he left many of his possessions to the Coe family. (H. L. Schultze Collection)

Plate 76

Plate 76. The living room at Gunantambu, the home of 'Queen' Emma Forsayth (see also plate 75, which completes the panoramic view of the large room). 'She had built for herself the house of her dreams. Gunantambu was admirably designed for tropical conditions, and it contained every device then known to provide for agreeable living. There was substantial material from Australia and from Europe, heavy carpets and curtains from the Orient, a hot-water system, lavish ornaments and decorations—she even acquired a dinner service of gold plate. Her servants wore livery.' R. W. Robson, *Queen Emma* (Sydney, 1965), p. 149. (S. Stephenson Collection)

Plate 77. Phoebe Parkinson translates the old man's story for her husband, Richard, shortly after they came to New Guinea in 1881 to join Phoebe's sister, 'Queen' Emma Forsayth. Phoebe was eighteen when she arrived with her son; her husband was twenty years older. Richard Parkinson helped Emma Forsayth establish a chain of plantations on the Gazelle Peninsula, a trading port at Ralum, and a magnificent bungalow, Gunantambu (see plate 74). Phoebe managed the bungalow, recruited labour and helped her husband with his anthropological work. Parkinson was honoured by German scientific bodies for his work, and for his notable book, *Dreissig Jahre in der Südsee* [*Thirty Years in the South Seas*]. When the E. E. Forsayth & Co. properties were being prepared for sale in 1907, the Parkinsons moved from their bungalow near Gunantambu to Kuradui, a kilometre away (see plate 78). Richard Parkinson died in July 1907, aged sixty-three, from injuries received in a buggy accident. Phoebe continued to live at Kuradui until the property was expropriated by the Australian government. She then remained in New Britain among her friends, the Tolai. 'She lived amongst them in a little house made of native materials and for years, despite her age, she earned an income by recruiting native labour for plantations.' (R. W. Robson, *Queen Emma* [Sydney, 1965], p. 223.) When the Japanese invaded New Britain in 1942, they told her to remain in a small village in New Ireland. She died there in 1944. (Mitchell Library)

Plate 77

Plate 78

Plate 78. Kuradui, the home of Phoebe and Richard Parkinson, near Raluana on Blanche Bay, New Britain, *c.* 1908. Lilian Overell, who was a guest of Phoebe Parkinson in this bungalow in 1920, described it: 'The bungalow was charmingly situated among the coco-nuts, indeed one palm was right in the middle of the house and served somewhat as the salt-cellar in days of old. On one side of the palm were kitchens and store-rooms, and on the other, facing Blanche Bay, was the main portion—the open-air dining room, bedrooms, drawing-room and the verandas where we chiefly lived.' Lilian Overell, *A Woman's Impressions of German New Guinea* (London, 1923), p. 36. (H. L. Schultze Collection)

Plate 79

Plate 79. A group of German citizens and local people at Makada, Duke of York Islands, *c.* 1890. From left to right: Hans Mannsfeld; Fritz Anacker; Herr Heydenreuter (Hernsheim manager at Makada); Frau Stehr (dressed Samoan style); Herr Goetch; behind Herr Goetch, Herr Schuster; Herr Steyr; Herr Steyr's youngest son, Franz; behind Franz Steyr, Herr Weimer; Herr Sturhan; [unidentified]. (M. von Hein Collection)

Plate 80

Plate 80. One of the trading stations of the firm Deutsche Handels-und Plantagen Gesellschaft (D. H. & P. G.) in the Bismarck Archipelago in the 1880s. See also plate 84. (National Library of Australia) ·

Plate 81. Scene on a farm owned by Hernsheim and Company on Blanche Bay, New Britain, 1891. This firm, formerly Robertson & Hernsheim, was based in Hamburg. Its first station was at Makada, the most northerly island of the Duke of York group, in 1879; later it transferred to Matupi on the north-eastern corner of New Britain and from this base a number of trading posts (about twenty altogether) were established along the north coast of New Britain, in the Duke of York Islands and in New Ireland. (National Library of Australia)

Plate 81

44

Plate 82

Plate 82. The trading station of Hernsheim and Company on Matupi Island in about 1900. Eduard Hernsheim, a German trader, came to the Duke of York Islands in 1876. There he established a trading depot on Makada Harbour and then transferred his activities to Matupi Island, where in 1874 an earlier unsuccessful attempt to set up a depot had been made by an agent of Godeffroy and Company. Hernsheim prospered at Matupi; at the beginning of the Australian military occupation of German New Guinea in 1914, the firm held 3362 hectares of land in the Bismarck Archipelago. Matupi Harbour near Hernsheim's depot became an important anchorage for European vessels. (Mitchell Library)

Plate 83. Raulai, the bungalow of the manager of Hernsheim and Company at Matupi, Rabaul, in 1905. (M. von Hein Collection)

Plate 83

45

Plate 84

Plate 84. No. 2 trading station of Deutsche Handels-und Plantagen Gesellschaft (D. H. & P. G.) on Mioko, Duke of York Islands, 1891. In 1878 this firm absorbed the firm of Godeffroy, which had its base in Samoa and had founded a settlement on the island of Mioko. D. H. & P. G. then extended its trading posts throughout the area. The firm bartered with the local people for copra, trepang and shell, but its chief activity was the enrolment of natives for its plantations in Samoa. Recruitment began in the early 1880s in the two vessels *Tonga Tabu* and *Ninafou*. In 1884 Adolph von Hansemann, who had brought about the D. H. & P. G. takeover of Godeffroy, formed a consortium that was to become known as the Neuguinea-Kompagnie (see plate 132). (National Library of Australia)

5 The Entry of the Christian Missions, Nineteenth Century

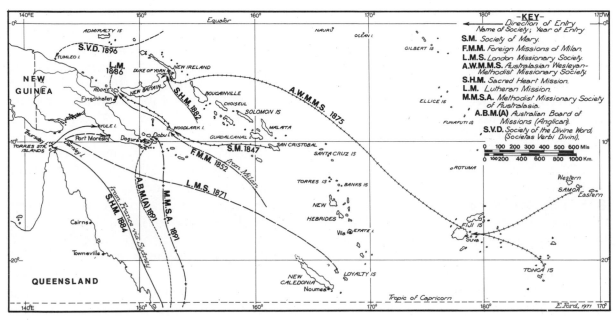

Plate 85

Plate 85. The entry of the Christian missions into eastern New Guinea in the nineteenth century. In general, the pioneer mission parties of the various societies followed existing shipping routes and established foundation stations contiguous with these, where supply would not be an insuperable problem. One feature common to many of the mission parties was the selection of an offshore island on which to begin work. In 1845, Bishop Epalle of the Society of Mary, while in Sydney preparing to enter New Guinea, saw 'great advantages in beginning at a place which we could master completely' before proceeding to the larger populations of the three main islands of New Guinea, New Britain and New Ireland. (Epalle to Colin, dated Sydney, 17 August 1845, *Archivio Padri Maristi* [Rome], A.P.M., O.M.M., 411.) Again, the Rev. Samuel Macfarlane, the pioneer of the New Guinea mission of the London Missionary Society, in explaining why a Torres Strait island was chosen as foundation head-

quarters in 1871 said: 'Prudence suggested the formation of stations on small islands off the coast, to be used as retreats, sanatoriums, and stepping-stones to the mainland — "cities of refuge", indeed, to secure the mission against total collapse at other points.' (Rev. S. Macfarlane, address to the Manchester Geographical Society, n.d., Mitchell Library reprint 279 846 A1, p. 23.)

THE CHRONOLOGY OF CHRISTIAN ENTRY

1847 *The Society of Mary* (S.M.) Under the leadership of Bishop Epalle, a party of Marist missioners came to San Christobal Island in the Solomons group in 1845 with a plan to advance from there towards New Guinea. In September 1847, under Bishop Epalle's successor, Bishop Collomb, S.M., a mission party established itself on Guasupa Harbour, Woodlark Island, and from there in 1848 a further advance was made to Rooke (Umboi) Island between New Britain and New Guinea.

1852 *The Foreign Missions of Milan* (F. M.M.) The F.M.M. took over responsibility for the mission on Woodlark and Rooke Islands from the Society of Mary and continued evangelical effort there until they withdrew in 1855.

1871 *The London Missionary Society* (L. M.S.) Under the leadership of the Rev. Samuel Macfarlane, an L.M.S. party made up of the Rev. A. W. Murray and some South Sea island teachers sailed from the Loyalty Islands to Darnley Island in Torres Strait. Teachers were placed on Darnley, Dauan and Saibai Islands, and in 1872 at Katau and at Redscar Bay on the Papuan coast.

1875 *The Australasian Wesleyan Methodist Missionary Society* (A.W.M.M.S.) Under the leadership of the Rev. George Brown, a mission party sailed from Sydney to Fiji where South Sea island teachers were recruited. From Fiji the party went to the well-known refreshment port on the Sydney to Canton sea route, Port Hunter on Duke of York Island. Here they established the headquarters of the New Britain mission.

1882 *The Sacred Heart Mission* (S. H. M.) Under the leadership of the Rev. Louis-André Navarre, a party of missioners of the Congregation of the Sacred Heart based in France came to Sydney and thence went to Port Breton (Gower Harbour), the capital of the Free Colony of New France. Finding the colony abandoned, the party crossed over to Matupi Island in Blanche Bay and then went to a site called Obei, near Nodup, where a French secular priest, the Rev. René-Marie Lannuzel, had previously worked. In 1883, Father Navarre purchased land at Kokopo on Blanche Bay; this was developed as mission headquarters and came to be called Vunapope. In October 1884, Father Navarre set up headquarters on Thursday Island in Torres Strait, under a plan of the Holy See to advance into Papua. In July 1885, Father Verjus was sent by Father Navarre to begin work on Yule Island.

1886 *The Lutheran Mission* (L.M.) Two Lutheran mission societies entered New Guinea. One based in Neuendettelsau, Bavaria, sent the Rev. Johann Flierl from Australia to Finschhafen, where he arrived in 1886. Finschhafen was the new headquarters of the Neuguinea-Kompagnie in Kaiser-Wilhelmsland. In 1887 the Rhenish Mission Society based in Barmen sent two missionaries to the Astrolabe Bay region and in November 1887 a permanent station was established at Bogadjim.

1891 *Methodist Missionary Society of Australasia* (M.M.S.A.) Formerly the Australasian Wesleyan Methodist Missionary Society, this society sent a mission party under the leadership of the Rev. W. E. Bromilow to Dobu Island in the D'Entrecasteaux group. In 1890 Sir William MacGregor had arranged with the L.M.S. and the Anglican and Methodist missions for each to work in an area of British New Guinea allocated to it. The entry of the Methodists into south-east New Guinea was undertaken as a result of this arrangement.

1891 *The Australian Board of Missions* (*Anglican*), A.B.M. Under the arrangement of 1890 between the L.M.S., the Methodists and the Anglicans, the latter sent a mission party from Sydney in 1891 under the leadership of the Rev. Albert Maclaren and the Rev. Copland King. The party landed at Kaieta on the north-east coast of south-east New Guinea, and land for the headquarters was purchased at nearby Dogura.

1896 *The Society of the Divine Word* (*Societas Verbi Divini*), S.V.D. This society, based in Steyl, Holland, was entrusted in 1896 with the newly erected Prefecture Apostolic of Wilhelmsland. In August 1896 a mission party led by Father Eberhard Limbrock arrived at Friedrich-Wilhelmshafen (Madang) and in the same year the first station was established on Tumleo Island near Aitape. (Map drawn by Edgar Ford)

Plate 86. Jean-Baptiste Epalle (1808–1845), missionary of the Society of Mary. Epalle served under Bishop Pompallier in New Zealand from 1838 to 1842 and, as his coadjutor, was sent to Europe to act as agent for the mission in France and in Rome. In August 1843, Epalle submitted a plan to the Sacred Congregation of the Propaganda, setting out a scheme for the evangelization by Roman Catholic missionaries of the islands of New Guinea, New Britain and New Ireland. On 19 July 1844, Pope Gregory XVI erected by brief the Vicariate Apostolic of Melanesia and Micronesia, and Epalle was consecrated vicar apostolic (bishop) in the same month. At the end of 1845 a party of seven under Epalle's leadership arrived in the south Solomon Islands. A base was established on San Christobal Island. On 16 December 1845, while exploring San Isabel Island, the party was attacked and Epalle suffered a head wound that proved mortal. (Mitchell Library)

Plate 86

Plate 87a. Jean-Georges Collomb (1816–1848), missionary of the Society of Mary, who arrived on San Christobal Island on 21 August 1847, as successor to Bishop Epalle. He found that the mission had been carried on in very difficult conditions, and decided to move towards New Guinea by advancing to Woodlark Island. Here, in September 1847, a station was established near Guasopa. When, in April 1848, another missionary arrived, Collomb decided to expand the mission by establishing a station on Rooke (Umboi) Island. From here Collomb planned to reconnoitre the three main islands, New Guinea, New Britain, and New Ireland, which had been the original intention of Bishop Epalle. However, before this could be done, Bishop Collomb died of illness on 16 July 1848. (Mitchell Library)

Plate 87a

Plate 87b

Plate 87b. The Rev. Samuel Macfarlane (1837–1911), founder of the London Missionary Society's New Guinea mission in 1871. Macfarlane served the L.M.S. in the Loyalty Islands until 1871, circumstances there leading to the L.M.S. decision to enter New Guinea. In 1870 the French authorities declared Macfarlane *persona non grata*. At the same time the French relaxed a prohibition against the use of Loyalty Island mission teachers outside French territory. In these circumstances, the board of directors of the L.M.S. decided to send Macfarlane and a group of Loyalty Island teachers to New Guinea.

After placing teachers on the Torres Strait islands in 1871, Macfarlane went to England for consultation. During his absence the Rev. A. W. Murray, who had accompanied Macfarlane on the pioneer voyage, conducted the mission.

Macfarlane returned in 1874 and set up the New Guinea mission headquarters at Somerset, a Queensland government station on Cape York. In 1877, when the New Guinea mission was divided into two branches for administrative purposes, Macfarlane set up headquarters for the western division on Murray Island. He retired from the mission in 1886. (Mitchell Library)

Plate 88. René-Marie Lannuzel (1846–c. 1886), French secular priest, was designated apostolic missionary to the Vicariate of Melanesia in September 1880, and accompanied colonists to Port Breton in southern New Ireland, arriving there in October 1880. After five weeks at Port Breton in adverse conditions, Lannuzel went to Sydney to confer with members of the Society of Mary who had long experience in mission work in the Pacific Islands. He returned to Port Breton in February 1881, but the colony was virtually abandoned; Lannuzel thereupon went to the Gazelle Peninsula, building a hut near Nodup and commencing mission work there. When Father Navarre arrived in New Britain in September 1882, he took up the mission site at Nodup, Lannuzel meanwhile having left for Europe to report the truth about the Marquis de Rays' colony (plate 94) to Church authorities in Rome. (Mitchell Library)

Plate 88

Plate 89. George Brown (1835–1917), founder of the Wesleyan Methodist mission in New Britain in 1875. From 1860 until 1874, Brown served in Samoa and then came to Sydney to present his plan for the New Britain mission to the executive of the Australasian Wesleyan Methodist Missionary Society. Brown's scheme was adopted and he left for Fiji, where indigenous teachers were recruited from the Methodist training institution. Brown and his party landed at Port Hunter on Duke of York Island on 15 August 1875, and from then, until he withdrew on 4 January 1881, he directed the work of the mission, although absent from August 1876 to August 1877, and from May 1879 to March 1880. On 2 December 1878 he was joined by the Rev. Benjamin Danks. In 1890 Brown negotiated with Sir William MacGregor for the establishment of a mission in Papua; as a result, accompanied by W. E. Bromilow, he led a party in June 1891 to Dobu Island (D'Entrecasteaux group) and supervised the establishment of a new mission. From 1887 to 1908 Brown held the position of general secretary of the Australasian Board of Missions of the Methodist Church. As such he exercised great influence on Methodist mission activity in New Guinea. (Mitchell Library)

Plate 90

Plate 89

Plate 90. Louis-André Navarre (1836–1912), missionary of the Congregation of the Sacred Heart. Navarre established the Sacred Heart mission on a permanent basis in New Britain, beginning work at Nodup in September 1882 and, shortly after, on land he purchased at Kokopo, which developed later into the head station of Vunapope. Sacred Heart mission stations were also founded by Navarre at Volavolo and Malaguna in 1884. In October 1884, Navarre set up his headquarters on Thursday Island and from there directed his fellow missionary Henry Verjus to Yule Island in July 1885, to establish the beginning of the Papuan mission. In May 1887 Navarre was designated vicar apostolic (bishop) of Melanesia and administrator of Micronesia. When a separation of the vicariates of New Britain and British New Guinea was made in 1889, Navarre was designated vicar apostolic of the latter with the rank of archbishop. He retired in 1907. (Mitchell Library)

Plate 91. Johann Flierl (1858–1947) of the Lutheran (Neuendettelsau) mission. From 1875 to 1885 Flierl worked among the Aboriginal people of inland Australia. After the entry of Germany into New Guinea, the Neuendettelsau mission decided to extend operations to that area and, on 12 July 1886, Flierl arrived at Finschhafen to begin work. The site chosen by Flierl and a fellow missionary named Tremel was at Simbang in the vicinity of Finschhafen. Here began the Lutheran mission in New Guinea which, under Flierl's leadership, extended operations throughout a considerable population in the Madang region. (Mitchell Library)

Plate 92

Plate 91

Plate 92. Henry Stanislaus Verjus (1860–1892), missionary of the Congregation of the Sacred Heart, joined Father Navarre on Thursday Island in February 1885. In July of the same year Verjus was sent by Navarre to establish a mission site on Yule Island, and it was through his unremitting efforts that the mission was given permanence. In April 1887 Verjus was designated vicar apostolic (bishop), and in January 1890 he was appointed coadjutor to Navarre. He died in Europe of illness contracted in New Guinea on 13 November 1892. (Mitchell Library)

6 The Free Colony of 'New France', New Ireland, 1880-82

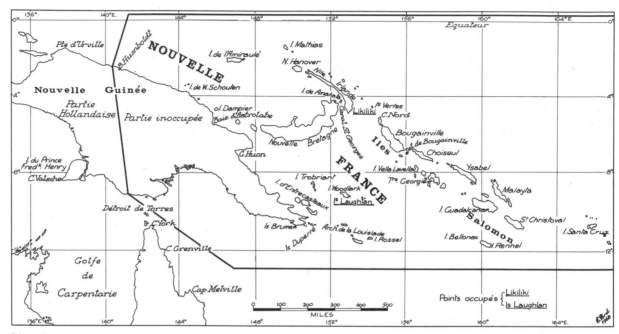

Plate 93

Plate 93. Nouvelle France, the territory claimed by the Marquis de Rays (see plate 94) in 1879 for his proposed Free Colony. In a speech to the Salon des Ouvres at Marseilles on 4 April 1879, the marquis said, 'But which part of the world will we choose? America and Asia are already taken. Africa with its unhealthy shores would not suit our purpose . . . . It is only Oceania which is still largely unoccupied . . . a suitable port has been found . . . in the south-east part of New Ireland which is an archipelago of New Britain. It is on the St George Channel and also on the long sea route between Australia and China.

'This port has been chosen wisely. It has been visited by Dumont d'Urville and commented on by Duperrey. Undoubtedly the French have greater right than any other nation to set themselves up there.

Furthermore we should not forget that we are at times merely individuals and that our government is in no way responsible for our actions.

'Our expedition can extend from Port Breton, today known as Port Praslin, over New Britain, the Louisiade Archipelago, which was discovered by our navigators, the Solomon Islands and New Guinea.

'The northern part of this last is already occupied by the Dutch who are our masters in this new type of colonisation. We could not miss out on these vast expanses of land.' Extract from a speech by the Marquis de Rays, 4 April 1879, to the Salon des Ouvres, Marseilles, in *La Colonie Libre de Port Breton: Nouvelle France en Océanie* (Marseilles, 1879), pp. 12–13. Translated from the French by Antoinette Wyllie. (Map drawn by Edgar Ford)

Plate 94. Charles Bonaventure du Breil, Marquis de Rays (1832–1893?); in France in 1879 he promoted a scheme for the founding of the Free Colony of New France with its capital at Port Breton (Port Praslin or Gower Harbour) in southern New Ireland (see plate 20). Between September 1879 and April 1881, the Marquis de Rays dispatched about one thousand colonists in four expeditions from Europe towards New Ireland. The marquis never visited the colony himself but relied on the reports of various French navigators, for example Bougainville and Duperrey, who had visited Port Praslin in 1768 and 1823 respectively. With the final failure of the colonization scheme in 1882, the public outcry in France led to the marquis being put on trial. He was sentenced to six years' imprisonment. (Hallstrom Pacific Library)

Plate 94

Plate 95. This engraving entitled 'Natives Cultivating Sugar Cane' was published in Brussels in 1882 in a book to advertise the advantages of buying land in Nouvelle France. The engraving had been published first in Paris in 1836, and the scene was set in Tahiti. (Mitchell Library)

Plate 95

Plate 96

Plate 96. The *Chandernagore*, commissioned by the Marquis de Rays to carry the first 150 of his colonists to Port Breton (Port Praslin) in southern New Ireland. She sailed in September 1879 from Flushing and arrived at Port Breton on 16 January 1880. The *Chandernagore* made a second voyage to Port Breton in August 1882, but by then the colony had been abandoned. The party of missionaries of the Congregation of the Sacred Heart on board who had embarked in Sydney for the colony were then landed on Matupi Island in Blanche Bay to begin work near there. (Mitchell Library)

Plate 97. The *Chandernagore* at the Laughlan Islands. In January 1880, during her first voyage from Europe to Port Breton, the *Chandernagore* called at the Laughlan Islands, which were within the territory of Nouvelle France claimed by the Marquis de Rays. The commander of the expedition, M. Titeu de La Croix (Baron de Villebranche), had a ceremonial meeting with 'King' Tomeo and had him recognize the Marquis de Rays as his liege lord. This is the scene in the engraving. Seventeen colonists were left on the Laughlan Islands to set up a trading post. They had only three months' supplies and suffered sickness and near starvation until they were evacuated by H.M.S. *Conflict* in June 1880. (Mitchell Library)

Plate 97

Plate 98

Plate 98. A contemporary sketch of Port Breton made at the end of 1881 by Captain Henry, governor of the colony. Irish Cove is on the left and English Cove, called Marie Bay by the colonists, on the right (see plate 43). The ships are the *Genil* on the left and the *Marquis de Rays* on the right. The buildings shown represent the full extent of building at Port Breton. (Mitchell Library)

Plate 99. The water race, quay and blockhouse at Port Breton (Irish Cove), on the site of what was planned by the Marquis de Rays to be the capital of New France. Still discernible today are the water race and the quay. (Mitchell Library)

Plate 99

54

Plate 100

Plate 100. Captain G. Rabardy, acting lieutenant governor of the Free Colony of Port Breton from August 1880 to August 1881. Rabardy, a Frenchman, sailed in command of the *Genil* in March 1880 with a party of Spaniards who were to act as a police force in the colony. He arrived at the Likiliki colony in August, where the remnants of the *Chandernagore* expedition were struggling to survive. Rabardy was supposed to prepare Irish Cove (see plate 20) for the arrival of the 340 colonists of the *India* expedition, which had sailed from Barcelona in July 1880. This expedition went on to Noumea, and Rabardy subsequently stayed in the area and became associated with Thomas Farrell in various trading activities. He provided help for Farrell in the punitive expedition against the people of Utuan Island in the Duke of York group, following the killing of the German naturalist Kleinschmidt in April 1881. Rabardy died in February 1882 at Farrell's station on Mioko Harbour, following the final abandonment of Port Breton. (Mitchell Library)

Plate 101

Plate 101. Captain Henry, commander of the fourth and final expedition to Port Breton and provisional governor of Nouvelle France, with two men of Lambon, Okela-menné and Tambrouk. Captain Henry arrived at Port Breton in September 1881 with about 150 colonists on board the *Nouvelle Bretagne*. Observing the deplorable state of the colony, which, since the departure of the *India* colonists for Noumea, had been left in charge of Captain Rabardy, Henry decided to sail for Manila to draw on funds there for additional necessary supplies. He took with him the two men of Lambon shown in the engraving. Henry found that in Manila there were no funds available as promised by the Marquis de Rays, and the financial difficulties of the colony led to Henry's arrest by a Spanish warship when he returned to Port Breton in January 1882. This warship, the *Legaspi*, evacuated about 60 sick colonists and took them to Manila. The remaining colonists negotiated with Thomas Farrell of Mioko in February 1882 for the sale of effects and their repatriation to Sydney in March. This was the final abandonment of the venture. (Mitchell Library)

7 European Claimants and Early Colonial Government

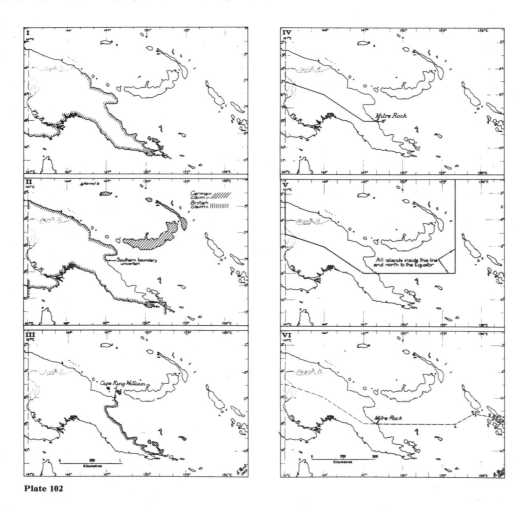

Plate 102

Plate 102. Maps I–VI: the partition of eastern New Guinea (1884–86) by Great Britain and Germany.

Background. On 24 August 1828, the Dutch flag was raised over Fort du Bus on Triton Bay (plate 39) and possession was taken on behalf of the Netherlands government of all that part of New Guinea as far to the east as 141° east longitude. In 1875 the Netherlands government defined its 1828 claim by fixing on the 140° 47′ east longitude as its eastern boundary in New Guinea. (See Paul W. van der Veur, *Search for New Guinea's Boundaries* [Canberra, 1966], pp. 10–13.)

Various proclamations by British officers taking possession of New Guinea territory, including those of Lieutenant C. B. Yule, R.N., at Cape Possession in 1846 (plate 28) and of Captain Moresby, R.N., at Hayter Island in 1873 (plate 103), were not acknowledged by the British government. The claim in 1880 by the Marquis de Rays to the whole of New Guinea and adjacent islands outside the Dutch possession for his free colony of Nouvelle France (see plate 93) was given no international recognition.

In 1883 the Queensland government, disturbed by the increasing German influence in the South Pacific, attempted to secure the territory of New Guinea outside the Dutch possession. Henry M. Chester, the resident magistrate at Thursday Island, was ordered to Port Moresby and there, on 4 April 1883, he proclaimed British sovereignty over the territory of New Guinea lying between 141° and 155° east longitude (see plate 104). This action was repudiated by the British government.

Map I. In acting thus the British government was much criticized in the Australian colonies; in response to such criticism it forwarded a proposal on 19 September 1884 to the German government in which was stated the intention to proclaim a protectorate '. . . over all the coasts of New Guinea not occupied by the Netherlands Government, except that portion of the north coast comprised between the 145th degree of east longitude and the Eastern Dutch Boundary.'

Map II. Official German reaction to this proposal led the British government to settle for the south coast east of 141° east longitude to East Cape, and the islands adjacent south of East Cape to Kosmann Island. This territory was proclaimed by Hugh H. Romilly in a premature ceremony at Port Moresby on 23 October 1884 (see plate 106) and later by Commodore Erskine in the official ceremony on 6 November 1884 (see plate 108).

At the same time the German government proclaimed its protectorate over the north coast of the mainland of New Guinea from the 141st meridian to the Huon Gulf and also the Admiralty, Hermit and Anchorite Island groups and New Britain and New Ireland with adjacent islands. Map II shows these British and German claims of 1884.

Map III. In 1885 Commodore Erskine was ordered to extend the British Protectorate over the territory between East Cape and the Huon Gulf up to Cape King William and including the D'Entrecasteaux group, Woodlark Island and the islands adjacent to the north coast including Long Island and Rooke (Umboi) Island. Flag-raising ceremonies and proclamation readings were held in early 1885 at various places in the newly proclaimed territory.

Map IV. In April 1885 the British and German governments arrived at a compromise regarding their boundary—starting from the coast in the neighbourhood of Mitre Rock on the 8th parallel of south latitude, and following this parallel to the point where it is cut by 147° east longitude, then in a straight line north-west to the point where the 6th parallel of south latitude cuts 144° east longitude, and continuing west-north-west to the point of intersection of the 5th parallel of south latitude and 141° east longitude. (See Paul W. van der Veur, *Search for New Guinea's Boundaries* [Canberra, 1966], pp. 18–20.)

Map V. In May 1855 the German government gave the Neuguinea-Kompagnie the following area of administration: the Bismarck Archipelago and all other islands north-east of New Guinea situated between the Equator and 8° south latitude and between 141° and 154° east longitude. The company was also given jurisdiction over that part of the mainland of New Guinea outside British or Dutch sovereignty.

Map VI. On 6 April 1886 an agreement was signed between the British and German governments fixing the spheres of influence of the two governments in the western Pacific. This laid down a line of demarcation that confirmed the previous boundary on the main island and then determined the division of the Solomon Islands group, placing Shortland Island, Choiseul and Ysabel under German authority. In 1904 this boundary was rectified by an Anglo-German agreement to acknowledge British protection over the Solomons south of Bougainville Island. (Maps drawn by Edgar Ford)

Plate 103. Hoisting the flag at Possession Bay, Hayter Island, south-east New Guinea, 24 April 1873. Captain Moresby read a proclamation. 'I, John Moresby, captain in the Royal Navy, commanding Her Majesty's ship *Basilisk* having discovered three considerable islands, from hence forth to be known as Moresby, Hayter and Basilisk islands . . . do hereby by right of discovery take possession of all the aforesaid islands.' The British Crown showed no more interest in this claim than it had in previous claims made by McCluer, Hayes and Yule. In 1791 Lieutenant John McCluer, an officer of the British East India Company's naval force, had surveyed the large inlet on the west coast that bears his name, and claimed that part of New Guinea for the Crown. Two years later, Lieutenant John Hayes of the Bombay Marine attempted to form a settlement at Dorei Bay. He renamed the harbour Restoration Bay and the region New Albion, and took possession of it on behalf of Britain. In 1846, Lieutenant C. B. Yule in H.M.S. *Bramble* took possession of New Guinea at Cape Possession (see plate 28). Yule's action probably stirred the Dutch to formalize their claim to west New Guinea in 1849, for in that year a combined Dutch and Malay expedition was dispatched to perfect the Dutch claim by the placing of markers bearing the Dutch coat of arms along the New Guinea coast. No additional claims were made by the Dutch until 1875, when the interior boundary of the Dutch claim was announced in the Kolonial Verslag as a straight line connecting the eastern shore of Humboldt Bay, 140° 47′ E., with the 141st meridian in the south. (Mitchell Library)

Plate 103

Plate 104

Plate 104. Henry Marjoribanks Chester (1832–1914), representing the Queensland government, proclaiming the annexation of south-east New Guinea in April 1883. 'On the afternoon of 3 April, the *Pearl* belonging to the Queensland Government arrived at Port Moresby with Mr H. M. Chester, police magistrate from Thursday Island, on board. At 10 o'clock next morning Mr Chester formally annexed New Guinea by reading a proclamation and hoisting the Union Jack. This was saluted immediately by the two guns of the *Pearl*. The Europeans present were Mr H. M. Chester, Revs W. G. Lawes and J. Chalmers, Messrs A. Goldie, C. Hunston, Walsh, Wilson, Exton and five men from the *Pearl*. There were about 200 natives present with the chief of Port Moresby, Boevagi.' (See plate 117.) The secretary of state for the colonies, Lord Derby, repudiated this action of the Queensland government. Text with the engraving from the *Australasian Sketcher*, 4 June 1883, p. 10. (National Library of Australia)

Plate 105. This cartoon comment in the Sydney *Bulletin* of 9 June 1883 looked at the Queensland annexation of New Guinea in 1883 against the background of the Queensland labour trade and the fate of that colony's Aboriginal people. (Mitchell Library)

Plate 106. 'I made rather an ass of myself or rather other people made an ass of me,' wrote H. H. Romilly of this premature flag-raising ceremony at the L.M.S. mission, Port Moresby, on 23 October 1884. Unknown to Romilly, Commodore Erskine was on his way to Port Moresby with a naval squadron, and the formal proclamation of the British Protectorate was made by him. (Mitchell Library)

Plate 106

Plate 107

Plate 107. The hoisting of the German flag at Mioko, Duke of York Islands, on 4 November 1884. On the previous day a similar ceremony had taken place at Matupi. Otto Finsch (see plate 67) was present on both occasions and recorded: '. . . It was then that we heard the happy tidings, namely, that the German possessions in the Archipelago of New Britain were to be placed under the protection of the Reich, which solemn act took place in Matupi with all due ceremony on November 3rd. It was a fine sight when 250 men landed expeditiously and in splendid formation took up their posts in the spacious grounds of the Hernsheim station. Then Captain Schering at His Majesty's behest read the short Proclamation, the troops presented arms and to the strains of *Heil Dir im Siegeskranz* [the German national anthem], the salute of guns and three cheers for His Majesty, the naval ensign was raised aloft and fluttered in the breeze.

'Next day the same ceremony was enacted at Mioko in the grounds of Handels-und Plantagen Gesellschaft in the presence of various chiefs from the Duke of York Islands who had been invited to attend.' Translated from the German by Marie von Hein. (Mitchell Library)

Plate 108

Plate 108. The proclamation by Commodore J. E. Erskine of the Royal Navy, Australia Station, of the British Protectorate over south-east New Guinea at Port Moresby on 6 November 1884. The proclamation read in part: 'To all to whom these Presents shall come Greeting: Whereas it has become essential for the protection of the lives and properties of the native inhabitants of New Guinea, and for the purpose of preventing the occupation of portions of that country by persons whose proceedings, unsanctioned by any lawful authority, might tend to injustice, strife and bloodshed, and who, under the pretence of legitimate trade and intercourse, might endanger the liberties and possess themselves of the lands of such native inhabitants, that a British Protectorate should be established over a certain portion of such country and the islands adjacent thereto.' The proclamation is being made from the veranda of the L.M.S. mission house of the Rev. W. G. Lawes. (Mitchell Library)

Plate 109

Plate 110

Plate 109. 'How happy I could be with neither' is the remark attributed to New Guinea as she is wooed by Germany and Britain. A Sydney *Bulletin* comment of January 1885. (Library of New South Wales)

Plate 110. A comment in the Sydney *Bulletin* on the proclamation of the British Protectorate over south-east New Guinea in 1884. (Library of New South Wales)

Plate 111. Bismarck, the German eagle, and the chickens of the South Pacific—a view of New Guinea in a dangerous world as commented on from Sydney in June 1886. (Library of New South Wales)

Plate 111

Plate 112. The proclamation of the British Protectorate over south-east New Guinea at Kerepunu by Commodore Erskine and the officers of H.M.S. *Nelson* in November 1884. (Mitchell Library)

Plate 112

Plate 113. This engraving, entitled 'Port Moresby Natives in Typical Attitudes', was published in the *Australasian Sketcher* in October 1885 and was, no doubt, an attempt by the artist to tell the Australian public something of the people to the north who in the previous year had come under the queen's protection. (National Library of Australia)

Plate 113

A. British New Guinea, 1884-1907

Plate 114. Sir Peter H. Scratchley (1835–1885), appointed special commissioner for the Protectorate of New Guinea on 22 November 1884, arrived at Port Moresby 28 August 1885, and visited various parts of the Protectorate. He died on board the S.S. *Governor Blackall* off Cooktown in December 1885. (Mitchell Library)

Plate 115. An engraving from the *Australasian Sketcher*, 21 October 1885, of a group on board the S.S. *Governor Blackall* in Port Jackson as Sir Peter Scratchley set out for New Guinea. The three men standing at left are, from left to right, Captain Lake of S.S. *Governor Blackall*; Colonel Roberts, R.A.; Mr Hugh Massey. The two women seated in front of the wheel are Mrs Massey (on the left) and Lady Scratchley; the man seated in front is Captain Shellard; the man standing at the back on the right is Mr Fort, Sir Peter Scratchley's private secretary, and to his right is Dr Glanville, Sir Peter Scratchley's physician; on the extreme right, Sir Peter Scratchley. (National Library of Australia)

Plate 114

Plate 115

Plate 116

Plate 116. Hugh Hastings Romilly (1856–1892), appointed deputy commissioner for the Western Pacific in 1881. He visited New Britain, New Ireland, the Admiralty Islands and New Guinea inquiring into the affairs of British subjects.

On this tour he held a magisterial inquiry into the Mioko massacre (Duke of York group, 1880). In 1883 during a second tour of duty Romilly stayed at E. Hernsheim's trading station on Matupi Island and inquired into the activities of British labour recruiters in the area. In November 1884, he was at Port Moresby at the proclamation of the British Protectorate over south-east New Guinea. After Sir Peter Scratchley's death he acted as special commissioner from December 1885 to the end of February 1886. Appointed deputy commissioner in New Guinea in 1887, he carried out his duties until he was superseded in September 1888, on the proclamation of British sovereignty. (Mitchell Library)

Plate 117

Plate 117. Boi Vagi, the chief of the Auna-patu or Port Moresby people in 1884, to whom Commodore Erskine, on the occasion of the proclamation of the Protectorate, presented a silver-mounted ebony stick as a symbol of authority committed to him by Her Majesty Queen Victoria. On his deathbed, Boi Vagi requested that his daughter, Kabadi, inherit the duties of his office. Kabadi felt unequal to the task, so the office was given to A-a-to, the next in lineal descent. Douglas wrote to Granville, 'I begged Kabadi, who is an estimable woman, to depend on my friendship, and I encouraged her to rely on me for assistance if she required it, in the Education of her children, exhorting them at the same time, to respect the memory and to emulate the virtues of the old chief, their grandfather.' Special Commissioner Douglas to Her Majesty's Secretary of State for the Colonies, Port Moresby, 16 July 1886. *Home Correspondence*, no. 34, p. 189. (Hallstrom Pacific Library)

Plate 118

Plate 118. In the course of his first journey on board S.S. *Governor Blackall*, eastwards from Port Moresby, Sir Peter Scratchley called at Kapa Kapa. He recorded: 'THURSDAY, SEPTEMBER 24th [1885]. We decided to take a rest at Kapa Kapa, and not to land today. Seventeen chiefs came on board and received presents. We had a long talk with them, because it appeared that there was a quarrel between the hill tribes and those on the coast. I told the chiefs that I insisted upon there being no fighting, and that they were to make up their differences. They agreed to, but we shall see whether they will keep their promises.' C. Kinlock Cooke, *Australian Defences and New Guinea: Compiled from the Papers of the Late Major-General Sir Peter Scratchley, R.E., K.C.M.G.* (London, 1887), p. 230. (London Missionary Society)

Plate 119. The Hon. John Douglas (1828–1904), appointed special commissioner for British New Guinea on 27 February 1886, following the death of Sir Peter Scratchley. Douglas held this appointment until the proclamation of sovereignty on 4 September 1888, when he was succeeded by Sir William MacGregor as administrator. (*Commonwealth Records* CRS A24, reproduced by permission of the Commonwealth Archives Office)

Plate 119

Plate 120

Plate 120. Sir William MacGregor, the first administrator of British New Guinea, at the time of his appointment, 4 September 1888. MacGregor was chief medical officer on Sir Arthur Gordon's staff in Fiji, where he gained experience in various aspects of colonial government. During his term in New Guinea, MacGregor laid down policies of lasting value. MacGregor retired in 1898 when arrangements for the transfer of control of the territory to Australia were being undertaken. (*Commonwealth Records* CRS A24, reproduced by permission of the Commonwealth Archives Office)

Plate 121. The Government Bungalow, Port Moresby, in the early 1900s; prefabricated in Townsville, the building was erected on a site chosen by Sir Peter Scratchley and was completed for occupation by the beginning of 1886. In July 1886, Special Commissioner Douglas informed Lord Granville, 'I have the honour to forward herewith, a copy of a communication addressed to me by Mr Assistant Deputy Commissioner Musgrave, giving a description of the Government Bungalow.

'It is beautifully situated on a healthy eminence commanding a magnificent view of the surrounding country, of Port Moresby, and of Fairfax Harbour, with Mt Scratchley in the distance to the northward.

'A rounded hill to the southward with an elevation of about 800 feet, I have named Goldie Law, in honour of Mr Goldie who is the oldest settler in New Guinea.' Douglas to Granville, 29 July 1886. *Despatches from Special Commissioner Douglas to H.M.'s Secretary of State for the Colonies,* pp. 191–2. (Mitchell Library)

Plate 121

Plate 122

Plate 122. Portrait of New Guinea magistrate M. H. Moreton, who served in British New Guinea from 1889 to 1905, first as assistant resident magistrate, Central Division, for a short term (1890–92) as private secretary to Sir William MacGregor, and then from 1892 to 1905 as resident magistrate in the Eastern Division (Samarai) and in the South-eastern Division (Bonagai). C. A. W. Monckton, a fellow magistrate, wrote in characteristic manner, 'Moreton, a younger brother of the present Earl of Ducie, had begun life in the Seaforth Highlanders: plucky, hard-working, and best of good fellows, he was fated to work on in New Guinea till, with his constitution shattered, an Australian Government chucked him out to make room for a younger man: shortly after which he died.' *Some Experiences of a New Guinea Resident Magistrate* (London, 1921), pp. 22–23. (*Commonwealth Records* CRS A24, reproduced by permission of the Commonwealth Archives Office)

Plate 123. Anthony Musgrave, appointed assistant deputy commissioner of British New Guinea in May 1885, and government secretary from 4 September 1888. Musgrave also acted as resident magistrate, Central Division, and as treasurer. He resigned on 30 June 1908. (*Commonwealth Records* CRS A24, reproduced by permission of the Commonwealth Archives Office)

Plate 123

Plate 124

Plate 124. Sir George Le Hunte, lieutenant governor of British New Guinea from 1898 to 1903 in succession to Sir William MacGregor. During Le Hunte's term of office, negotiations went on between the Colonial Office in London and the Australian colonies about whether British New Guinea should be under joint control or Australian control. The Papua Act, which decided in favour of the latter, was not passed until 1905. (Mitchell Library)

Plate 125. Captain F. R. Barton, administrator 1904–07, assumed office shortly before the death by suicide of the acting administrator, C. S. Robinson, on 16 June 1904. He held the post until succeeded by J. H. P. Murray in March 1907. Barton was commandant of the Armed Native Constabulary before his appointment as administrator. (Mitchell Library)

Plate 125

Plate 126. The officers of the Papuan administration in 1906. Left to right, Messrs F. Weekley and C. A. W. Monckton; Judge Murray; Captain F. R. Barton (administrator); Messrs D. Ballantine, A. M. Campbell, W. Whitten and W. Little. (Information and Extension Services, Administration of Papua New Guinea)

Plate 126

Plate 127. Andrew Goldie, pioneer explorer, storekeeper and gold prospector of New Guinea. Born in Ayrshire in 1840, Goldie came to Port Moresby in 1875 as a botanical collector and subsequently opened a store near Hanuabada village. He carried out trading and exploration trips along the coast from Port Moresby and discovered Alice Meade Lagoon, Millport Harbour and Port Glasgow. He also explored the hinterland of Port Moresby and discovered the first gold in New Guinea in the basin of the Goldie River in 1877. Goldie acted as collector for many of the world's museums and supplied them with specimens of Papuan ethnology. He was agent for Burns, Philp and Company in Port Moresby until 1891 when he sold out to that firm. (*Commonwealth Records* CRS A24, reproduced by permission of the Commonwealth Archives Office)

Plate 127

Plate 128. Henry Ogg Forbes arrived at Port Moresby in August 1885 in command of an exploration expedition under the auspices of the Royal Geographical Society, the Royal Scientific Geographical Society and the British government. He established a base camp at Sogeri, but Sir Peter Scratchley's death caused postponement of exploration. He was appointed by Douglas as deputy commissioner at Dinner Island (Samarai), and later became government meteorologist at Port Moresby. In 1887 Forbes resumed his exploration work and penetrated to the headwaters of the Goldie River. He observed the peak of the Owen Stanley Range that Sir William MacGregor later named Mount Victoria. (Mitchell Library)

Plate 129. The Royal Commission of 1906 at Samarai; seated, left to right, W. E. Parry-Okeden, formerly police commissioner of Queensland; Colonel J. A. K. Mackay, chairman, member of Legislative Council of New South Wales; C. E. Herbert, formerly government resident and judge in the Northern Territory and member for the Northern Territory in the South Australian parliament. Standing on the left, George Belford, government guide, and on the right, E. Harris, secretary to the Royal Commission. A member of the Armed Native Constabulary is on the extreme right and the others in the group are men from the Samarai region. The Royal Commission was asked by the Commonwealth government to inquire into 'the present conditions, including the methods of Government of the territory now known as Papua, and the best means for their improvement'. The Commissioners arrived at Port Moresby in September 1906 and spent two months travelling in Papua, returning to Melbourne in early December. The report of the Commission, published in 1907, said that the policy of the future should be to encourage enterprise in Papua and to pursue economic expansion. (Mitchell Library)

Plate 128

Plate 129

Plate 130. Members of the Royal Commission at Kokoda. Left to right, Mr Justice Herbert, Mr Charles Monckton, government officer at Kokoda, Colonel J. A. K. Mackay, chairman of the Commission. (Mitchell Library)

Plate 131. The *Merrie England*, the government vessel used by Sir William MacGregor to make contact with the coastal peoples of British New Guinea in an endeavour to bring the new subjects of the queen under her protection. The difficulties of overland travel meant that great dependence was placed on this vessel. The *Merrie England* was used by members of the Royal Commission for their tour of Papua in 1906. (Mitchell Library)

Plate 131

Plate 130

B. German New Guinea, 1884-1914

Plate 132

Plate 132. Adolph von Hansemann (1827–1903), the director of the Disconto-Gesellschaft and the founder of the Neuguinea-Kompagnie. In 1878 von Hansemann arranged for the absorption of the firm of Godeffroy by the Deutsche Handels-und Plantagen Gesellschaft (D.H. & P.G.). Under his guidance, a consortium was then formed. On 26 May 1884, with Bismarck's banker Bleichroder and two other political personalities, Ekardstein-Protzel and Hammacher, von Hansemann founded the Neuguinea-Kompagnie. Herr Hansemann's brother-in-law, Heinrich von Kusserow, was Bismarck's chief adviser in the Foreign Office. The consortium commissioned Dr Otto Finsch (see plate 67) to establish footholds in New Guinea by negotiating land from the New Guineans. In August 1884, Bismarck, who had been converted to protectionism and an active colonial policy, guaranteed the protection of the Reich to all areas occupied by the Neuguinea-Kompagnie. On 17 May 1885 Bismarck granted a charter that delineated the rights of the company. Dr H. Schnee said that von Hansemann 'tried to run New Guinea from his office desk in Berlin as if it were a feudal estate in Brandenburg'. H. Schnee, *Als Letzter Gouverneur in Deutsche-Ostafrika: Errinerungen* (Heidelberg, 1964), p. 26. (Landeshauptstadt und Universitätsstadt, Mainz, Stadtbibliothek)

Plate 133

Plate 133. The house of the district controller of German New Guinea in Finschhafen in the 1880s. From November 1885 until March 1891, Finschhafen was the centre of German administration. Von Schleinitz, who administered the Protectorate until March 1888, combined in his person powers of supreme administrative, judicial and commercial head, and his successor, Kraetke, combined the same powers until November 1889. There was then a separation of officers of the administration of the Protectorate from the commercial management; Imperial Commissioner Rose became supreme official, and Arnold the director-general of the Neuguinea-Kompagnie. After Arnold's death, Rose took over the office of director-general until July 1890, when Ed. Wissman became director-general. Wissman died in office in February 1891, an epidemic at this time leading to the abandonment of Finschhafen for Stephansort, where Rose continued in office again as administrative head and director-general of the Neuguinea-Kompagnie. (National Library of Australia)

Plate 134

Plate 134. German employees of the Neuguinea-Kompagnie at Finschhafen in the 1880s. Finschhafen was the first centre from which the Kompagnie administered Kaiser-Wilhelmsland, Neu Pommern (New Britain), Neu Mecklenburg (New Ireland) and Neu Lauenburg (Duke of York Islands). It was founded on 5 November 1885, named after the man who selected the site, Dr Otto Finsch (see plate 67), and abandoned in March 1891 on account of high mortality. In 1891 there was an epidemic at Finschhafen which, within six weeks, claimed the lives of eleven employees of the Kompagnie, including the medical officer. Stephan von Kotze, a nephew of Bismarck and surveyor in the German Protectorate, said that the two most frequented spots in Finschhafen were the cemetery and the hotel. 'I am one of the few to get out of that malaria-hole Finschhafen with a whole skin,' he wrote, 'because I treated the fever with alcohol instead of quinine, and the orders of the Neuguinea-Kompagnie similarly—with alcohol instead of respect.' S. von Kotze, *Aus Papuas Kulturmorgen* (Berlin, 1905). (National Library of Australia)

Plate 135. The Imperial District Court of Law on Kerawera, the most southerly island of the Duke of York group. Von Schleinitz, administrator of German New Guinea from 1886 to 1888, combined the powers of supreme administrative, judicial and commercial head, and established his headquarters on Kerawera. He tried to start a coffee plantation in New Britain, but a tidal wave destroyed it before planting could begin. His successors, Kraetke (administrator), Rose (imperial commissioner) and Arnold (director-general of the Kompagnie), continued the search for suitable plantation sites. In 1890 Kerawera was abandoned because of its small area and the Kompagnie established itself on Blanche Bay (Herbertshöhe station) to grow cotton. By 1891 branch stations had been established to experiment in growing tobacco at Hatzfeldthafen, cotton and copra at Konstantinhafen, cotton on the Maclay Coast and cotton and tobacco at Stephansort. In the end the enterprises in the Bismarck Archipelago proved far more prosperous than those on the mainland. (Staatsbibliothek, Berlin)

Plate 135

Plate 136. The house of the Neuguinea-Kompagnie administrator, Müller, about 1912, in Stephansort (Bogadjim). Stephansort was founded in August 1888 and became the centre for German administration of the Protectorate in mid-March 1891 when Finschhafen was abandoned. It was hoped that Stephansort would have a healthier climate, but it was soon found to be even less healthy than Finschhafen, for it claimed the lives of twenty-five Europeans before it was abandoned in September 1892 for Friedrich-Wilhelmshafen (Madang). (Hallstrom Pacific Library)

Plate 136
Plate 137

Plate 137. The trade store in Stephansort, about 1912. After the failure of cotton as a commercial venture, German planters thought to replace cotton by kapok and sisal. Stephansort was the centre of German administration of the Protectorate from March 1891. By 1895 Stephansort had a hospital, a Chinese store, a residence and offices for the landeshauptmann (district commissioner), a club house, a park with a shooting stand, a number of private European houses, and twenty labour houses, each accommodating about fifty Chinese, Javanese or Melanesians. (Hallstrom Pacific Library)

Plate 138

Plate 138. Kurt von Hagen, who from 1893 was manager of the Astrolabe Kompagnie and director-general of the Neuguinea-Kompagnie, and from October 1896, provisional administrator based at Stephansort. He died in office on 14 August 1897, murdered by one of the two Buka Islanders, Ranga and Opia, who accompanied Otto Ehlers and W. Piering on their tragic attempt to make a coast-to-coast crossing of New Guinea in 1895 (see plate 554). Ranga and Opia were charged with the murder of Ehlers and Piering, and were held at Stephansort to await trial. They escaped and in August 1897 they were reported to be in Gorib. Von Hagen set out with four German officials and thirty New Guineans to capture them. As they approached the village a shot was fired, and von Hagen fell, mortally wounded. Ranga and Opia escaped but were later killed by Gaib people. (Landeshauptstadt und Universitätsstadt, Mainz, Stadtbibliothek)

Plate 139. A ceremonial peace ceremony concluded between Europeans and people of Friedrich-Wilhelmshafen (Madang), German New Guinea, 1898. (M. von Hein Collection)

Plate 139

Plate 140

Plate 140. Dr Runge, a German medical practitioner, rests on the veranda of his bungalow in Friedrich-Wilhelmshafen (Madang) in 1894. Dr Runge was taken prisoner by the Allies in World War I, but was returned to Germany in 1916 when an exchange was arranged between him and an English prisoner of war held in Germany. (Mitchell Library)

Plate 141

Plate 141. A street in Friedrich-Wilhelmshafen (Madang) about 1912. (Hallstrom Pacific Library)

Plate 142. The mess in Friedrich-Wilhelmshafen (Madang) about 1912. Friedrich-Wilhelmshafen became the centre for German administration of the Protectorate from September 1892 when Stephausort was abandoned. It remained the main station until the autumn of 1896, when Stephansort once again became administrative headquarters. (Hallstrom Pacific Library)

Plate 142

Plate 143

Plate 143. Dr Albert Hahl (1868–1945), who was appointed imperial judge at Herbertshöhe (Kokopo) at the age of twenty-eight. For three years he was the only imperial representative in the eastern part of the Protectorate. His next appointment was as deputy governor of German New Guinea, with his seat at Ponape in the east Carolines. Hahl held this position from July 1899 to June 1901, when he became acting governor of German New Guinea, replacing the ailing von Benningsen. Shortly after taking up this appointment he was striken by blackwater fever and returned to Europe to recover. On 20 November 1902, he was appointed governor of German New Guinea. His career in New Guinea was cut short by the outbreak of World War I. After the war he was appointed director of the Neuguinea-Kompagnie, a position that became largely honorary following the expropriation of German properties. Dr. Hahl's policy in New Guinea was to give equal weight to indigenous and European interests and to establish a plantation economy that would ultimately benefit the local societies as well as the Europeans. (Landeshauptstadt und Universitätsstadt, Mainz, Stadtbibliothek)

Plate 144. A headman with his two brothers in Neu Pommern (New Britain) about 1896. A man like this *Häuptling* was selected in each community for his energy and wealth by Dr Albert Hahl (see plate 143) and installed in the office of *luluai*. The Germans themselves always referred to the *luluais* as chiefs, magistrates or constables. The first three chiefs were appointed in August 1896 near Ralum. Others were appointed in the Duke of York Islands and in the Gazelle Peninsula. Hahl recorded: 'It is not difficult to persuade the inhabitants of the nearby villages to elect one of their clan leaders as their *luluai*, as their acknowledged head who would be responsible to me. He would come to me with their disputes immediately if they were of a serious nature, otherwise he would settle them himself and report to me on the great court days from time to time.' Albert Hahl, *Gouverneurs Jahre in Neuguinea* (Berlin, 1937), pp. 35–6. (Staatsbibliothek, Berlin)

Plate 144

Plate 145. Dr H. Schnee, who succeeded Dr Albert Hahl (see plate 143) as imperial judge at Ponape in February 1899. Schnee was extremely critical of the Neuguinea-Kompagnie's administration and particularly of its director, Adolph von Hansemann (see plate 132). On his way to Ponape, Schnee stopped briefly at Friedrich-Wilhelmshafen and Stephansort and was appalled to see machinery lying about going to rust and tobacco plantations covered with weeds. 'I did not know whether to pity the futility of it all or to be amazed that an experienced man of affairs like Hansemann should have failed so utterly,' he wrote. H. Schnee, *Als Letzter Gouverneur in Deutsche-Ostafrika: Errinerungen* (Heidelberg, 1964), p. 27. (Troponinstitut, Hamburg)

Plate 145

Plate 146. Headquarters of Hernsheim and Company in New Britain, *c.* 1910. (M. von Hein Collection)

Plate 146

Plate 147

Plate 147. A group of Germans from the Kavieng district in 1910. At centre left is Boluminski, district officer at Kavieng; on Boluminski's left in the centre row is Curt Schultze (Lebrechtshof plantation), and to his left in the front row is Captain Macco (Ulul Nono plantation). In the front row on the extreme left is Franz Kirchner, local manager for Hasag. (H. L. Schultze Collection)

Plate 148

Plate 148. The medical officer of the German administration, Dr Wilhelm Wendland, in front of the hotel building at Herbertshöhe (Kokopo) in 1906. (Mitchell Library)

Plate 149. Dr Albert Hahl (centre front), governor of German New Guinea (see plate 143), with leading businessmen and officers from a visiting cruiser. (M. von Hein Collection)

Plate 149

Plate 150

Plate 150. Leading businessmen farewelling Dr Albert Hahl before his departure for Europe. Dr Hahl is seen at top of steps, centre. Rabaul, April 1914. (M. von Hein Collection)

Plate 151. The sanitarium built by the German administration at Toma, in the mountains behind Rabaul, 1905. This was a cool weekend retreat for Europeans, who could enjoy here the novelty of sleeping under blankets. (M. von Hein Collection)

Plate 151

Plate 152

Plate 152. A detachment of German indigenous police in naval-style uniform. The photograph was taken in 1901 by E. S. Merriett, an American tourist in New Britain. (R. Clark Collection)

Plate 153. Bernhard Frommund, police inspector and harbourmaster at Friedrich-Wilhelmshafen (Madang) from 1905 to 1908. He related his experiences in German New Guinea in *Deutsch-Neuguinea*, sub-titled *A Pearl of the Pacific*. (M. von Hein Collection)

Plate 154. The German residency at Kaewieng (Kavieng), Neu Mecklenburg (New Ireland), about 1900. The district office here administered the northern section of New Ireland and Neu Hannover (New Hanover). This photograph shows the eastern aspect of the residency, which stood on a high hill and looked towards the island of Nusa. The government coconut plantation lay at the foot of the hill, so that the residence overlooked the tallest palms. (Mitchell Library)

Plate 154

Plate 153

Plate 155

Plate 155. The western aspect of the German residence at Kavieng, New Ireland (see plate 154). The centre portion of the residence is seen at the top of the eighty stone steps that led down to the waterfront. To the right of the main office, at centre, were the district office and the rooms of the chief officer; to the left of the main office were the clerks' offices, the police offices, the police barracks and the gaol. The residence was built by Boluminski, a district officer of the German administration. Boluminski had been a sergeant of police in German East Africa and he was sent from there to New Guinea as district officer. (B. Backus Collection)

Plate 156. The district office of the German administration at Kavieng, New Ireland. (M. von Hein Collection)

Plate 156

8 The Founding of European Towns

Plate 157

Plate 157. The beginning of European settlement at Port Moresby, a view *c.* 1880 from Elevala Island. Hanuabada village is on the right. The building nearest the shore on the right is Andrew Goldie's first store. The other buildings include the London Missionary Society's mission house on the left and the church at the rear. (Mitchell Library)

Plate 158

Plate 158. Port Moresby in 1886, a view looking towards Paga Point from the Government Bungalow. This photograph was taken by an English traveller, Reginald Gallop, who stayed at the Government Bungalow in 1886, and is the left-hand photo of a group of four, which together form the first panoramic view of Port Moresby and Fairfax Harbour. (Mitchell Library)

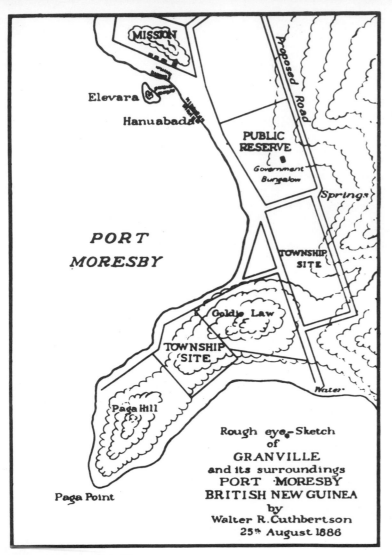

Plate 159

Plate 160

Plate 159. Walter Cuthbertson was a South Australian surveyor who, on instruction from Special Commissioner Douglas, surveyed the town site of Granville (Port Moresby) as shown here. Cuthbertson reported on 21 September 1886: 'I have the honour to make the following report in connection with the surveys that I have completed—viz., the townships of Granville East and West, public reserves, native and mission reserves, cemetery, etc. . . . The township of Granville West, situated near Paga Point, or, I should say, between Paga Hill and Goldie Law, and extending from the Port Moresby beach to Ila Beach, comprises about 50 acres of land. . . . The township of Granville East lies about eighty chains north-easterly from Granville West, and is so far cut up into eight sections. . . .' Cuthbertson to the Deputy Commissioner, 21 September 1886, in *British New Guinea Report for the Year 1886* (Brisbane, 1887), appendix C, no. 1, pp. 11–12. (Mitchell Library)

Plate 160. Samarai in the early twentieth century. Established as a government station in 1886, Samarai became the administrative centre for the Eastern District of British New Guinea and remained an important commercial centre until World War II. W. D. Pitcairn, who visited Samarai in the early 1890s, wrote of its beginning: 'There is a swamp of seven acres in the middle, the home of malarial fever, thus making this island one of the most unhealthy spots in New Guinea. A government agent is located there and has charge of the customs. In the time of the Protectorate, a large wooden bungalow was built on top of the highest hill by Rooney and Co. of Townsville costing the sum of £900. About 60 natives lived on the island which had been their home for many years. In August, 1888, just previous to the acquisition of New Guinea as a British possession, they were all driven away, or ephemistically [*sic*] got notice to quit. . . . The natives were naturally incensed at being thus rudely driven from their island home, where they had lived for so many years. . . . They will never forget it, and would retaliate, but know that they are powerless to act.' W. D. Pitcairn, *Two Years Among the Savages of New Guinea* (London, 1897), pp. 47–9. (Mitchell Library)

Plate 161. Early development of Granville West as Port Moresby's commercial centre. In 1886, Andrew Goldie was granted allotments on the waterfront at Granville West by Special Commissioner Douglas. His first store at Hanuabada became a schoolhouse for the London Missionary Society. (I. Stuart, *Port Moresby Yesterday and Today* [Sydney, 1970], p. 46.) Goldie built a jetty and store at Granville West and on his retirement in 1891 sold his property to Burns, Philp and Company. This firm built a store, a manager's two-storeyed house, a workman's house (not shown in photo) and a wharf storage-shed. The wharf was improved and a tramway built from the wharf to the store. This view of these developments was probably taken in 1896. (Burns, Philp and Company Ltd)

Plate 161

Plate 162. The wharf of Burns, Philp and Company at Granville West, Port Moresby, *c*. 1896. Burns, Philp and Company were trading into Port Moresby as early as 1883. The Port Moresby correspondent of the *Sydney Mail* reported at the end of 1883: 'We are growing in importance and dignity. We have a monthly mail from Thursday Island. The *Elsea*, a schooner belonging to Messrs. Burns, Philp and Co., is here for the second time. She has been advertised for some time as a monthly boat to Port Moresby . . . all honour to Messrs. Burns and Co., the captain has instructions not to leave any grog here.' (*Sydney Mail*, 5 January 1884, p. 15.) In 1886 an agreement was negotiated between Special Commissioner Douglas and James Burns for the firm to run a regular steamship service to Port Moresby and Samarai. (*British New Guinea Report for the Year 1886* [Brisbane, 1887], p. 3 and appendix AD. 10.) This run proved unprofitable and ceased in 1888. Thereafter the firm served Port Moresby with a schooner of the type shown here, the *Myrtle* of 160 tonnes, on a bi-monthly service. (Burns, Philp and Company Ltd)

Plate 162

Plate 163. James Burns (1846–1923), co-founder of the firm Burns, Philp and Company Ltd. Born in Scotland, Burns came to Queensland in 1862 and over twenty years built up extensive interests in commerce and shipping. In 1883 his various business interests were amalgamated under the name Burns, Philp and Company Ltd, with Burns as chairman. In the same year the firm began trading along the coast of Papua and this was the beginning of the important and continuing influence it exerted in New Guinea's economy. (Burns, Philp and Company Ltd)

Plate 163

Plate 164. The site of Rabaul was reclaimed from the wasteland of a mangrove swamp. Here a labour gang constructs the landing place at the Norddeutsche Lloyd line depot in 1905. The first building in Rabaul is shown in the background. (Mitchell Library)

Plate 164

Plate 165

Plate 165. Beginnings at Rabaul. A view of Rabaul in 1904 showing the Norddeutsche Lloyd company wharf and depot. The cutting for the road to Herbertshöhe is seen to the left. In January 1910 the seat of government and the High Court were transferred from Herbertshöhe to Rabaul. (Mitchell Library)

Plate 166. The Norddeutsche Lloyd line depot house at Simpson Harbour (Rabaul) in 1905. (Mitchell Library)

Plate 166

9 Social Life and Commerce to 1920

Plate 167

Plate 167. Friends and relatives gathered at Kokopo to farewell Mrs Emma Kolbe ('Queen' Emma) on the eve of her departure for Europe in 1911. (See also plate 72.) After a holiday in Europe, Emma Kolbe retired to Mosman, New South Wales, but in 1913 she left to join her husband at Monte Carlo, and died there. When this photograph was taken, Emma was sixty-one years old. Douglas Rannie met her when she was thirty-seven: 'She was a handsome and very striking figure when I first met her. She was dressed in white satin, with a long train, which was borne behind her by half a dozen dusky little maidens, natives of the Solomon Islands, all dressed in fantastic costumes. Above her jet-black hair she wore a tiara of diamonds—her whole carriage was queenly. She was accompanied on this occasion by a number of female cousins and other relations from Samoa, mostly part-Samoan, and all highly educated and beautiful women.' R. W. Robson, *Queen Emma* (Sydney, 1965), p. 181. (Mitchell Library)

Plate 168

Plate 168. An interior at Gunantambu, home of 'Queen' Emma (Forsayth) Kolbe. Note the personally signed portrait of the German emperor on the wall. Before her marriage to Kolbe, Emma Forsayth's American citizenship helped her to win a legal battle with the German Neuguinea-Kompagnie over the validity of her land purchases. (H. L. Schultze Collection)

Plate 169. Section of the living room at Gunantambu. (S. Stephenson Collection)

Plate 169

Plate 170. Something of the social life surrounding 'Queen' Emma is revealed by this photograph of her niece, Miss Hurgren, taken at Gunantambu in the 1890s. (H. L. Schultze Collection)

Plate 170

Plate 171

Plate 172

Plate 172. An anniversary celebration of the Macco family in the hotel at Kavieng (New Ireland) in 1919. In front, left to right: the Macco children, Herr Engelke, Rudolf Richter, [unidentified]. Next row (seated): Ad. Jahn, [unidentified man and woman], Mrs Kettnis, Herr Macco, Mrs Macco, Mrs Furter, the district officer, [two unidentified men]. Next row (standing): Gushie Peper, Fritz Hoffmann, Mrs Hoffmann, Her Kirchner, Mrs Kirchner, [unidentified]. Back row (standing): [unidentified], Herr Furter, Herr Kettnis, [five unidentified men]. At far back: Herr Eidelbach. (M. Von Hein Collection)

Plate 173. The manager of Hernsheim and Company, Emil Timm, fifth from the left, with some of his employees and officers of the *Cormoran* at Raule, *c.* 1905. (M. von Hein Collection)

Plate 174. Members of the Parkinson family, New Britain, 1910. Seated, left to right, Phoebe Parkinson, wife of Richard Parkinson, and Nelly Parkinson, who married Herr Diercke. Standing, Phoebe Parkinson's son, Carl, and Rudolf, a son of Nelly Diercke. (Mitchell Library)

Plate 173

Plate 174

Plate 175

Plate 175. Friends relax outside the Kokopo Hotel, 1916. Phoebe Parkinson is seated at the extreme left and in front of her is her niece, Mrs Carolina Schultze, and Mr and Mrs Rosenbaum. Rudolf Spangenberg, with hat, is kneeling behind Mrs Rosenbaum. Those standing at the back are Walter Weichmann on the left, and Herr Wiemer on the right. (M. von Hein Collection)

Plate 176

Plate 176. Left to right, Jonny Mercier, Walter Weichmann and Fritz Hauser enjoying a large brandy after having undergone the Chinese custom of being dropped into the water following the launching of the *Matupi*, *c.* 1912. (B. B. Perriman Collection)

Plate 177

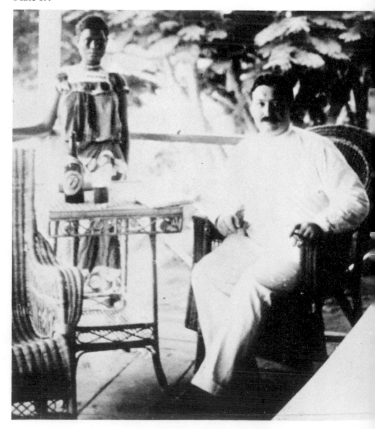

Plate 177. Ernst Paatzsch, a clerk employed by the German firm of Hernsheim and Company, relaxes on the veranda of his bungalow, 1915. After World War I, Paatzsch stayed on in Rabaul and lived in Chinatown, where he became the social nucleus for the remaining German population. Paatzsch and Furter established a store in Rabaul, the second storey of which became the German Club. Hitler appointed Paatzsch German consul. During World War II, Paatzsch was interned in Australia. He died at Mona Vale, New South Wales, in 1948. (Mitchell Library)

Plate 178

Plate 178. Mrs Phoebe Parkinson, seated left, with her family in the garden of her plantation, Kuradui, near Rabaul, in 1920. Seated also are her daughter Dolly and child. Standing at the back, her son-in-law, Herr Euchtritz, and her son Edward; in front, her younger son Paul. (S. Stephenson Collection)

Plate 179. Paul Parkinson, son of Richard and Phoebe Parkinson, and 'Big Bell(y)', a descendant of one of the twenty Buka people the Parkinsons brought to New Britain for protection against the Tolai. (Mitchell Library)

Plate 179

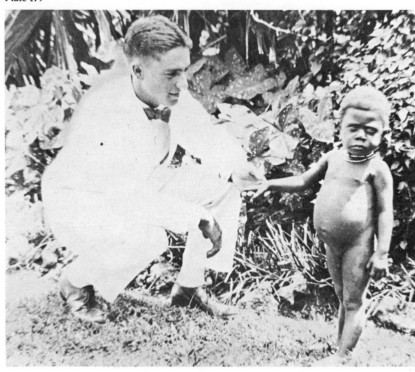

Plate 180

Plate 180. Phoebe Parkinson photographed on the veranda of the bungalow at her plantation, Kuradui, in 1920. Lilian Overell, a guest in her house at this time, described her first meeting with 'Missus Kuradui', as she was known locally. 'Mrs Parkinson was a personality. Simply dressed in white, her kindly face wearing a pleasant smile, her dark eyes flashing with wit and humour, and with an air of quiet dignity, she was indeed a delightful person to meet.' Lilian Overell, *A Woman's Impressions of German New Guinea* (London, 1923), p. 33. (Mitchell Library)

Plate 181. Mrs Phoebe Parkinson on her plantation, Kuradui, near Ralum, New Britain. This photograph, taken after the death of her husband Richard (see plate 77), shows her in her carriage—the term used for buggy—visiting labourers and their families. On this occasion, in 1920, an Australian guest in her home wrote: 'The people came running out of the villages as they heard the carriage. Everywhere Miti [Mrs Parkinson] was recognized and glad cries of "Miti, Miti," resounded. Mothers held up their children that they might see her, withered old women got as near to her as they could, and the *luluais* shook hands gravely. Miti knew everybody, inquired after their families and circumstances, sympathised with their griefs and smiled benevolently on them all.' Lilian Overell, *A Woman's Impressions of German New Guinea* (London, 1923), p. 88. (Mitchell Library)

Plate 181

Plate 182. Phoebe Parkinson holding 'court' with *luluais* and other New Britain people on her plantation, Kuradui, about 1920. A guest in the house of Mrs Parkinson at this time described a court session on the plantation: 'One night Miti [Mrs Parkinson] held court on the veranda. She sat in her big chair, heard the evidence and gave the verdict with judicial impartiality. In English and Australian police courts there is often levity and cheap witticism even when cases of serious import are being tried. There was nothing but the utmost gravity here. The sewing woman was on trial and the husband insisted that her lover should pay *tambu*. . . . Eventually it was decided that the young man should pay 10s. fine, half of what the husband demanded. This was paid, they shook hands, and the three went off together, the best of friends!' Lilian Overell, *A Woman's Impressions of German New Guinea* (London, 1923), pp. 73–5. (Mitchell Library)

Plate 182

Plate 183. Friends relax at the plantation bungalow of Constantini, New Ireland, 1911. Herr Wolf ('Lupus') and Herr Spangenberg ('Maste Bombe') are on the right. Constantini came to German New Guinea as a missionary with the Sacred Heart mission at Vunapope. He inherited a wealthy estate in Italy and left the Church to establish a plantation on New Ireland. (M. von Hein Collection)

Plate 184. Relaxing on the veranda of the Hernsheim and Company mess, Matupi, in 1911: Captain Meyer, (left foreground) and, sleeping between Hermann and Wilhelm Bolten, Herr Westphal. (M. von Hein Collection)

Plate 183

Plate 184

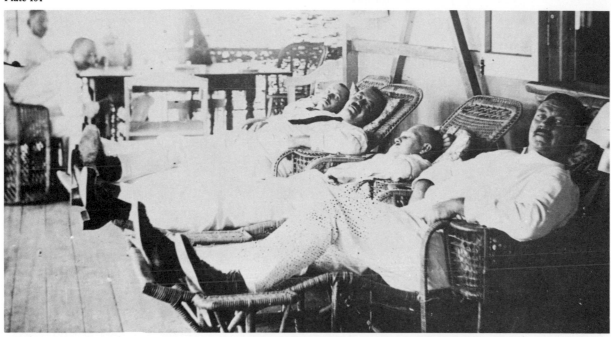

Plate 185

Plate 185. The Rabaul manager of Hernsheim and Company, Rudolf Spangenberg, takes a bath on the veranda, 1915. Spangenberg, known to the locals as 'Maste Bombe', was a popular member of the German expatriate community. (M. von Hein Collection)

Plate 186. A group of German nationals in playful mood pretend to be wounded as a result of the 'Copra War'. Hans Mannsfeld recalls, 'In 1914 we jokingly called the defence of our Colony the "Copra War". At the time, of course, we could not have known that this was in actual fact a very accurate description, since the Australian Administration was bent on expropriation from the word go; we were kept there solely to manage the plantations for them, otherwise the native labourers would have run off to their respective villages and the plantation left to run wild, for the Australian Administration lacked both the necessary experience and labour.' Recollections of Hans Mannsfeld, in correspondence with the authors, June 1973. (M. von Hein Collection)

Plate 186

Plate 187

Plate 188

Plate 187. Employees of Hernsheim and Company, Matupi, 1914. Left to right, Hans Mannsfeld, Herr Paatzsch, Herr Class, Captain Käferlein, Robert von Blumenthal ('Lord Bob'), Herr Wiemer, Herr Timm, Herr Spangenberg, Herr Heymann, Emil Goetsch, Herr Sturhann, [unidentified], Jonny Mercier. (M. von Hein Collection)

Plate 188. The Kokopo Hotel bar, about 1919. The skipper of the *Montoro*, Captain Hillman, stands at the extreme left. (B. B. Perriman Collection)

Plate 189

Plate 189. Employees of Hernsheim and Company relaxing at Rabaul in 1915. (M. von Hein Collection)

Plate 190. In February–March 1914, the managers of the various branches of Hernsheim and Company throughout the Bismarck Archipelago met at Rabaul to draw up a balance sheet of the company's trading. In the back row, left to right, are Jonny Mercier, Captain Käferlein, Captain Lehmann, Fritz Anacker, Herr Heydenreuter, Walter Weichmann, Hans Mannsfeld, Theodor von Hein, Herr Drege, Herr Sturhann. Front row, left to right, Ernst Paatzsch, Rudolf Richter, Herr Schuster, Emil Goetsch, Herr Wiemer, Herr Heymann. (M. von Hein Collection)

Plate 190

Plate 191

Plate 191. One of the several rock grottos below 'Haus Kirchner' at Kavieng provided a cool retreat for this party in October 1919. The Europeans from left to right are Miss Sommerhoff, governess employed by the Kirchner family; Geoffrey Furter, manager for Hasag at Rabaul; Mrs Kirchner; Franz Kirchner, Hasag manager at Kavieng; Georg Kirchner. Franz Kirchner, Furter and Eidelbach, in partnership, established Kimadan plantation on the east coast of New Ireland. (S. Stephenson Collection)

Plate 192

Plate 192. The living quarters of Ulul-Nono plantation, twenty-nine kilometres east of Kavieng, New Ireland, in 1917. The sleeping quarters, not shown, are to the right and are similar in structure to the buildings at the left. Ulul-Nono was one of the biggest plantations in German New Guinea, as the land was taken up before Dr Hahl brought in the regulation that limited any single land purchase to 243 hectares. It was famous for its Macassar ponies and for its cattle, which constituted the biggest herd on New Ireland. At the time of this photograph Ulul-Nono was owned by Captain Macco (see plate 147); after World War I, Franz Kirchner bought it from the Expropriation Board. (M. von Hein Collection)

Plate 193

Plate 193. A gathering at Ulul-Nono plantation, Kavieng, New Ireland, for a *sing-sing*, 1920. (S. Stephenson Collection)

Plate 194. A New Guinean with his catch of birds of paradise. Skins of these birds brought a good price. Coconut planters used the returns from the skins to support themselves during the years that plantations were unproductive, and to buy land for plantations. A professional hunter could equip an expedition for about six months in the interior at a cost of one hundred pounds. Before major gold strikes were made, Europeans combined the shooting of birds of paradise with gold prospecting in the interior of New Guinea. (M. von Hein Collection)

Plate 194

Plate 195. The home of Heinrich Rudolf Wahlen on Maron Island. Wahlen came to New Guinea in 1895 as a clerk in the service of Hernsheim and Company, and was sent to the Northwest Islands. By 1905 he had bought out the rights of Hernsheim plantations and had started a rich trade in trochus shell. In 1909 he arranged for the purchase by Hasag of nearly all the interests of E. E. Forsayth and Company, and, as New Guinea director of the firm, moved into 'Queen' Emma's residence, Gunantambu (plate 74). Wahlen left New Guinea in 1913 for Hamburg, where he died in 1968. (S. Stephenson Collection)

Plate 195

Plate 196

Plate 196. A coffee plantation in the Sogeri district in 1909. (Hallstrom Pacific Library)

Plate 197. Ploughing by steam tractor at Katea plantation, Papua, 1912. (Hallstrom Pacific Library)

Plate 197

Plate 198. Tapping para rubber at Itikinumu plantation in the Sogeri district, 1912. Messrs Greene and Garrioch introduced the first para rubber plants into the Territory. In December 1903 they planted 3·3 hectares at Sogeri and the following year another 2 hectares. The government imported 100 000 seeds in 1906. (Hallstrom Pacific Library)

Plate 199. The radio-telegraph station at Port Moresby in 1912. (Hallstrom Pacific Library)

Plate 198

Plate 199

Plate 200

Plate 200. Bales of sisal hemp ready for export from Papua, 1912. Sisal hemp plants were brought into Papua by the administration in 1893. In November of that year Special Commissioner Douglas reported to Granville the loss of these plants and requested more. The plant, sisalana, produces fibres from 50 to 130 centimetres long, which are used chiefly to make binding twine. Sisal is harvested once or twice a year. The soil, drainage and rainfall in the Port Moresby district were suitable for the production of sisal hemp, but the scarcity of labour meant that plantations did not get proper attention and many attempts had to be abandoned. In May 1906, Douglas reported that attempts to produce hemp from the pandanus seemed doomed because pandanus could not be found in sufficient quantities to encourage its exploitation. (Hallstrom Pacific Library)

Plate 201

Plate 201. A steam tractor with its heavy load at Bomana in the 1920s. (A. A. Speedie Collection)

Plate 202

Plate 203

Plate 202. The plantation house at Ogamobu, Kikori River, in 1920. Mrs Robinson, wife of the owner, is in the foreground, with her daughter Penelope seated in the middle. It was to this plantation that Jack Hides and Jim O'Malley made their way in 1935, ill and exhausted after their expedition from Daru to the Mandated Territory border and back to the south coast. (D. Mercer Collection)

Plate 203. The entire white population on the Kikori River in 1926. At the back are Percy Robinson, owner of Ogamobu, and A. Lyston-Blythe, chief officer of Kikori Government Station. Mrs Blythe is in the centre, and Penelope Robinson and Mrs Robinson on the lower step. (D. Mercer Collection)

Plate 204

Plate 204. Sluicing alluvial gold, Yodda goldfield, Kumusi Division, 1909. The field was proclaimed in July 1900. In that year the yield was 1935 kilograms, valued at £255 450. The strike at Yodda brought prospectors to this area at a time when British-Australian administration had not extended control very far from the coastal fringe. British New Guinea consisted of three divisions: Western, Central and Eastern. The opening of the Yodda field forced the establishment of a Northern division. (Hallstrom Pacific Library)

Plate 205

Plate 206

Plate 205. Some of the miners at Woodlark Island, *c.* 1906. Miners received between £5 and £6 per week. At this time there were twenty-three Europeans on Woodlark engaged in mining for wages, and twenty-five working their own claims. The township consisted of a hospital, two licensed liquor stores and a collection of miners' humpies. (Hallstrom Pacific Library)

Plate 206. Kulumadau gold mine, Woodlark Island, *c.* 1906. This mine was started in 1901. By 1907 there were three other mines operating on the island: Woodlark King, at Karavakum, and Murua United and Federation Lease at Busai. The yield from Kulumadau mine was restricted because the lease ran through the property of the Woodlark Island Pty, but in 1907 the two mining interests amalgamated. In the year 1908–09, 3660 tonnes of ore were treated for 60 kilograms of gold valued at £7252. The total quantity of gold won from all the mines on Woodlark for this year was 180 kilograms, valued at £19 721. (Hallstrom Pacific Library)

Plate 207

Plate 207. Dubuna Mines, Astrolabe copper field, 1912. This field was proclaimed in December 1906, embracing 2500 square kilometres on the south-west side of the Astrolabe Range. In the absence of railway communication with Port Moresby the ore had to be brought to the coast by pack mules, a distance of 8 to 25 kilometres. The area actually worked was 80 square kilometres, as costs prohibited the use of the northern end of the field. The total value of copper exported in 1912 was £31 423. (Hallstrom Pacific Library)

Plate 208. T. L. Sefton, manager of Koitaki rubber plantation, with two of his 'houseboys' about 1923. (R. Speedie Collection)

Plate 209. T. L. Sefton, manager of Koitaki rubber plantation, with Mr Burton and Mrs Carson, relaxing in the garden of the plantation bungalow, about 1923. (R. Speedie Collection)

Page 164

Plate 208

Plate 209

101

10 The People
Facing Change

Plate 210

Plate 210. A New Guinea head-hunter poses proudly with his trophy. Jorge de Meneses, who was perhaps the first European to set foot in New Guinea (1526), recorded that the Devil walked with the people. Hernando de Grijalva said of the people he contacted in 1537, 'Most of them eat men's flesh, and are witches, so given to devilishness, that the devils walk among them as companions.' (A. Galvano, *Discoveries of the World* [London, 1862], p. 202.) Their opinion was echoed by numerous other Europeans making fleeting contacts with the people over more than three centuries. Not all the New Guinea peoples were head-hunters or cannibals, but most were involved in constant warfare with one another. The insistence of the early European settlers in New Guinea that warfare should cease made for tremendous social change. War was a necessary part of the social system. The traditional social structure through which the New Guineans gained status, and thus satisfaction, was weakened by the imposition of the white man's authority. (B. B. Perriman Collection)

Plate 211

Plate 211. A Tench Islander, 129 kilometres due north of Kavieng, New Ireland, takes his first close look at a European. He swam out to the boat and, as he pulled himself up the side and stared into the strange face of schooner skipper Les Bell, the lens caught his awe and wonder. (H. L. Schultze Collection)

Plate 212

Plate 212. A group near Blanche Bay in the 1870s. The Rev. George Brown, who visited Raluana in 1897, recorded, 'Changes noted; all were naked [in the 1870s] men, women, children—now all clothed—not a single naked native is visible within the sphere of mission influence.' (Mitchell Library)

103

Plate 213

Plate 213. A group of Motuans at Port Moresby in 1884 at the time of the proclamation establishing the British Protectorate over south-east New Guinea. (Mitchell Library)

Plate 214. A group of Koiari men and women at the time of first contact with Europeans, *c.* 1885. The Koiari, who lived in the Owen Stanley foothills to the north-east of Port Moresby, had a reputation for fierceness toward the first Europeans who penetrated their region. This photograph was taken by the Rev. W. G. Lawes of the London Missionary Society. (Mitchell Library)

Plate 214

Plate 215

Plate 215. A family on Duke of York Island about 1882. In September 1883, H. H. Romilly reported, 'Muskets and Snider rifles are much in demand among the natives. To obtain a Snider a native will work for a year . . . it is, to my mind, an improper practice on the part of the German [traders] to supply them with these articles.' (Mitchell Library)

Plate 216. A house near Blanche Bay in the 1870s. When the Rev. George Brown, who took this photograph, visited Raluana in 1897 he recorded, 'Changes noted; they lived in poor miserable houses [in the 1870s]; now there are numbers of houses built in Tongan, Fijian and Samoan shapes and a genuine New Britain house or hut will soon be a curiosity anywhere near our stations.' (Mitchell Library)

Plate 216

Plate 217

Plate 217. The Rev. R. H. Rickard took this photograph at Raluana on Blanche Bay in 1885 and gave it the caption, 'A Superior Native Residence at Raluana'. It reflects the change alluded to by the Rev. George Brown (see plate 216). (Mitchell Library)

Plate 218

Plate 218. Pottery at Hanuabada village ready for shipment in the annual *Hiri* to the Papuan Gulf, *c.* 1890. Captain F. R. Barton wrote that he was informed by Dr Lawes that 'in 1885 four *lakatoi* left Port Moresby, each carrying an average number of 1628 pots. In 1903 the Kwaradubuna *iduhu* (idibana and laurina) equipped a *lakatoi* named 'Bogebada', consisting of 4 *asi*. The total number of pots carried in this *lakatoi* was 1294, giving an average therefore of 324 pots per *asi*. Assuming that twenty *lakatoi* sailed that year, and that each was composed of four *asi*, the total number of pots taken was 25,920.' F. R. Barton, 'The Annual Trading Expedition to the Papuan Gulf', in C. G. Seligman, ed., *The Melanesians of British New Guinea* (Cambridge, 1910), p. 114. (London Missionary Society)

Plate 219

Plate 219. Sago mills at Purari River, Gulf Division. The word *sago* is said to be derived from a Malayan word *sagu* or *sago*, signifying food. Trees grow along the low-lying river banks and in swampy country principally in the Western Gulf and Mambare Divisions. Sago was the staple diet of the coastal people of the Western and Gulf Divisions and was traded for hundreds of kilometres along the coast. (Hallstrom Pacific Library)

Plate 220

Plate 220. Men bringing a wharf pile into position at Ogamobu plantation, Kikori River, 1920. (D. Mercer Collection)

Plate 221. The colonial relationship of the races is typified in this photograph taken in Rabaul in 1923 of a domestic servant, and Pam and Margaret Roscoe, daughters of an Australian ex-army officer. (S. M. Matthews Collection)

Plate 222

Plate 221

Plate 222. Interior of a labour house on Kuradui plantation, New Britain, 1920. (S. Stephenson Collection)

107

Plate 223

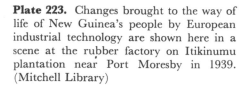

Plate 223. Changes brought to the way of life of New Guinea's people by European industrial technology are shown here in a scene at the rubber factory on Itikinumu plantation near Port Moresby in 1939. (Mitchell Library)

Plate 224. A hospital on the plantation at Ralum, New Britain, 1920. (S. Stephenson Collection)

Plate 224

Plate 225

Plate 225. The native hospital run by the Australian (Mandate) Administration, Rabaul, about 1925. The hospital was originally built and operated under the German administration. (B. B. Perriman Collection)

11 The London Missionary Society, Papua, 1871-1900

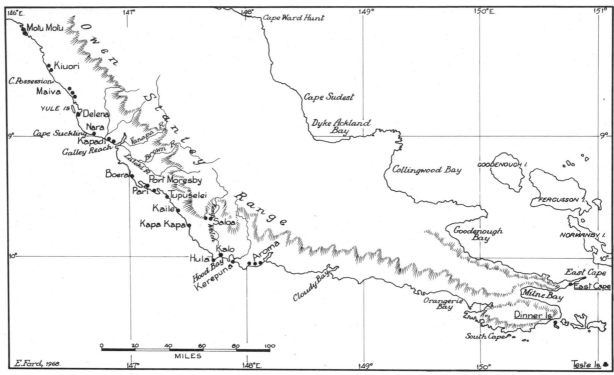

Plate 226

Plate 226. Mission stations of the London Missionary Society in Papua in 1884. The New Guinea mission of the London Missionary Society was established by decision of the London board of directors in 1869. In 1871, the Rev. Samuel Macfarlane and the Rev. A. W. Murray installed the first teachers of the New Guinea mission on Darnley Island in Torres Strait and on Dauan and Saibai Islands near the Papuan coast.

In the following year teachers were placed at Katau about forty-eight kilometres east of Dauan Island and at Manu Manu on Redscar Bay. At the end of 1873 the first teachers were installed at Anuapata on Port Moresby and early in 1874 at Boera. With the installation of the Rev. W. G. Lawes at Port Moresby in 1874 there came the first European missionary to the eastern part of the mainland.

Two teachers were placed on Yule Island at the end of 1875 but were withdrawn after about ten months following the murder of two Europeans at Hall Sound. The mission intended that this would be a temporary withdrawal, but the setting up of the mission on Yule Island by the Congregation of the Sacred Heart in 1885 precluded further effort in this place by the London Missionary Society. Meanwhile, the society continued expansion of mission stations along the coast west of Port Moresby. In 1881 the Rev. James Chalmers and the Rev. W. G. Lawes surveyed the Delena area and visited the Maiva, Roro and Nara villages. (Percy Chatterton, 'The History of Delena', in *The History of Melanesia*, Second Waigani Seminar [Canberra, 1969], pp. 283–95.) In 1882, Raratongan mission pastors were installed at Delena and Maiva. Some of these later transferred to Motu-motu in the Kerema district. Also in 1882 pastors were installed at Hula, Kerepunu and Aroma to the east of Port Moresby.

In 1875 the board of directors of the London Missionary Society learnt of Captain Moresby's discoveries in the China Strait region of south-east New Guinea and the decision was made to extend mission work to this area. Messrs Macfarlane, Lawes and Chalmers visited the area and mission stations were set up on Teste and Stacey Islands (South Cape).

The 'spheres of influence' policy devised by Sir William MacGregor set the pattern of Christian mission distribution in British New Guinea. The Congregation of the Sacred Heart, based on Yule Island from 1885 onwards, was not permitted to encroach on the coastal areas within the London Missionary Society's sphere of influence. By necessity, therefore, the main thrust of the Sacred Heart mission was into the hinterland behind Yule Island, leaving only a small portion of the coastline within its domain. The London Missionary Society's sphere of influence was recognized as the coastline from East Cape to the Torres Strait region in the west. By the turn of the century, London Missionary Society activity was taking place in the Fly River delta region.

The 'spheres of influence' policy brought the Anglicans and Methodists into British New Guinea in the 1890s. The Australasian Methodist Missionary Society was given its sphere of influence in the Louisiades and in the D'Entrecasteaux group, while the Anglican mission was given its sphere on the mainland from Cape Ducie westwards to the Mambare River (see plate 329). (The map in this plate was adapted by Edgar Ford from one drawn by Rev. W. G. Lawes in 1884 in a letter to Rev. R. W. Thompson [Port Moresby, 16 June 1884], in 'Papua Letters 1882–85', Folder 4, Box 3. Microfilm reel 93, FM 4/422, Mitchell Library)

Plate 227

Plate 228. The six pioneer teachers of the New Guinea mission of the London Missionary Society, with their families. Recruited by the Revs S. Macfarlane and A. W. Murray in the Loyalty Islands, these teachers were installed on Darnley, Dauan and Saibai Islands in Torres Strait in 1871. At the end of the following year the first teachers were installed on the New Guinea mainland. (London Missionary Society)

Plate 227. The first mission station of the London Missionary Society on the mainland of New Guinea at the mouth of the Binaturi River. The Rev. A. W. Murray placed the first two teachers at Katau River in November 1872. The engraving of the teacher's house at Mawatta (Katau) was published in 1884. The Rev. S. Macfarlane and the Rev. A. W. Murray visited the region to the east of Saibai Island in 1871 in the course of their pioneer voyage to Torres Strait and the south coast of Papua. They recorded, 'We made our way some distance up the river and dropped anchor opposite the settlement of Katau . . . at our first approach the natives looked shy and distrustful . . . confidence soon spread, and large numbers appeared on the beach. . . . We made it our special business of course to try to give the chief and people some idea of our object in visiting them and their neighbours. We told them of the teachers we had left at Tauan [*sic*] and Darnley Island . . . the chief declared his approval and his wish to have teachers to live with him.' Report by A. W. Murray and S. Macfarlane, 'First Voyage to New Guinea from Loyalty Islands', pp. 70–6. 'London Missionary Society, Papua and Australia Reports', Box 1, 1871–76. Microfilm FM 4/388, Mitchell Library. (Hallstrom Pacific Library)

Plate 228

Plate 229

Plate 229. The mission station on Darnley Island in Torres Strait, the site of the beginning of the London Missionary Society's New Guinea mission in 1871. It was here that the Revs S. Macfarlane and A. W. Murray installed the first Loyalty Islands teachers of the New Guinea mission. (London Missionary Society)

Plate 230. An engraving of 1878 showing the London Missionary Society's station at Port Moresby. The Rev. A. W. Murray reported to London on the selection of the site and the first building in 1874: 'The place on which we had fixed and which we succeeded in obtaining, is a beautiful spot— a more beautiful it would, I should think, be difficult to find in any part of the world. It lies between the villages on Anuapata and Elevara . . . it is near the sea on a ridge of land which rises to an elevation of 110 to 130 feet . . . on November 24th [1874] the building of the dwelling-house commenced. . . . The result of all is that in the short space of four days and a half the house is so far complete as to be in a habitable state, and very shortly, all being well, Mr & Mrs Lawes will take up their abode in their new home.' (Mitchell Library)

Plate 230

Plate 231

Plate 231. William George Lawes (1839–1907), missionary of the London Missionary Society. Ordained in 1860, Lawes was appointed to Samoa in 1861, and later served on Niue (Savage) Island until appointed to the New Guinea mission in 1874. On 21 November 1874, Lawes was installed as the first European missionary at Port Moresby. He lived at Port Moresby for many years during his service, but also travelled extensively along the south coast supervising the extension of the mission's activities. Work in language was Lawes's notable contribution and in 1891 he completed the translation of the New Testament into Motu. Lawes spent the last ten years of his service at Vatorata near Kapa Kapa, at the training college for local teachers that he had helped to establish (see plate 250). He retired in 1906 and died in 1907. (Mitchell Library)

Plate 232. The rigours of missionary travel in Papua: the Rev. W. G. Lawes on an expedition into the interior accompanied by Polynesian teachers and their wives in 1875. The expedition was organised by O. C. Stone and left Port Moresby on 7 December 1875. Lawes was accompanied also by Hargrave, Broadbent and Pettard. The man illustrated on the end of the rope is probably Hargrave. The drawing comes from the *Illustrated Sydney News* of 3 March 1876 (Mitchell Library).

Plate 232

113

Plate 233

Plate 234

Plate 233. A London Missionary Society group, Port Moresby, 1889. From left to right, E. B. Savage, H. M. Dauncey, F. W. Walker, A. Pearse, W. G. Lawes, ·Hirst [?], and J. Chalmers. (London Missionary Society)

Plate 234. Four Samoan teachers of the London Missionary Society, Port Moresby, *c.* 1885; the society made extensive use of teachers from the South Sea Islands in its work in Papua. Opinions about them varied. For example, in 1887 the Rev. L. A. Navarre of the Sacred Heart mission at Yule Island expressed the view: 'They [the London Missionary Society island teachers] are not trained, and they differ little in morals or training from the savages amongst whom they live. They have no fixed object in view, as far at least as I could see. They are not under direction or supervision and their life and their works are without control or nearly so. I know a large number of them. There are amongst them some good fellows, but they are very bad teachers.' (Navarre to Douglas, 5 May 1887, in *British New Guinea Report for the Year 1887*, Appendix E, pp. 25–6.) Douglas, on the other hand, expressed the view in the same year: 'A great and noble enterprise has been conducted by a set of most self-sacrificing men who have carried the message of Christ to a savage race of inhuman murderers. The first stages of this transmutation have been effected at the cost of a great sacrifice of life among the devoted South Sea Island teachers who have been the chief instruments in the partial conversion of these interesting though bloodthirsty savages.' J. King, *W. G. Lawes of Savage Island and New Guinea* (London, 1909) pp. 258–9. (Mitchell Library)

Plate 235

Plate 235. The station of the London Missionary Society at Stacey Island (South Cape), south-east New Guinea, in 1884. This station was established in December 1877 by the Rev. Samuel Macfarlane and the Rev. James Chalmers. Macfarlane reported the founding of the station: 'Mr Chalmers and I went ashore before dinner and had a look round deciding to form the mission station at the village on Stacey Island situated in the pass between that island and the mainland. . . . We found no difficulty in securing a portion of the largest house in the village for the use of the teachers until they get one built. . . . On the following morning we selected a site and commenced the erection of a house for Mr and Mrs Chalmers. The natives entered into the spirit of the thing, cutting and carrying in timber. In less than a week we had completed the frame of a commodious, substantial house, which when neatly covered in with platted pandanus leaves will make a comfortable temporary dwelling.' 'London Missionary Society, Papua and Australia Reports', Reel II, Box I, 1871–76. Microfilm FM 4/338, Mitchell Library; 'Report of the Voyage of the *Bertha* from Murray Island to the East End of New Guinea, 1877', Rev. S. Macfarlane to Rev. J. Mullens, p. 23. (State Library of Victoria)

Plate 236

Plate 236. Ruatoka (1846–1903), a pioneer missionary teacher of the London Missionary Society, with his wife and family. A Raratongan, Ruatoka was educated at Raratonga Institution of the London Missionary Society and in 1871 joined the founding party of the New Guinea mission. He was installed in 1872 at Manu Manu on Redscar Bay and in the following year at Port Moresby by the Rev. A. W. Murray. He served the mission at Port Moresby until his death in 1903. Ruatoka was associated with most of the important events of the settlement, acting as liaison between the Europeans and the local people. He accompanied James Chalmers on some of his important journeys of exploration. A street in Hanuabada bears his name. (London Missionary Society)

Plate 237. The house of Dr William Turner, medical missionary of the London Missionary Society at Port Moresby, 1874–75. (London Missionary Society)

Plate 238

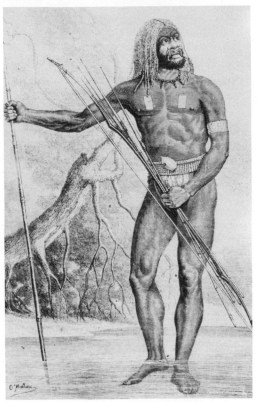

Plate 237

Plate 238. 'Papuan of New Guinea', depicted in 1874 by the artist of a missionary journal for British supporters of missions abroad. Financing of the London Missionary Society's efforts in Papua from 1872 depended to a large extent on contributions from the British public. (Mitchell Library)

115

Plate 239

Plate 239. A portrayal of the Rev. James Chalmers in the role of peacemaker. His biographer, Cuthbert Lennox, wrote in 1902, 'Tamate entered every strange village with shouts of "Peace, peace, peace."' (*James Chalmers of New Guinea* [London, 1902], pp. 64–5.) In a short time it became known that Chalmers tried everywhere to make peace, and many a feud was terminated through his mediation. In this connection we may quote the testimony of Dr Doyle Glanville, who visited New Guinea in 1885 as a member of a Special Commission appointed by the British government: 'Whatever might be its origin *Tamate* meant a great deal . . . if I said [to the natives] What is *maino*?—*maino* meaning peace, remember—they would say, *Tamate* because Tamate settled their quarrels, soothed their strife. Was it not Tamate who turned their quarrels into peace? Had not Tamate been known when two opposing tribes were approaching, to go and take the two hostile chiefs, like two turbulent children, and insist upon their being friends, and not fighting?' (Hallstrom Pacific Library)

Plate 240

Plate 241

Plate 240. The London Missionary Society mission house at Port Moresby in 1890. (Mitchell Library)

Plate 241. Four missionaries of the London Missionary Society. From left to right, Rev. Frederick Walker, who arrived in Papua in 1888 and served at Suau, in association with Abel—Walker resigned from the London Missionary Society in 1897 and in 1906 formed the Industrial Training Mission at Badu in Torres Strait; Rev. Harry Dauncey, who arrived in Port Moresby in 1888 and served at Delena from 1894 to 1928; Rev. Albert Pearse (1841–1911), who arrived in Port Moresby in 1887 and served at Kerepunu 1887–1907; Rev. Charles Abel (1862–1930), who arrived in Port Moresby in 1890, and joined Walker at Suau. He established Kwato as the central station for the Eastern Division and in 1918 converted this to the Kwato Extension Association. (Mitchell Library)

Plate 242

Plate 242. Missionaries of the London Missionary Society among the people somewhere in Papua in the 1890s. The Rev. James Chalmers is the missionary on the left of the group and the Rev. J. H. Holmes is on the right of the two seated. The woman and the other European man have not been identified. (London Missionary Society)

Plate 243. The London Missionary Society's church at Kaile (Gaile) on the coast east of Port Moresby in the early 1880s. The Rev. W. G. Lawes recorded in 1881–82: 'We anchored the first night at Kaile, a village where we have a Nive teacher. This is one of the places where the Port Moresby people used to plunder and kill. Only since the coming of the missionaries have these little villages enjoyed anything like peace. . . . We went ashore, or, more correctly perhaps, we boarded the village, for it stands in deep water even at low tide. . . . The teacher has lately built a shaky sort of bridge to connect the church, so that the people can come to the services without swimming.' (London Missionary Society)

Plate 243

Plate 244

Plate 244. A village scene at Kalo, *c.* 1897, with London Missionary Society teacher and Christian church. Kalo was visited first by the Rev. W. G. Lawes in 1877, and it was he who named the Kemp Welch River nearby, after the treasurer of the London Missionary Society. In 1878 teachers were placed at Kalo, but the mission in this area received a severe check when, in April 1881, the four teachers stationed there, together with two wives and four children, were murdered by the villagers. Following punitive action by Commodore Wilson of the Australian Station in the same year, the mission was restored.

The Rev. W. G. Lawes visited Kalo again in 1897. 'We entered the river [the Kemp Welch], and landed at the spot where the massacre had occurred. . . . [We] were welcomed by the pastor of the Kalo Church, a Roratongan related to the murdered teachers . . . we then visited the large building which had been erected for Christian worship, where the people now gather on Sundays and read the words of the Gospel of Peace. . . .' J. King, *W. G. Lawes of Savage Island and New Guinea* (London, 1909), pp. 181–2. (London Missionary Society)

Plate 245

Plate 245. The first Papuan students of the London Missionary Society college at Vatorata near Port Moresby, soon after its opening in 1896. The Rev. W. G. Lawes was appointed as principal and continued in that position until his retirement from the mission in 1906. (London Missionary Society)

Plate 246. A class at the London Missionary Society school at Port Moresby, *c.* 1890. A traveller to Port Moresby in 1883 visited the school and wrote of it: '. . . There were about seventy children present. All were very young, though there were a few girls approaching maturity. They were divided into nine classes. The male and female Polynesian teachers set a good example by their dress. One or two Papuans who had classes were, however, quite naked. The course of instruction was in reading and writing of a very primitive kind. The teacher, squatted on the floor in the centre of the class, listened to the alphabet or words of one syllable repeated alternately by the children around. In the higher "forms" short sentences were being read, which were all of a Scriptural character. Around Port Moresby the bringing up in the fear of the Lord was the beginning of all education.' Julian Thomas, *Cannibals and Convicts* (London, 1886), p. 396. (London Missionary Society)

Plate 246

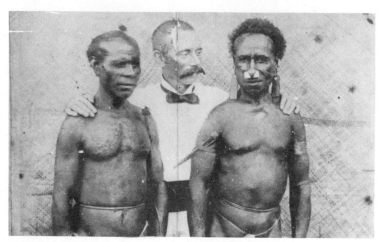
Plate 247. 'The Rev. J. H. Holmes of the London Missionary Society and his Orokolo "Chums" ' was the original caption of this photograph taken in 1897. Holmes arrived in Papua in 1893. He served for four years at Jokea, and then at Orokolo until 1906 when he moved to a station on the Purari delta. He retired from the mission in 1920. (London Missionary Society)

Plate 247

Plate 248. The church at Kabadi (Gabadi) near Cape Suckling about 1895, with the Rev. H. M. Dauncey and three South Sea Island teachers. The Rev. James Chalmers recorded the placing of the first London Missionary Society teacher at Gabadi in 1884. '. . . For some time, owing to raids by the Motumotu and Lese natives, the coast villages of Kabadi had been nearly deserted, and the natives had been living on their plantations, very much scattered. We had one teacher for the coast, and one for the villages inland, on the right bank of the Aroa River. The natives were glad to see us, and promised to finish the house for the teacher immediately. We slept one night there, and the following morning walked inland where great joy was expressed on seeing their teachers. . . .' (J. Chalmers, *Pioneering in New Guinea* [London, 1887], p. 246.) Gabadi came under the Rev. H. M. Dauncey's control from his central station at Delena. (London Missionary Society)

Plate 248

Plate 249

Plate 249. Missionary travel, Papua, *c.* 1894; the Rev. H. M. Dauncey and Mrs Dauncey of the London Missionary Society at breakfast on a beach in the Delena area of the Papuan coast. Dauncey's responsibility extended over the villages from Manu Manu (Morabi) in the east to Kivori (near Cape Possession) in the west, with the exception of those Roro and Mekeo villages coming within the sphere of influence of the Sacred Heart mission on Yule Island. (Mitchell Library)

Plate 250. The London Missionary Society college at Vatorata near Port Moresby, *c.* 1896. In 1897 the Rev. R. Wardlaw Thompson wrote of his visit to the college: 'Vatorata is a new district, very much smaller than any other in the Mission. . . . It has been sliced off the large district of Port Moresby because it contains the new training institution at Vatorata, which is henceforth to be a place of education for all natives who become teachers in connection with the whole Mission.' (London Missionary Society)

Plate 251. Pupils of the London Missionary Society school at Port Moresby in 1922, in a photograph from the *Sydney Mail*. The caption read, 'The work of the London Missionary Society is beyond praise. To see 300 native children drilling and to hear them singing "God Save the King" is an experience to be long remembered.' (Library of New South Wales)

Plate 250

Plate 251

Plate 252

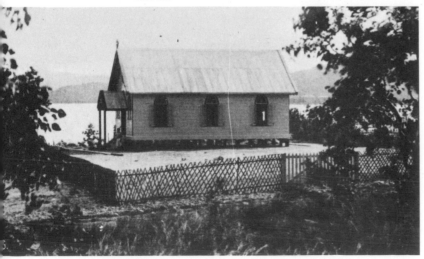

Plate 252. The 'English' church (Ela church) at Port Moresby. Erected in 1890 and costing £274 4s 6d, the church was built to minister to European Protestants in the town. The Rev. W. G. Lawes of the London Missionary Society raised the money for its construction and it was used as an interdenominational Protestant church until the building of the first Anglican church in 1915. (London Missionary Society)

Plate 253

Plate 253. An early Christian wedding in Papua at the
London Missionary Society station, Port Moresby, about
1890. (Mitchell Library)

12 The Methodist Mission, New Britain, 1875-1925

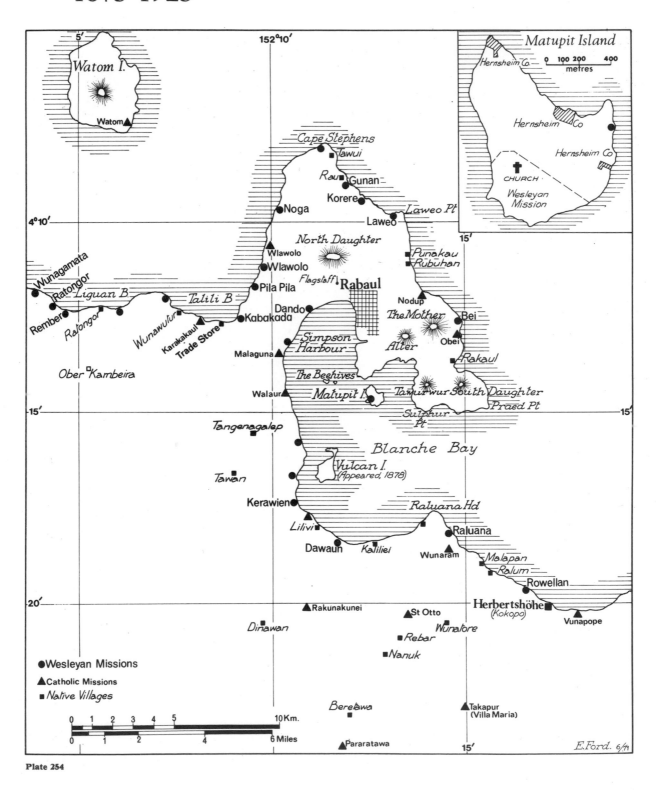

Watom I.
Watom

152°10'

Matupit Island

0   100 200   400
metres

Hernsheim Co
Hernsheim Co
Hernsheim Co
CHURCH
Wesleyan Mission

Cape Stephens
Tawui
Rau   Gunan
Korere
Noga   Laweo Pt.
Laweo

4°10'

North Daughter
Wlawolo
Wlawolo
Flagstaff   Rabaul
Pila Pila

15'

Punakau
Rubuhan

Wunagamata
Ratongor
Rember   Liguan B.   Talili B.
Ratongor   Wunawuiur   Dando   Nodup
Karakakaul   Kabakada   The Mother   Bei
Trade Store   Obei
Ober Kambeira   Simpson   Alter
Malaguna   Harbour   Rakaul

The Beehives
Walaur   Matupit I.   Tavurwur South Daughter
Praed Pt.
Sulphur
Pt.

15'

Tangenagalep

Blanche Bay

Tawan

Vulcan I.
(Appeared, 1878)

Kerawien   Raluana Hd.
Lilivi   Raluana
Dawaun   Kaliliei   Wunaram   Malapan
Ralum
Rowellan

20'

Rakunakunei   Herbertshöhe
(Kokopo)
Dinawan   St Otto
Wunalore   Vunapope
Rebar
Nanuk

● Wesleyan Missions
▲ Catholic Missions
■ Native Villages

Berelawa   Takapur
(Villa Maria)
0 1 2 3 4 5   10 Km.
0 1   2   4   6 Miles
Pararatawa

E.Ford. 6/71

15'

Plate 254

122

Plate 254. The distribution of Roman Catholic and Protestant Christianity in the Gazelle Peninsula, *c.* 1910. Before the coming of European government in 1884, the two mission societies—the Roman Catholic Congregation of the Sacred Heart, and the Protestant Australasian Wesleyan Methodist Missionary Society—were free to establish stations wherever it was thought necessary and land could be purchased. Rivalry does not appear to have been overt, but from the beginning each Christian group expressed definite views about the presence of the other. Father Navarre of the Sacred Heart mission reported to his superior soon after his arrival in 1882: '. . . Many obstacles stand in the way. The Protestant missionary societies have stationed in each village catechists who are natives either of the Fiji Islands or of Tonga, and they are most hostile to us. One of them has been sent to Beridni (Obei) but can find nothing to do here, Tolitoro having told him repeatedly that he wants none but missionaries with long gowns. We have confidence in Our Lady of the Sacred Heart, who has it in Her power to crush out all heresy.' (L. A. Navarre to Jules Chevalier, Beridni, New Britain, 3 October 1882, in *The Australian Annals of Our Lady of the Sacred Heart*, 1 November 1890, vol. 1, no. 12, pp. 275–8.)

The response of the Rev. Isaac Rooney, who in 1882 was chairman of the Wesleyan Methodist New Britain mission, was: '. . . In view of the advent of the French Priests and their intention to settle on New Britain I have decided to remove at once to Matupit where I can watch their movements and render more efficient help to our Teachers than I could do from D. of York. . . . As it is probably in and around Blanche Bay that the priests will strive to get a footing, Bro. Danks and I agreed that Matupit is the proper place for me to reside. So please do not allow anything to interfere with our wishes in this matter, unless indeed you intend to retire in favour of the priests.' (Rev. I. Rooney to the General Secretary, Duke of York, March 1882. 'The Journal and Letter Books, 1865–88, of the Rev. Isaac Rooney', pp. 144–7 of letter book, 19 Sept. 1881–25 Aug. 1882. Microfilm FM 4/2346, Mitchell Library.)

In 1890 the German government began negotiations with the two missions, with the intention of rationalizing missionary activity on the Gazelle Peninsula. The Rev. R. H. Rickard, who was chairman of the Wesleyan Methodist mission in 1890, negotiated with the local authority and attempted to have the whole of the Gazelle Peninsula allocated to his society and New Ireland allocated to the Sacred Heart mission. This proposal was rejected by the Colonial Department of the Imperial German Foreign Office in 1891, and the directive was issued that both missions would be free to operate in the Gazelle Peninsula but that the Roman Catholics were to concentrate their activities in the southern part of the peninsula and the Methodists in the north. This arrangement seems to have applied to future expansion of mission activities. There does not appear to have been any direction to give up stations where the two missions were in proximity. (Map drawn by Edgar Ford)

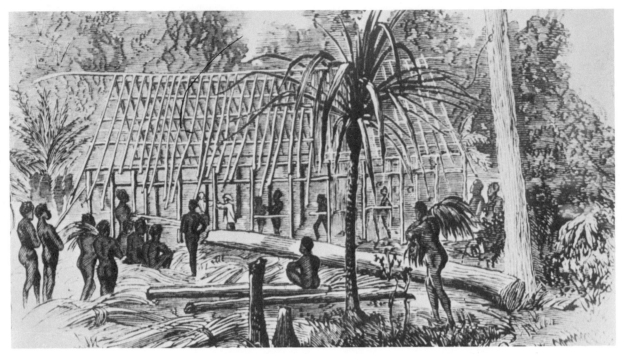

Plate 255

Plate 255. The building of the first church of the New Britain mission of the Australasian Wesleyan Methodist Missionary Society; a view published in Sydney in 1875. The Rev. George Brown reported in 1876: '*Friday, January 28th*, Duke of York Island. A great day here and one which I trust will long be remembered as that on which the first Christian Church on these Islands was opened for Divine Worship. . . . I wished the natives to know that the church was theirs and not mine, and that they must be prepared to do something themselves to help in the work, and so by urging them to it repeatedly, going round to their houses and talking with them, and by lending axes and going into the bush with them to get the logs, we at last succeeded in getting it finished without making any formal payment.' (Mitchell Library)

Plate 256. The mission scene in New Britain as portrayed in the *Illustrated Sydney News* in 1875. The engraving shows the Rev. George Brown and his South Sea Island teachers at the beginning of the Australasian Wesleyan Methodist Missionary Society's work on Duke of York Island in 1875. (Mitchell Library)

Plate 256

Plate 257

Plate 257. Talili, the first of the Tolai leaders who sought to oppose European penetration of the Gazelle Peninsula. Talili's country was inland from Kabakada (see plate 254) and it was here that four Fijian teachers of the Wesleyan Methodist mission were killed by Talili's followers in April 1878. In retaliation the Rev. George Brown armed the few Europeans in the mission area, engaged local auxiliaries at Nodup and then waged war against Talili over a period of six days. Several villages were burnt and Brown estimated that his party killed about sixty men. Talili took no part in the subsequent peace negotiations and remained an opponent of the mission.

In July 1879 it was alleged by the mission teacher at Kabakada that Talili burnt down the mission house and threatened the lives of the mission teachers. This allegation was made by a Fijian mission teacher to the Rev. B. Danks, acting head of the mission. It was also reported to Danks that Talili had 'been purchasing a large stock of Snider Rifle cartridges to suit his breech loading Snider Rifle . . . while purchasing them [he said] that he expected a fight soon with the missionaries.' (*Methodist Church Papers*, Rev. B. Danks, 'Daily Journal, New Britain, 1878–82', Mitchell Library MS., Meth. Ch.

616, entry for 12 August 1879, pp. 72–6.) Danks reported Talili's actions to Captain Richards of H.M.S. *Renard*, then in the area. The subsequent punitive action was recorded by Danks: 'About eight o'clock on Saturday morning two boats put off from the *Renard* . . . went ashore and burnt two houses, also cut down about 100 banana trees. Mr Lieutenant Tipping fired a war rocket far inland in the direction of Talili's inland town and which I afterwards learned went a little to one side of the town knocking down a Cocoa Nut tree and burning much grass. They then returned to the ship and all was quiet again. . . .' (Ibid., p. 75.)

In his autobiography Brown wrote of Talili: 'I took his likeness several times and often look at it with deep interest. I really liked the man, though I fear he was a big rascal, but we got to be great friends, and after I left the Group I used to receive very kindly messages from him. He was finally deported by the German Government to New Guinea and died there an exile from his own land, and I for one, felt very sorry indeed when I heard he had passed away.' G. Brown, *George Brown D.D., Pioneer Missionary and Explorer: An Autobiography* (London, 1908), p. 287. (Mitchell Library)

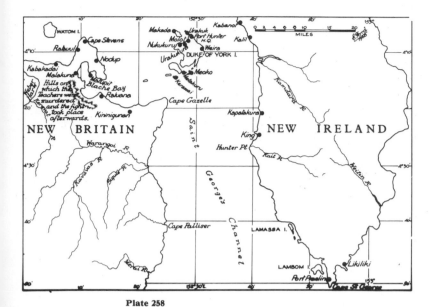

Plate 258

Plate 258. The mission stations of the New Britain District of the Wesleyan Methodist mission in 1880, together with the sites of the Free Colony of New France, Port Praslin and Likiliki in southern New Ireland. The map shown here has been adapted from a series of maps drawn by the Rev. Benjamin Danks to illustrate the five-year history of the mission, 1875–80. (*Methodist Church Papers*, Rev. B. Danks, 'Letters from New Britain, 1880–81', Mitchell Library MS., Meth. Ch. 617, pp. 75–7.) It will be noticed that Danks gives prominence to the place where the teachers were killed in 1878 (inland from Kabakada on the Gazelle Peninsula) and where subsequently the action was fought between Talili's people and the Europeans and their auxiliaries.

In July 1880 Danks recorded his view of mission influence in the same area. 'I started about 6 o'clock for Tarlili's [*sic*] place to hold a service there. It was market day on the coast and as I travelled through crowd after crowd of natives who had come down from the bush to attend the market, I got a glimpse of the mighty population which dwells in ignorance and sin within a radius of about seven miles from the mission house [at Kabakada]. How my heart sank within me as I went from one group of men to another and tried to tell them of the God who made them, and was met by the sneer and laugh and ill concealed disgust and contempt. How dark and sullen some of them seemed to be, many refusing to answer when I spoke to them. O God give me patience to work and wait, give me great love to Thyself and these people to sustain me; give me wisdom to guide me and Thy arm to protect me.' *Methodist Church Papers*, Rev. B. Danks, 'Daily Journal, New Britain, 1878–82', Mitchell Library MS., Meth. Ch. 616, entry for 18 July 1880, pp. 214–6. (Map drawn by Edgar Ford from the originals)

Plate 259. The first mission house of the Wesleyan Methodist mission at Raluana on Blanche Bay. The Rev. Isaac Rooney reported in 1883: 'Brother Rickard was strongly in favour of Raluana as being further removed from the volcano, and, as we had land already purchased, it was decided to erect the New Mission House there. There is a large native population within easy reach and it is more central than Kabakada. Raluana is the native name; Schulze Point is the name on the chart. The *Upolu* having landed our goods at Port Hunter, Brother Rickard went in her to Blanche Bay to superintend the landing of the timber for the New House and make preparation for its erection.' Rev. I. Rooney to Rev. W. Kelynack, Port Hunter, 23 [month obscured] 1883, in 'The Journal and Letter Books, 1865–88, of the Rev. Isaac Rooney', pp. 268–9. Microfilm FM 4/2346, Mitchell Library. (Mitchell Library)

Plate 259

Plate 260. South Sea Island (Fijian, Samoan and Tongan) teachers at a Raluana meeting in the mid-1880s. In 1883 the Rev. Isaac Rooney, chairman of the New Britain mission, reported to headquarters in Sydney: 'In view of the facts:—1st that we have sixteen stations this year which were previously occupied but which are now left vacant owing to deaths and to the large numbers of teachers we have been compelled to return to their homes; 2nd, that several opportunities now present themselves which, if we had teachers, we could seize with lasting advantage to the Mission; 3rd, that we regard the present as offering special opportunities for activity on our part, as the agents of Popery have temporarily suspended their efforts, and as we have reason to expect more determined opposition on their part, this District Meeting begs the Brethren, in Fiji, Tonga and Samoa to help us under these special circumstances by making a special effort to secure for us a strong reinforcement of young married men . . . for a stated term of say five or six years.' (New Britain District Minutes, 1881–83, in 'Methodist Church of Australasia: Department of Overseas Missions Papers', Mitchell Library MS., Meth. Ch. O.M. 20.)

Teachers were paid £7 per annum, catechists £10 per annum, and ministers £15 per annum in 1885. They were furnished with food, housing and clothing. Rooney's 1884 order to Sydney included one dozen white military coats and three dozen alpaca umbrellas. (Mitchell Library)

Plate 260

Plate 261

Plate 261. Pioneer missionaries of the New Britain Methodist mission are included in this group photographed in Sydney early this century. Standing, from left to right, Rev. George Brown, founder of the mission; an unidentified South Seas missioner; the Rev. Benjamin Danks, who served on Duke of York Island and at Kabakada from 1878 to 1886; seated, Aminio Bale, the pioneer Fijian missionary who went with Rev. George Brown to the Duke of York Islands in 1875; and Rev. Halse Rogers, then secretary general of the Board of Missions of the Methodist Church of Australia.

Plate 262. A New Ireland custom, *c.* 1892. A photograph by Rev. R. H. Rickard of a girl confined in a *buck*. Rickard described this in the *Australasian Methodist Missionary Review*, vol. I, no. II (4 March 1892), p. 7: 'One day we heard of a girl in a buck, so we went to see her. A buck is the name of a little house, not larger than an ordinary hen-coop, in which a little girl is shut up, sometimes for weeks only, and at other times for months. This custom is called a *Kihal*, the particulars of which are more suitable for a scientific society than for general readers. Briefly stated the custom is this. Girls on attaining puberty or betrothal, are enclosed in one of these little coops for a considerable time. They must remain there night and day. We saw two of these girls in two coops. The girls were not more than ten years old, still they were lying in doubled-up position, as their little houses would not admit them lying in any other way. These two coops were inside a large house, but the chief in consideration of a present of a couple of tomahawks, ordered the ends to be torn out of the house to admit the light, so that we might photograph the buck. The occupant was allowed to put her face through an opening to be photographed, in consideration of another present. It is pleasing to note that in the *lotu* towns of this district this custom is quite extinct.' (Mitchell Library)

Plate 262

Plate 263. A group of South Sea Island mission teachers at Raluana about 1890. (Mitchell Library)

Plate 263

Plate 264

Plate 264. 'Raluana School Boys, 1885'. In October 1885 the Rev. R. H. Rickard reported from Raluana, 'We have completed another year's work and now write a little on it. Would that we always remembered that we were making history! . . . Firstly: we have succeeded in establishing our Institution in which we have twenty young men from the other towns to live here to study with a view to future usefulness as teachers. This effort was attended with difficulties and has been rewarded with success. The students have built their houses, have planted about ten acres of ground, and have attended school daily.' Raluana Section Report, New Britain District Reports for 1885, 21 October 1885, signed by R. H. Rickard, in Mission District Minutes, 1884–87, 'Methodist Church of Australasia: Department of Overseas Missions Papers', Mitchell Library MS., Meth. Ch. O.M. 21. (Mitchell Library)

Plate 265. This photograph of 1885, captioned by Rickard 'Leading Men at Raluana', shows the changes noted by Brown under plate 212. (Mitchell Library)

Plate 265

Plate 266. Two Fijian preachers of the Wesleyan Methodist mission on New Britain 'setting out for inland for Sunday morning services' in 1885. The Rev. Isaac Rooney reported to Sydney headquarters in 1886: 'In carrying on mission work in a country like this, native helpers are an absolute necessity. They are the hands and feet of the missionary. Multiply the native agents and you multiply in proportion the missionary's influence and his power to reach the people—you multiply the channels by which the waters of life are conveyed to the arid wastes of heathenism, and you cause the desert to rejoice and blossom as the rose.' New Britain District Reports, October 1886, signed by I. Rooney, in Mission District Minutes, 1884–87, 'Methodist Church of Australasia: Department of Overseas Missions Papers', Mitchell Library MS., Meth. Ch. O.M. 21. (Mitchell Library)

Plate 266

Plate 267. Aminio Baledrokadroka (Bale), catechist, and his class on Duke of York Island, *c.* 1884. Aminio Bale was recruited in Fiji and accompanied the Rev. George Brown to New Britain in 1875. He served the mission for many years. The Rev. Benjamin Danks wrote of him in 1901: '. . . [His] life told powerfully upon the people of Molot in particular, and of Duke of York in general! Under him great victories were won for the Lord Jesus. Entering Molot when there was not a single Christian native in it, he left it without a single heathen.' (Mitchell Library)

Plate 268. The newly completed mission house at Kabakada in 1879. The Rev. Benjamin Danks served there from 1879 to 1886. He was to recall later, '. . . Our own work at Kabakada was carried on in the midst of heathen rage, cannibalism and immorality. There was fighting between the natives, between German men-of-war and the people, threats against ourselves and the teachers, attempts on life and property and opposition from Romish priests.' (Mitchell Library)

Plate 267

Plate 268

Plate 269

Plate 270

Plate 271

Plate 269. The Rev. W. J. Chambers and a group of mission students at the Raluana station of the Australasian Methodist Missionary Society about 1895. Chambers began work at Raluana in 1893, worked at Kabakada, and was appointed to New Ireland where he organized the expansion of the mission until 1900. (Mitchell Library)

Plate 270. 'The missionary's wife's sewing class; these women and girls made the garments they are wearing.' The date and location are not stated but it is likely these are 1885 and Raluana respectively, and the missionary's wife would be Mrs R. H. Rickard. Clothing for the hitherto naked was of importance in missionary endeavour. In January 1884 the Rev. Isaac Rooney, as mission chairman, ordered from Sydney: '1 bale fancy prints—good quality—assorted patterns; 2 lengths Brown Calico—30 in.—1 length white calico—good; 2 lengths Turkey Red; 2 doz. Crimean Shirts about 55/-; 1 doz. Crimean Shirts better quality'. Rev. I Rooney to Rev. G. Waterhouse, Duke of York, 8 January 1884, in 'The Journal and Letter Books, 1865–88, of the Rev. Isaac Rooney', pp. 310–12. Microfilm FM 4/2346, Mitchell Library. (Mitchell Library)

Plate 271. The Reverend Richard Heath Rickard (1859–1938), Methodist missionary in New Britain 1882–92. Rickard arrived at Port Hunter at the end of 1882; after a short period he took up residence at Raluana on Blanche Bay and worked there until his retirement from the New Britain mission in 1892. Rickard did valuable work in the Kuanua language and published a dictionary in 1888 that was used extensively by the mission in its educational work. As district chairman in 1890 he negotiated with the German authorities to arrange spheres of operation for the Methodist and Sacred Heart missions. In 1891, Rickard aided the Rev. George Brown in the founding of the new mission at Dobu in Papua. This photograph was taken in 1881. (N. Rickard Collection)

Plate 272

Plate 273

Plate 272. The Rev. Isaac Rooney, appointed superintendent of the New Britain mission of the Australasian Wesleyan Methodist Missionary Society early in 1881. He arrived at Port Hunter on 23 June 1881. Rooney succeeded the Rev. George Brown as superintendent and served on the Duke of York Islands until 1887. In addition to his administration of the mission, Rooney collaborated with Brown and Danks in the compilation of the Duke of York language dictionary. (Mitchell Library)

Plate 273. The Rev. H. Fellman and his pupils at Raluana in the early 1890s. (Mitchell Library)

Plate 274. Mr and Mrs George Pearson, who were selected by British Methodists in 1901 to go to New Ireland in response to an appeal from the Australasian Methodist Missionary Society. (Mitchell Library)

Plate 274

Plate 275

Plate 275. A group of schoolgirls, the pupils of Sister Mary Woolnough of the Methodist mission, at Watnabara, Duke of York group, 1918. (A. V. Noall Collection)

Plate 276

Plate 276. A group at Government House, Rabaul, at the time of the jubilee celebrations of the New Britain Methodist mission in 1925. The group includes mission personnel, Rabaul residents, and visitors from Australia. In front, from left to right, Rev. W. H. Cox, chairman of the New Britain District of the Methodist mission; Brigadier General E. Wisdom, administrator; Mrs Wisdom; Rev. W. B. Burton, general secretary, Board of Missions of the Methodist Church of Australia. (A. V. Noall Collection)

Plate 277

Plate 277. Mr E. Noall, the first principal of the Methodist Teacher Training College on Watnabara Island in the Duke of York group in 1925, and four of his assistant teachers. This institution was moved to New Britain in 1927. (A. V. Noall Collection)

13 The Mission of the Sacred Heart, New Britain, 1881-1932

Plate 278

Plate 278. The Sacred Heart mission station at Malaguna on Blanche Bay about 1905. The site for the station was acquired in 1883 by Father Navarre, and was occupied at the end of the same year after a fire caused the temporary abandonment of Kiningunan (later Vunapope). As early as 1881 Father Lannuzel, who had built a house at Nodup after leaving the Port Breton colony, had worked in the Malaguna region. In 9 September 1881, the Rev. Isaac Rooney of the Wesleyan Methodist mission wrote, 'On Tuesday we left Kabakada and walked overland to Blanche Bày striking the Bay at Malakuna, a town where formerly we had a good cause and everything seemed promising . . . but the teacher died. . . . A priest belonging to the French Colony finding the coast clear stepped in and baptized a number of people, and now he claims them as Catholics . . . so there is trouble in store for us—for wherever [these priests] set their foot in Polynesia they make trouble.' 'The Journal and Letter Books, 1865–88, of the Rev. Isaac Rooney', pp. 50–1. Microfilm FM 4/2346, Mitchell Library. (Mitchell Library)

Plate 279. Louis Couppé, M.S.C., head of the New Britain mission of the Congregation of the Sacred Heart from 1890 to 1923. Couppé was ordained priest in 1874 and entered the Congregation of the Sacred Heart in 1880. In 1884 he accompanied the Rev. Henry Verjus to Sydney and worked there under Father Navarre's direction as the Sacred Heart mission advanced from Thursday Island to Yule Island in 1885. Couppé joined the mission at Yule Island in 1886 and worked with Navarre and Verjus in the first difficult years.

On 10 May 1889 the Holy See erected the Vicariate Apostolic of New Britain and in 1890 Couppé was named as vicar apostolic of New Britain and titular bishop of Léro. Couppé served in New Britain with notable success from 1890 until his retirement in 1923. In that period his firm leadership created a strong organization for mission work throughout the Bismarck Archipelago. (Mitchell Library)

Plate 280. Missionaries of the Sacred Heart with some of their pupils, New Britain, 1903. (M. von Hein Collection)

Plate 281. Mission pupils with their teachers at St Paul's Mission, Baining Mountains, New Britain, 1899. (M. von Hein Collection)

Plate 279

Plate 280

Plate 281

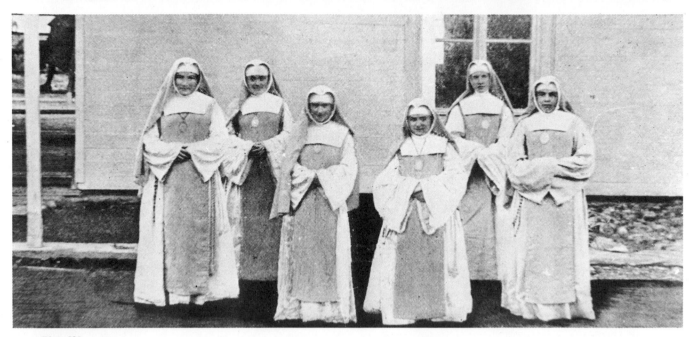

Plate 282

Plate 283

Plate 284

Plate 282. A group of mission sisters at Vunapope in 1898. In 1884 the Rev. L. A. Navarre had applied to the Mother Superior of the Sisters of Our Lady of the Sacred Heart for sisters to be sent to New Britain. Navarre had seen the need in the following terms: 'They can begin by introducing fashion among our coloured parishioners, for the only fashion they have hitherto adopted is a little too primitive and urgently necessitates a prompt reform.... But the charitable care of the sisters must above all be lavished on the children. These poor little creatures live in an atmosphere so remote from all that elevates the soul and touches the heart, that they are in a pitiful state.' Rev. L. A. Navarre to the Mother Superior of Our Lady of the Sacred Heart, Sydney, 24 February 1884, in *The Australian Annals of Our Lady of the Sacred Heart*, vol. 3, no. 8 (1 July 1892), p. 180. (Hallstrom Pacific Library)

Plate 283. Vunapope mission station, New Britain, 1903. (M. von Hein Collection)

Plate 284. St Paul mission station in the Baining Mountains of the Gazelle Peninsula and (inset) its founder, Father Matthaus Rascher, M.S.C. St Paul station was established in November 1896 and was the first Christian mission to enter the area. This photograph was published in 1907. In 1904, St Paul was the scene of bloodshed when Father Rascher, together with another priest, three mission brothers and five mission sisters, was killed by a band of Baining men. (Mitchell Library)

Plate 285

Plate 286

Plate 287

Plate 285. The Sacred Heart mission at Vunapope, New Britain. A view from Blanche Bay, December 1914. (Australian War Memorial)

Plate 286. St Paul mission in 1932. (Reproduced by permission of the Commonwealth Archives Office)

Plate 287. '*Canaque de la Nouvelle-Bretagne*' was the caption to this engraving published in *Annales de la Propagation de la Foi* (Paris, 1884). This journal of the Society for the Propagation of the Faith was circulated among the friends of the missions in France and Western Europe. Roman Catholic missionaries in all parts of the world sent news of their activities, and donations from the interested faithful helped in their support. The Sacred Heart mission in New Britain was one of the missions supported by the society. Note in the engraving the steel axe-head, the tobacco pipe and the pipe-cleaner. (Mitchell Library)

138

Plate 288

Plate 288. Students and staff of the Roman Catholic catechist school at Taliligap near Rabaul in 1927. (Reproduced by permission of the Commonwealth Archives Office)

Plate 289. Mission education, 1928. A class at St Paul's College for catechist students at Taliligap near Rabaul. (Reproduced by permission of the Commonwealth Archives Office)

Plate 289

Plate 290

Plate 290. Five veteran brothers of the Sacred Heart mission in New Britain in 1927. (Reproduced by permission of the Commonwealth Archives Office)

Plate 291. The Sacred Heart mission station at Nakanai, New Britain, in 1927. (Reproduced by permission of the Commonwealth Archives Office)

Plate 291

Plate 292

Plate 293

Plate 292. The headquarters of the Sacred Heart mission at Vunapope near Kokopo in New Britain in 1932. (Reproduced by permission of the Commonwealth Archives Office)

Plate 293. The cathedral of the Sacred Heart at Vunapope, the headquarters of the Sacred Heart mission in New Britain, about 1932. This cathedral was destroyed by Allied bombing in 1943. (Reproduced by permission of the Commonwealth Archives Office)

14 The Mission of the Sacred Heart, Papua, 1885-1935

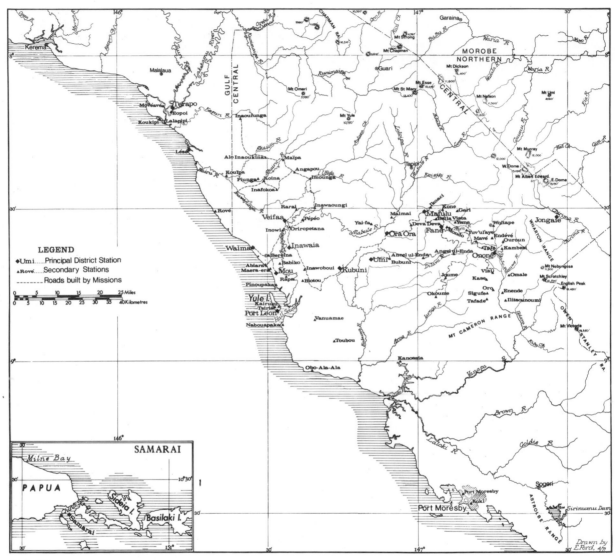

Plate 294

Plate 294. The mission of the Congregation of the Sacred Heart in Papua, *c.* 1935, showing the territorial spread of the mission in the first fifty years of its existence. Between 1885, the year of the founding of the mission at Port Léon on Yule Island, and 1889, Fathers Navarre and Verjus (see plates 90, 92) overcame the difficulties of a pioneer mission. By 1889 the base on Yule Island was secure and supply from Australia assured. After preparatory exploration in 1886–87 in the district of the Roro and Mekeo, the first mission station of the Congregation was established at Mou in September 1889. In the following year Inawaia was established as a station for the Mekeo and, from 1891 to 1896, Vunuamae for the Polao. The coastal station of Waima was founded in 1897.

142

By the end of the century the coast east and west of Yule Island and the hinterland had been brought under the influence of the mission. The next phase of expansion was penetration into the rugged terrain of the Papuan mountains. In 1896, Sacred Heart missioners began explorations of the mountain area in the Kouni district and in 1899 Kubuni and Oba Oba (Ora Ora) were established, followed by Mafulu in 1905 and Ononé (Ononghé) in 1913. Problems of supply in the rugged terrain would explain the time between the founding of stations; it was necessary to build a secure base station in each newly entered area before further penetration was possible. In 1914 and 1932 the Sacred Heart Mission entered Port Moresby and Samarai respectively in order to minister to the European settlers in those towns and to the local people.

The geographical pattern of the Sacred Heart mission was affected by the 'spheres of influence' policy that the government of British New Guinea attempted to implement from 1890 onwards. The Anglican, Methodist and London Missionary Society missions approved of this policy but the French Catholic missionaries of the Congregation of the Sacred Heart did not. Bishop Navarre as head of the mission said that the policy was an attempt by government to restrict the mission's field of activity. The 'spheres of influence' policy caused the Sacred Heart mission to concentrate its efforts, during the important period of expansion at the turn of the century, on the region shown in the map. In 1903 Father de Boismenu, as coadjutor to Monsignor Navarre, laid down a policy of expansion towards the interior rather than along the coast, which was left within the London Missionary Society's sphere of influence.

It is clear that the success of the Sacred Heart mission in its first fifty years came from the quality of its leaders: Louis-André Navarre from 1885 to 1907, and Alain de Boismenu from 1908 to 1945. Navarre, assisted by the energetic and able missioners Henry Verjus and Louis Couppé, and de Boismenu himself, established the firm foundation of the mission. De Boismenu consolidated the mission by carrying out a planned reorganization of its administrative and financial structure.

In 1898 the mission was made up of five districts covering about 8000 people, and of these 2400 were baptized Catholics; 800 children were in the mission's schools. In 1935 there were about 60 000 people under mission influence. About 20 000 of these were regarded as Christian and about 6000 children were in the schools. (Map drawn by Edgar Ford, adapted from end-paper map in André Dupeyrat, *Papouasie: Histoire de la Mission, 1885–1935* [Paris, 1935])

Plate 295

Plate 296

Plate 295. The Yule Island mission of the Sacred Heart (Port Léon) as pictured for the faithful in France in 1890. (Mitchell Library)

Plate 296. On 28 January 1889, Fathers Verjus and Hartzer set out from Yule Island to extend the Sacred Heart mission to the mainland. The place chosen was Mou, a village of the Roro people. They arrived there on 28 February, and a mission house and church were constructed near the Roro meeting house (pictured), as the missionaries called it. This engraving was published in Paris in 1890. (Mitchell Library)

Plate 297. Alain Marie Guynot de Boismenu (1870–1953), missioner of the Sacred Heart. Born in France, de Boismenu was ordained in 1895 and became counsellor to Archbishop Navarre. In March 1900 he was consecrated as bishop coadjutor and succeeded Navarre on his retirement in January 1908. During his long term in charge of the mission until 1945, de Boismenu directed its expansion to Ononé in 1913, to Port Moresby in 1914, to Toaripi in 1927 and to Samarai in 1932. De Boismenu expanded the training of native catechists from 9 in 1908 to 219 in 1933, and also created an indigenous priesthood (see plate 312). In 1918 he established the Handmaids of the Lord, an indigenous sisterhood. (Mitchell Library)

Plate 298. Marie-Thérèse Noblet and members of the Papuan sisterhood of the Sacred Heart at Florivel convent, Kubuni (see plate 294), in 1921. The first Papuan girls were admitted as postulants in 1918 and in 1919 the newly erected convent at Kubuni was occupied by the sisterhood. Mother Marie-Thérèse Noblet was brought out from Europe in 1920 by Bishop de Boismenu and commenced her notable career in the mission by taking charge of the Florivel convent. (Mitchell Library)

Plate 297

Plate 298

Plate 299

Plate 299. A view of part of the Sacred Heart mission station on Yule Island in 1924. (Father Coltré Collection)

Plate 300

Plate 300. The visit of the apostolic delegate to Yule Island about 1930. Seated, left to right, Sister James; Bishop de Boismenu; the apostolic delegate; Monsignor King of Sydney; Sister Zita, and Sister Albertine. (Father Coltré Collection)

Plate 301. School children and teachers at the Yule Island headquarters of the Sacred Heart mission. This photograph probably dates from the 1930s. (Reproduced by permission of the Commonwealth Archives Office)

Plate 301

Plate 302. Pupils and staff of St Patrick's School, Yule Island, 1928. (Father Coltré Collection)

Plate 302

Plate 303. Missioners of the Sacred Heart at Yule Island in 1928. Front row, seated, left to right, Brother Henry, Rev. Father Vitale (who arrived with Bishop Verjus), Rev. Father Chabet, Rev. Father Fastre (Superior of the Mission Fathers), and Rev. Father Guilbau. Standing, Rev. Fathers Bodet, Reus, Moyon, Fradette, Lang, Lepaire, Dubuy and van Campenhaut. Back row, Rev. Father Caudron, Brother Alexis, Fathers Coltré and Van Neck, Brothers Boviert and George Garred (Australians), [unidentified]. (Father Coltré Collection)

Plate 304. The problem of supply for mission stations in rugged mountainous country is indicated here. A caravan of horses is seen arriving at the Oba Oba mission station in 1924. (Father Coltré Collection)

Plate 303

Plate 304

Plate 305

Plate 305. A photograph taken in 1928 of recent converts to Christianity in the Ononé district. These men were baptized and confirmed by the founder of the Ononé mission station, Father Jules Dubuy. (Father Coltré Collection)

Plate 306. The mission house at Ononé with the founder of the station, Father Jules Dubuy, on the veranda. The roof is covered with pandanus thatch. The station was established in 1913 and its extreme isolation and the rugged terrain caused difficulties. Even so, by 1918 the mission claimed four hundred converts amongst the local people and within a few years Father Dubuy had established a school with fifty pupils. (Father Coltré Collection)

Plate 306

Plate 307

Plate 307. A photograph taken at the moment of Benediction of the Blessed Sacrament on the feast of Corpus Christi at Ononé, 1928. The altar is on the veranda of the mission house. (Father Coltré Collection)

Plate 308. Representatives of Church and State at Yule Island, about 1930. Left to right, Father Chabet, Sir Hubert Murray, Mr Pinney, Mother Rosalie, Mrs Pinney, Lady Murray and Captain Planson. (Father Coltré Collection)

Plate 309. A scene at Oba Oba mission station in 1928. Fathers Denees, Rossier and Caudron and Brothers Paul and John are resting on the veranda of the fathers' house after a Corpus Christi procession. (Father Coltré Collection)

Plate 308

Plate 309

Plate 310

Plate 311

Plate 312

Plate 310. Girls of the Oba Oba mountain region (Kouni district) with a sister of Our Lady of the Sacred Heart in 1928. Oba Oba mission station was established in 1899–1900 by Father Armand Pages. (Father Coltré Collection)

Plate 311. The twenty-fifth anniversary of Bishop de Boismenu's consecration is recorded in this photograph taken in 1925. It shows Bishop de Boismenu, Archbishop Duhig of Brisbane and Monsignor Byrne, vicar-general to the archbishop, with the missioners of the Sacred Heart and some local men and boys. (Father Coltré Collection)

Plate 312. Louis Vangeke, the first indigenous Roman Catholic bishop, was born at Beipa in the Mekeo in 1905. In 1928 when this photograph was taken, he was about to leave Papua to study at a seminary in Madagascar, encouraged to do so by Bishop de Boismenu. After ordination in 1937 he returned to Papua. In 1971 he was consecrated bishop in Sydney by Pope Paul VI. (Father Coltré Collection)

Plate 313

Plate 313. Transport in the mountainous area of the Sacred Heart mission was difficult. In this photograph Sister Saint Florent is about to start on her rounds, *c.* 1930. (Father Coltré Collection)

Plate 314

Plate 314. Much of the success of the Sacred Heart mission in the Papuan mountains depended upon the hard work of the mission brothers who organized the industrial side of the mission. This photograph shows four brothers with two of their local helpers who worked the mission sawmill at Aropokina in the 1930s. (Father Coltré Collection)

15 The Lutheran Mission, Mainland New Guinea, 1886-1945

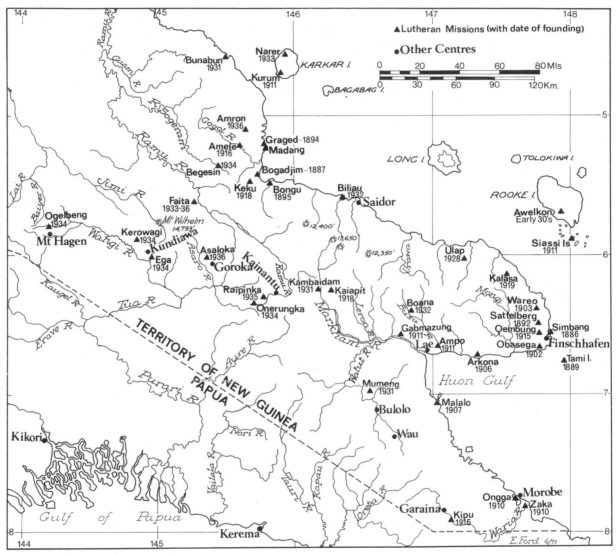

Plate 315

Plate 315. The Lutheran mission in New Guinea, 1886–1939. From its beginning at Simbang near Finschhafen in 1886 the mission followed in the wake of German settlement, and, in the first period of expansion to 1900, stations were established in the regions of Finschhafen and Madang. Near Finschhafen, stations were placed on Tami Island and at Sattelberg, and near Madang the stations of Bogadjim, Graged and Bongu were established. Two mission societies of the Lutheran Church contributed funds and missionaries to New Guinea: the mission society based on Neuendettelsau in Bavaria and the Rhenish Mission Society based on Barmen. These two societies were responsible for the New Guinea mission until the Australian government assumed the mandate in 1921.

The first decade of the twentieth century was a period of consolidation for the mission. In 1910–11 expansion led to

Siassi Island in Vitiaz Strait, to Lae and Gabmazung on the Markham River and to Ongga and Zaka near Morobe. Problems of sickness and local opposition in the Madang area confined the mission to this area until 1910, but in 1911 the founding of Kurum, on Karkar Island, led to the mission's permanent presence there.

World War I presented difficulties for the mission in obtaining supplies from Germany and arranging alternative supplies. Nevertheless, important explorations were carried out. In 1916 an expedition reconnoitred the country between Finschhafen and the Ramu River and another in the Morobe district looked at the country near the Bulolo and Watut Rivers. The founding of a mission station at Kaiapit in 1918 resulted from such exploratory journeys.

After the war the mission was restricted in its activities while the future of German New Guinea was subject to negotiation and the status of German missionaries was considered by the Australian authorities. The United Evangelical Lutheran Church in Australia assumed some responsibility for the mission, in conjunction with the Evangelical Lutheran Synod of Iowa. When Germany joined the League of Nations in 1927 the position of the Neuendettelsau and Barmen societies in the mission was restored. In 1930 the mission area was divided into areas of responsibility. The Rhenish (Barmen) society assumed responsibility for the Madang region, the Iowa Synod for the Finisterre region (Rai Coast, Sio Island, Siassi Island, Kaiapit), and the Neuendettelsau society for the Finschhafen region.

The 1920s were important for the future expansion of the mission into the Highland region. In 1920 a mission party from Kaiapit penetrated the Eastern Highlands. In the period 1922 to 1929, explorations were made as far as the Bena Bena Valley and as a result Kambaidam was established in 1931. Three years later this station was advanced to Onerungka.

In 1933 a survey flight as far as Mount Hagen led to land exploration westwards from Onerungka in the same year. From these explorations came the knowledge that led the mission into the central Highlands. Kerowagi was established in 1934, as were Ega and Ogelbeng.

By 1939 the Lutheran mission in New Guinea was well established along the coastline from Karkar Island to Astrolabe Bay and thence to the Huon Gulf and to Morobe. Inland, the hinterland of Madang, the Huon Peninsula, and the Markham and Waria Rivers had been occupied; in the last stage of expansion before World War II the Highlands as far as Mount Hagen had been taken up in a series of mission stations. (Map drawn by Edgar Ford)

Plate 316

Plate 316. Simbang II mission station, 1906. The original station established by Johann Flierl and Karl Tremel in 1886 was eight kilometres south of Finschhafen. In 1891 Flierl decided to relocate the station on an elevated position away from the coast. This was an active centre until 1906. (Mitchell Library)

Plate 317. A group at Deinzerhöhe mission station in the early twentieth century. The missionary is Johann Decker, who served the mission from 1895 to 1943, mostly at Deinzerhöhe. The station, situated between Finschhafen and Arkona on the Huon Gulf, was established by missionary Bamler in 1899. It was destroyed in World War II and was not rebuilt. (Mitchell Library)

Plate 317

154

Plate 318. A conference of Lutheran missionaries in 1900 (at Simbang?). Seated, left to right, Georg Bamler (1887–1928), Adam Hoh (1892–1914), Johann Flierl (1886–1930), Konrad Vetter (1889–1906), Richard Hansche (1899–1907). Standing, left to right, Friedrich Held (1897–1901), Johann Decker (1895–1943). The dates in parentheses are the periods of service. (Mitchell Library)

Plate 319. Missionary Georg Pfalzer (1899–1914) at Pola (Finschhafen), outside the church in 1914. Pola, on Finschhafen harbour, was an important mission station until World War II when it was completely destroyed. Missionary Pfalzer established Pola in 1903 and spent the remaining years of his office there. (Mitchell Library)

Plate 318

Plate 319

155

Plate 320

Plate 320. The influence of national educational ideas in European education of New Guineans is shown in this photograph of a teacher and his pupils at a Lutheran mission school somewhere in Kaiser-Wilhelmsland about 1916. A feature of German education up to World War I was an emphasis on gymnastics and drill (*Turnen*) for boys. (Mitchell Library)

Plate 321. 'Missionary Zahn Preaching to the Heathen' was the caption given this photograph by the Rev. Johann Flierl (J. Flierl, *Forty-Five Years in New Guinea* [Columbus, Ohio, 1931], p. 132). Heinrich Zahn served the New Guinea mission from 1902 to 1932 and was notable for establishing the Hopoi Teachers' Training College in 1924 near Arkona on the Huon Gulf. Zahn contributed to mission literature in the Yabem language, including a dictionary and a translation of the New Testament. (Mitchell Library)

Plate 321

Plate 322

Plate 322. Frau Boettger and her pupils at Malalo, *c.* 1910. Malalo, on the Huon Gulf south-east of Lae, was established in 1907 by missionaries Mailaender and Boettger. The mission worked among the Buang people to the west. The station was rebuilt after World War II. (Mitchell Library)

Plate 323. Wareo mission station, early in the twentieth century. Established in 1903 by missionaries Zwanziger and Wagner, this station was active up to World War II, when it was totally destroyed. For twenty years Wagner conducted a middle school at Wareo. (Mitchell Library)

Plate 323

Plate 324

Plate 324. Sattelberg mission station, *c.* 1920s. This station was established in 1892 by Johann Flierl and served as a place where missionaries could recover from fever contracted on the coast. Sattelberg developed as one of the most important of the Lutheran mission stations. A notable missionary at Sattelberg was Dr G. Pilhofer, who served the mission from 1905 to 1939. It was Pilhofer who translated the New Testament into the Katê language. Sattelberg was the scene of bitter fighting during World War II and was totally destroyed. (Mitchell Library)

Plate 325. A group of Christian converts at Sattelberg mission, early twentieth century. The first baptisms were conducted at Sattelberg as early as 1905 by missionary Keysser. (A. C. Frerichs, *Anutu Conquers in New Guinea* [Columbus, Ohio, 1957], p. 42.) '. . . Soon after that ten enrolled in a catechetical class. It was the beginning of a great work, the blessings of which extended to the valleys beneath, to the hills and mountains beyond, and reached even to Mt Hagen in the far interior. It was Sattelberg whose natives had given the impetus.' Ibid., p. 78. (Mitchell Library)

Plate 325

Plate 326

Plate 326. The founder of the Lutheran mission, senior missionary Johann Flierl, near the end of his long service (1886–1930) in New Guinea. The caption to this photograph in Flierl's own work (J. Flierl, *Forty-Five Years in New Guinea* [Columbus, Ohio, 1931], p. 104) was 'Senior John Flierl and Some of His Spiritual Children'. Flierl in 1920 saw one success of the mission as the establishment of '. . . a new good order of a young Christian people, their own order, not that of the white missionaries . . . no antagonism between Christian and heathen but rather a united people with only one aim—to do away with the old heathendom with its wicked rites and to establish a new order, not the strange one of the European Church, but rather a genuine Papuan civil order rooted in their own community.' J. Flierl and A. I. Hopkins, 'Native Life in the South-West Pacific from Two Points of View', in *International Review of Mission*, vol. 17 (1920), p. 540. (Mitchell Library)

Plate 327. The dedication of the first school at Kerowagi in the Chimbu, 4 July 1937. Kerowagi mission was established in September 1934 from Madang and by 1937 was firmly established. Restrictions imposed by the Administration on the use of indigenous evangelists and teachers in 1935–36 prevented the anticipated expansion of the work of the Kerowagi station. The killing of a Roman Catholic priest and a brother was one reason for the restrictions. Another reason advanced was friction between the Lutheran and Roman Catholic missions. A. C. Frerichs, *Anutu Conquers in New Guinea* (Columbus, Ohio, 1957), pp. 63–4. (Mitchell Library)

Plate 327

Plate 328

Plate 328. The ruins of Sattelberg, November 1943, at the time of its reoccupation by Australian troops. Sattelberg mission station was a battleground as Australian troops fought to dislodge the Japanese who had entrenched themselves on the site. Damage at Sattelberg was typical of that caused to many Lutheran stations in the battle areas of Markham, Finschhafen and Madang. (Australian War Memorial)

16 The Methodists and Anglicans, North-east Papua, 1891-1940

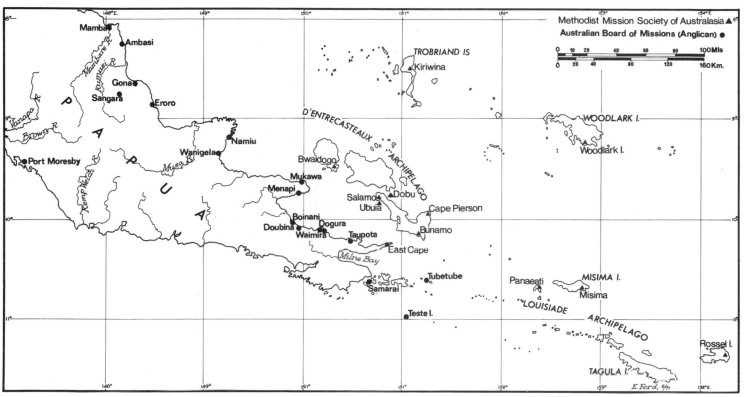

Plate 329

Plate 329. The mission stations of the Methodist Missionary Society of Australasia and of the Australian Board of Missions (Anglican) in Papua, 1891–1930.

In June 1890, Sir William MacGregor, lieutenant governor of British New Guinea, invited representatives of the London Missionary Society, the Methodist Missionary Society of Australasia and the Anglican Board of Missions to confer with him about the prospects of extending mission influence throughout the Possession. From this emerged a policy whereby the London Missionary Society was to consolidate its position along the south coast from South Cape to the Papuan Gulf, the Methodist Mission Society would enter the D'Entrecasteaux Islands, the Trobriands and the Louisiades, and the Anglican mission would work in the area of the north-east coast from Cape Ducie to the border with German New Guinea at Mitre Rock.

The Anglican Mission. Following the assumption by Great Britain of sovereignty over British New Guinea in 1888, the General Synod of Australia resolved: 'That the recent annexation of portion of New Guinea imposes direct obligation upon the Church to provide for the spiritual welfare both of the natives and of the settlers.' (Quoted in A. K. Chignell, *Twenty-One Years in Papua* [London, 1913], p. 5.) In the following year the Rev. A. A. Maclaren was appointed as the first missionary to New Guinea and in 1890 he visited the north-east coast to reconnoitre the region allotted to the mission by Sir William MacGregor. Joined by the Rev. Copland

King, Maclaren arrived at Samarai in August 1891, and land was purchased at Dogura for the first mission station. Extension of the mission was slow because of sickness. Maclaren died at the end of 1891 and Copland King had to withdraw to Australia. The Board of Missions in Sydney discussed the mission's future, which was considered to be uncertain, but in March 1892 King was able to return to Dogura and complete the building of the mission house. Two South Sea Island teachers recruited in Queensland joined the mission in May 1893 and it was possible to place them at Taupota and at Awaiama. An attempt to place a teacher at Menapi in July 1893 was unsuccessful and this station was not permanently manned until 1904. In 1894 a teacher was placed at Boiani.

In 1895 Sir William MacGregor urged extension of the mission to the Musa River in Dyke Ackland Bay, but mission finances did not permit this. In June 1897 the executive council of the Australian Board of Missions considered a letter from Mac-Gregor in which they were asked to '. . . face the question and declare their inability to extend and their willingness to cede a portion of the territory allotted to them, and allow him to invite some other body to take up the work'. (A. K. Chignell, *Twenty-One Years in Papua* [London, 1913], p. 54.)

This challenge led to the appointment of the Right Reverend Montagu John Stone-Wigg as bishop of New Guinea, with responsibility for financing mission work in his diocese. Stone-Wigg had ten years as head of the mission and under him the mission expanded to extend its influence throughout its allotted area. In 1898 Wanigela and Mukawa on Collingwood Bay were established and the following year Mamba, at the mouth of the Mambare River, was founded. By 1901 eleven coastal stations had been firmly established and the mission had extended its influence along its 480 kilometres of coastline.

The Methodist Mission. The Methodist Missionary Society of Australasia took up its option of the north-east coast from East Cape to Cape Ducie and the D'Entrecasteaux, Trobriand and Louisiade island groups in 1891. The mission party that sailed to Dobu in the D'Entrecasteaux group was led by the Rev. William E. Bromilow and was made up of four European missionaries and twenty-two South Sea Island teachers from Fiji, Samoa and Tonga. Also in the party were the Rev. Dr George Brown, founder of the New Britain mission in 1875 and in 1891 the general secretary of the Methodist Missionary Society, and the Rev. R. H. Rickard of the New Britain mission.

In June 1891 the pioneer party landed on Dobu Island and a headquarters station was established with efficiency and expedition; soon teachers were stationed at several points on Dobu and on Fergusson Island nearby. On the advice of Sir William MacGregor the island of Panaete to the west of Misima Island was chosen for the central station of the Louisiade Archipelago, and the Rev. S. B. Fellows and the Rev. J. Watson went to establish a station there in August 1891. At the same time two Samoan teachers were installed at Teste Island which, under the arrangements arrived at with Sir William MacGregor and the London Missionary Society, was now included in the Methodist sphere of influence. At the request of the people of Tubetube Island in the Engineer Group, the Rev. J. T. Field was installed there as missionary, also in 1891.

In September 1892 the Rev. W. E. Bromilow visited the Trobriand Islands, but it was not until 1894 that it was possible to install a missionary there. The Rev. S. B. Fellows was transferred from Panaete to establish the first station at Kiriwina. At about the same time a South Sea Island teacher was installed at Bwagbwaga, on Misima Island in the Louisiades.

After the discovery of gold on Woodlark Island in 1897, Bromilow decided to extend the mission to that island to fulfil the needs of the miners as well as those of the island people. In 1897 a European lay missionary named Glew was established in the mining camp. South Sea Island teachers were maintained on Woodlark to work among the island people after the gold mining came to an end.

An important development in the mission's history was the creation at Salamo on Fergusson Island of a central training institution. In 1919 the synod of the New Guinea mission acceded to the request of the Rev. M. K. Gilmour, who had urged the setting up of a training institution at Salamo on a site that he advised was most suitable for the purpose.

In October 1920, Gilmour went to live at Salamo and in 1922, after land purchase had been properly legalized, building operations began on a mission site with an area of 247 hectares, much of which was put under cultivation for the support of the student community.

The Rev. J. W. Burton, general secretary of the Methodist Missionary Society of Australasia, writing in 1926, saw the institution at Salamo as one of the great achievements of the New Guinea mission. J. W. Burton, *Our Task in Papua* (London, 1926), pp. 79–84. (Map drawn by Edgar Ford and adapted from that in J. W. Burton, *Missionary Survey of the Pacific Islands* [London, 1930], p. 60)

Plate 330

Plate 330. The mission ship *Lord of the Isles* at anchor off Dobu Island in the D'Entrecasteaux group in June 1891, at the founding of the Papuan mission of the Australasian Methodist Missionary Society. (Mitchell Library)

Plate 331. The building of the mission house at Dobu, June 1891. The Rev. George Brown wrote of this, 'It will give some idea of the work done, if it is considered that the land had to be cleared, temporary storehouses erected for furniture and stores; 126 hardwood piles, many of them 9′ and 10′ in length, cut and boated over from Normanby, erected in position on the ground and levelled, all the timber for 2 large houses to be landed; houses for teachers to be erected; and a large mission house, 66′ long and 35′ wide, to be built. All this was done in a short space of 3 weeks, and the missionaries were in possession of the house, which, though not finished, was quite habitable when we left for New Britain.' (Mitchell Library)

Plate 331

Plate 332

Plate 332. Dobuan boys watching the landing of the first missionaries, members of the Methodist mission party, in June 1891. The Rev. R. H. Rickard took this photograph and labelled it 'Dobu boys watching us land. . . .' The Rev. William Bromilow, leader of the mission, wrote in 1929, 'I shall refer in a sentence only to the licentiousness of the Dobuans in common with Papuans as a whole. Up to the time of marriage the women are undisguisedly unmoral, and afterwards the restraints are doubtfully observed. Among the men no moral code can be said to exist; children are initiated to vice at a terribly early age.' W. E. Bromilow, *Twenty Years Among Primitive Papuans* (London, 1929), p. 98. (Mitchell Library)

Plate 333. Different ideas from the two cultures about suitable dress for the tropical climate are represented in this photograph of two unidentified missionaries of the Methodist mission with a group of Dobu Islanders. Probable date, about the turn of the century. (Mitchell Library)

Plate 333

Plate 334

Plate 334. The New Guinea synod of the Methodist mission at Dobu in about 1900. The missionary behind the unoccupied chair is the Rev. W. E. Bromilow, the founder and chairman of the mission. On his left is the Rev. M. K. Gilmour, and seated in front of Gilmour is his wife. The Gilmours were the founders of a new mission station at Salamo on Fergusson Island in 1922. This became the training centre for the mission. Bromilow retired from the mission in 1908 and was succeeded in the chairmanship by Gilmour. The woman second from the right is Bessie Corfield, a mission sister, and the last on the right is Janet Gibb, a mission teacher. The other members of the group have not been identified. (Mitchell Library)

Plate 335. The Rev. S. B. Fellows of the Methodist mission and Enamakala, at Kiriwina (Trobriand Islands) in the late 1890s. Enamakala was recognized by his European contemporaries as paramount chief of the Trobriands. C. A. W. Monckton wrote: 'The old paramount chief never walked, but was always carried on the backs of men, and was invariably accompanied by his sorcerer and a sort of grand vizier. Before the old chief, women crawled on their bellies, and men bent almost to the ground.

'I have lately received from Dr Seligman a book written by him entitled, *The Melanesians of British New Guinea*, in which he flatly contradicts a statement made by Sir William MacGregor that Enamakala was the paramount chief of this group of islands. . . . I have no hesitation in saying that he [Seligman] is not right.' C. A. W. Monckton, *Some Experiences of a New Guinea Resident Magistrate* (London, 1921), p. 162. (Mitchell Library)

Plate 335

Plate 336. The Rev. S. B. Fellows of the Methodist mission with his pupils at Kiriwina (Trobriand Islands) in the late 1890s. Fellows was at the founding of the mission at Dobu in 1891 and shortly after began a station on Panaete Island, west of Misima Island in the Louisiade Archipelago. In 1894 he transferred to Kiriwina, where he opened the head station of the mission at Kawataria. In 1901 he returned to Australia and his colleagues put it on record: 'The synod [Dobu synod] would place on record its appreciation of the earnest, efficient and successful work of Brother Fellows—first at Panaeiti and then at Kiriwina. At both of these stations his personal influence and preaching ability have done great good to a large number of people and his special work amongst the youths and children has been greatly blessed.' (1901 Dobu Report.) An entry for 15 November 1891 in Fellows's diary while he was serving at Panaete Island indicates some missionary values: 'Had a good service and showed picture of Queen. Spoke of duties of natives as subjects— honour placed by Britishers on Queen and pleaded for lightening of labours of native women. As I did so several women cried out, "Ubada iwaidi", while Kaiwai, the chief, sulkily said, "If women did not work in gardens there would not be enough food!" I then went on to speak of Albert the Good as having only one wife, and bashed Polygamy.' Diary of Rev. S. B. Fellows, Mitchell Library MS. (Mitchell Library)

Plate 337. A Methodist mission congregation in the D'Entrecasteaux group in the early 1920s. (Mitchell Library)

Plate 338. A Methodist mission congregation at Dobu, *c*. 1926. (Mitchell Library)

Plate 336

Plate 337

Plate 338

Plate 339

Plate 339. A Methodist mission meeting with the offering in the form of coconuts, somewhere in north-east Papua in the 1920s. (Mitchell Library)

Plate 340. Salamo on Fergusson Island, the central training institution for the Methodist mission. Established in 1922 by the Rev. M. K. and Mrs Gilmour, Salamo was designed to train Papuan teachers and missionaries. In 1926, J. W. Burton, the general secretary of the Methodist Missionary Society of Australasia, said of Salamo: 'It is to be a great Training Centre. No need in Papua is greater than this. We must train men and women to make unnecessary, some day, the white missionary, and the South Sea Island teacher who costs so much in travelling expenses to and from his island home.' J. W. Burton, *Our Task in Papua* (London, 1926), p. 82. (Mitchell Library)

Plate 340

Plate 341

Plate 341. The Rev. A. A. Maclaren (1853–1891), founder of the Anglican New Guinea mission, was accepted by Bishop Barry, primate of Australia, in 1889 as the first missionary of the Church of England in New Guinea. Maclaren visited the country in 1890 and travelled with Sir William MacGregor in the region allotted by him to the mission from Cape Ducie to Mitre Rock. On his return to Australia he raised funds for the intended mission and recruited the Rev. Copland King to join him in the project.

Maclaren and King sailed to New Guinea in July 1891, and in August land at Dogura was bought as the site for the first mission station. Both Maclaren and King contracted malaria, and the latter was forced to return to Australia. Maclaren fell ill in December 1891 at Samarai and died on board the government vessel *Merrie England* en route to Cooktown. (Mitchell Library)

Plate 342 **Plate 343**

Plate 342. The Rev. Copland King was associated with the Rev. A. A. Maclaren in the founding of the first Anglican mission in New Guinea. King went with Maclaren to Dogura in August 1891, but in November illness forced him to withdraw to Australia. He returned to New Guinea in March 1892 and was appointed acting head of the mission; the continuance of the mission depended largely on him until the appointment of the Right Rev. Montagu John Stone-Wigg as bishop of New Guinea in 1898. In 1899 King went to Mamba, a newly established mission station on the Mambare River, and served there, and at Ambasi, until 1913.

The success of the Anglican mission in overcoming formidable difficulties in the early years was due largely to the work of Copland King, who provided the stability and experience that the mission needed. (Mitchell Library)

Plate 344

Plate 343. The Right Rev. Montagu John Stone-Wigg, the first Anglican bishop of New Guinea, consecrated in January 1898. Stone-Wigg assumed financial responsibility for the mission, which he governed for ten years. During his bishopric the mission expanded throughout the region of its responsibility and when he retired in 1908 was in a strong position to ensure permanent influence. (Mitchell Library)

Plate 344. The church at Wanigela on Collingwood Bay, 1904. The founding of the Wanigela mission in 1898 resulted from the strong pressure exerted by Sir William MacGregor to have the mission occupy that part of the coast allotted to it by the 1890 arrangement and not yet taken up. Bishop Stone-Wigg responded to this. The founding party of 1898 first attempted to establish the station of Sinapa on a site chosen by Sir William MacGregor. This site proving to be unsuitable, Bishop Stone-Wigg chose Wanigela. (Mitchell Library)

Plate 345

Plate 345. Thomas Kasiko, a pupil-teacher of the Anglican mission, and his class at Wanigela on Collingwood Bay, c. 1908. Kasiko received a wage of fourpence a week in addition to food, according to the Rev. A. K. Chignell, the missionary at Wanigela. He usually taught a class of about thirty-five big boys and girls. 'His class had read and re-read all the printed matter that is available, and now he has got them translating from Ubir into Wedauan and back again into Ubir, with a running commentary of his own in the English he so persistently affects and so intelligently uses.' Chignell commented on mission education generally: '. . . The establishment of schools is no easy matter. We have taken it for granted, apparently, that what is supposed to be good for English children must also of course be suitable for children in Papua, and so we have been trying to give everywhere along this coast, a sort of European primary education, consisting of the "three Rs" with the addition of a fourth "R"—Religion.' A. K. Chignell, *An Outpost in Papua* (London, 1911), pp. 88–103. (Mitchell Library)

Plate 346. The Church of St Peter and St Paul at Dogura, *c.* 1909. This church was constructed in 1904 and served in place of the chapel that had been built as a part of the mission house established in 1892. The Church of St Peter and St Paul served the mission until the building of the Dogura cathedral in the late 1930s. (Mitchell Libráry)

Plate 347. The Rev. C. Miller and students at Eroro on Oro Bay in 1933. (E. Miller Collection)

Plate 346

Plate 347

Plate 348

Plate 348

Plate 348. The Cathedral of St Peter and St Paul at Dogura in the 1960s. The proposal to build the cathedral, using voluntary labour and locally raised funds, was first put forward in 1933. In January 1934 a lay missionary, Mr Robert Jones, submitted a building plan based on the architectural sketches of Professor Wilkinson of Sydney University. A legacy of £605, made up to £1800 by local subscriptions, formed the basic finance for the project. The materials used in construction were reinforced concrete and local timber. The work force consisted of local labourers who worked for three months for no wages and were fed and housed by the mission. (S. M. Matthews Collection)

17 The Society of the Divine Word, Mainland New Guinea, 1896-1940

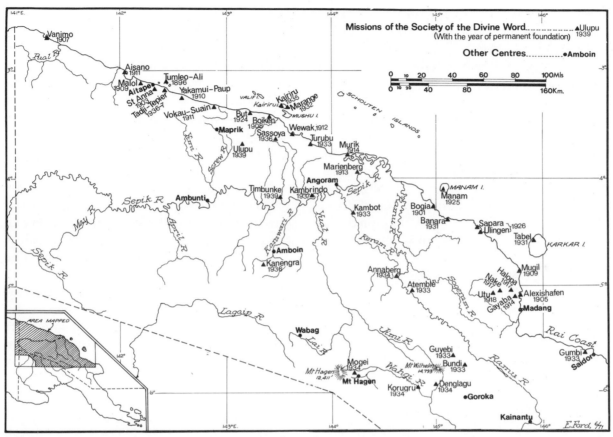

Plate 349

Plate 349. The mission stations of the Society of the Divine Word (*Societas Verbi Divini*) in New Guinea, 1896–1939. The Society of the Divine Word was founded in 1875 at Steyl in Holland. In 1896 the society was entrusted by the Holy See with a mission field, the newly erected Prefecture Apostolic of Wilhelmsland, that part of the New Guinea mainland under German control. The pioneer mission party, under the leadership of Father Eberhard Limbrock, arrived at Friedrich-Wilhelmshafen (Madang) on 13 August 1896.

The mission's intention was to establish its first station at Friedrich-Wilhelmshafen, but the presence there of the Lutheran (Rhenish Mission Society) mission proved to be a hindrance to the Society of the Divine Word. Father Limbrock then visited Berlinhafen (Aitape) and subsequently purchased land on Tumleo Island from the Neuguinea-Kompagnie. Land was purchased also on the mainland, and in 1896 the first Society of the Divine Word missionaries were installed on the island site. In 1900 Father Limbrock was authorized by the governor of German New Guinea to seek land on the coast extending from Eitel Friedrichhafen (Ulingen) to Potsdamhafen (near Bogia). Two hundred and three hectares of land were purchased at Prinz Albrechthafen (Bogia) and it was planned to develop this site as the central station for the mission. Shipping difficulties forestalled this plan and in 1904 Governor Hahl sanctioned the purchase of land at Alexishafen, which was developed as mission headquarters. In the following year Dr Hahl sanctioned land purchases at St Anna near Aitape and at Dallmanhafen (Wewak), and extensions to mission sites at Potsdamhafen, Bogia and Alexishafen.

An early policy of the mission was to secure enough land for the laying down of coconut plantations. (See R. M. Wiltgen, S.V.D., 'Catholic Mission Plantations in Mainland New Guinea: Their Origin and Purpose', in *The History of Melanesia*, Second Waigani Seminar [Canberra, 1969], p. 329.) This policy aimed at making the mission as independent as possible of financial sources overseas, mainly in Europe, and was pursued as coastal and offshore island sites were consolidated and increased in the first decades of the twentieth century. At the same time some penetration of the hinterland went on, notably to the west of Alexishafen (Halopa, Nake, Utu and Gayaba) and along the Sepik River (Marienberg, 1913).

The 1930s was a period of great development for the mission. From its strong position on and near the coast it played a notable role in the opening up of the New Guinea Highlands. In 1933 Father Alfons Schäfer and Brother Anton Baas crossed the Ramu River and established mission stations at Guyebi and at Bundi. About the same time the explorer of the Mount Hagen area, Michael Leahy, urged Father William Ross, stationed at Alexishafen headquarters, to come to Mount Hagen and establish a mission in the midst of an extensive population.

Leahy's suggestion was taken up by Father Ross and in 1934 he led a mission party from Bogadjim on Astrolabe Bay to the Ramu River and thence to the Society of the Divine Word station at Bundi. The party arrived at Wilya, Mount Hagen, on 28 March 1934. The mission station at Mogei (Mount Hagen) was established by the end of 1934, as well as an intermediate station between Bundi and Mount Hagen at Mingende (Korugru). (Map drawn by Edgar Ford)

Plate 350

Plate 351

Plate 352

Plate 350. This shelter at Alexishafen, without doors, windows or walls, was used as a house for eight to ten weeks by the Divine Word missionaries who founded the station there. The floor, forty centimetres above ground, was made of rough strips of the betel palm. Sago palm leaves were used for the roof. On 3 July 1905 the missionaries moved into the house shown in plate 351. A shipping crate served as an altar in this first shelter and here Mass was said each morning. The same crate served as a table for meals and as a desk for work. Father Eberhard Limbrock, S.V.D., head of the New Guinea mission, lived in the shelter with Brother Canisius Hautkappe and Brother Sylvester Litzenburger until the better house was built. Those in the photograph are, from left to right, Brother Baldomer Stiene, Brother Pontianus Hennecke, Brother Sylvester Litzenburger, Deputy District Officer Sigwanz, Prefect Apostolic Father Eberhard Limbrock, Father Constantin van den Hemel, and an unidentified New Guinean. The photograph was taken by Mr Kastner, a German government official at nearby Friedrich-Wilhelmshafen, and was published in Germany in September 1906. (*Societas Verbi Divini*)

Plate 351. The first building erected at Alexishafen by Divine Word missionaries. At left are schoolchildren from Sek Island. At right, young men from Monumbo who assisted in the foundation of the Alexishafen mission. Photograph taken between 1905 and 1907. (*Societas Verbi Divini*)

Plate 352. Nake village. On the left, Father Heinrich Wortel, S.V.D. (1863–1926), who came to New Guinea in 1903, and Father Richard Nowak, S.V.D. (*Societas Verbi Divini*)

Plate 353

Plate 354

Plate 353. Father Franz Vormann, a Divine Word missionary (1868–1929) who came to New Guinea in 1896, with a New Guinean friend. (*Societas Verbi Divini*)

Plate 354. Father Heinrich Buschoff, S.V.D., with twenty of his pupils from Sek Island in 1907 or earlier. (*Societas Verbi Divini*)

Plate 355. Missionary sisters with schoolchildren at the Catholic mission on Tumleo Island between 1905 and 1907. Left to right, seated, Sister Veronica König, Sister Superior Valeria Dietzen, Sister Josephine Steiger; standing, Sister Cherubina Frings, Sister Chrysostoma Wehner, Sister Pacifica Schmitz, Sister Valentina Steinkeller. (*Societas Verbi Divini*)

Plate 356. A group of Divine Word missionaries in New Guinea in late 1906 or early 1907. Left to right, seated, Father Theodor Schlüter, Father Joseph Erdweg, Father Constantin van den Hemel; standing, Father Andreas Puff, Father Joseph Reiber, Father Jakob Wendel, Father Theodor Averberg, Father Joseph Schmidt. (*Societas Verbi Divini*)

Plate 355

Plate 356

Plate 357. Sawmill built at Alexishafen Catholic mission in late 1905. The large steam-engine at far right was transported to Alexishafen on two boats lashed together. The mission was opened in mid-1905 and on 5 December 1905 the first planks were cut at the sawmill. At far left, Brother Wunibald Rindfleisch, S.V.D. (1869–after 1913), who came to New Guinea in 1902, stands at the brick-making machine. The first manager of the sawmill was Brother Eustochius Tigges (1864–1906) who came to New Guinea in 1896. Photograph taken between 1905 and 1907. (*Societas Verbi Divini*)

Plate 357

Plate 358

Plate 358. Sister Cherubina Frings (1877–1915), who came to New Guinea in 1905 as a Holy Spirit missionary sister. She became directress of the printing press established on Tumleo Island near Aitape and taught the trade to schoolgirls. Photograph taken in 1907 at the latest. (*Societas Verbi Divini*)

Plate 359

Plate 359. Father Constantin van den Hemel, S.V.D. (1873–after 1919), who came to New Guinea in 1903, was sworn in by Governor Hahl as a chartered surveyor and in 1905 began surveying mission property at Bogia. He is shown here with his equipment and his assistants. By 1909 he had mapped out the entire mainland coast from Aitape eastwards to Nightingale Bay between Wewak and the Sepik River. The German Admiralty used this data in its official map of the coast, and the map was also used by Allied forces during World War II. (*Societas Verbi Divini*)

Plate 360

Plate 360. Brother Antonius Baas, S.V.D., bagged this water buffalo, which had gone wild in the vicinity of Alexishafen. (*Societas Verbi Divini*)

Plate 361. Centre, Father Josef Niedenzu, S.V.D. (1877–1939), who came to New Guinea in 1911, with the chief of police of Aitape on his right, the postmaster of Aitape on his left, police boys at his rear and children at front. (*Societas Verbi Divini*)

Plate 362. Divine Word Fathers and brothers on the occasion of an official visit by Father Kost, at a date between 1929 and 1932. Left to right, seated, Father Andreas Puff (1905); Monsignor Joseph Lorks (1900); the prefect apostolic of central New Guinea, Father Theodor Kost; Father Franz Wiesenthal (1910); Father August Becker (1907); standing, Brothers Kunibert Cebulla (1929), Cletus Egbers (1902), Siegbertus Komar (1929), and Cletus Mainzer (1928). Dates in parentheses indicate the year the missionary arrived in New Guinea. (*Societas Verbi Divini*)

Plate 361

Plate 362

Plate 363. Divine Word missionaries who pioneered in the Bismarck Mountains. From left to right, Fathers Heinrich Aufenanger (1933), Alfons Schäfer (1929), and Antonius Cranssen (1932); Brother Antonius Baas (1923). In November 1933 the three on the right entered the Chimbu Valley. (*Societas Verbi Divini*)

Plate 364. Father William Ross, S.V.D. (1895–1973), with schoolboys from Rempi mission. Fr Ross arrived at Alexishafen on 19 November 1926. He taught in the Central School there and also cared for the Rempi mission. (See plate 365.) (*Societas Verbi Divini*)

Plate 363

Plate 364

Plate 365

Plate 366

Plate 365. Pioneer Divine Word missionaries in the Wahgi Valley on 1 April 1934. Left to right, Fr William Ross, Fr Heinrich Aufenanger, Fr Alfons Schäfer, Br Eugene Frank, Fr Wilhelm Tropper. Of this occasion, Fr William Ross wrote: 'We arrived at Wilya, Mount Hagen on March 28, 1934, met Mick and Dan Leahy, who had completed a small airstrip and were expecting the first plane to land at the Mogei airstrip on Easter Sunday, 1st April, 1934. . . . The first plane on the Mogei airstrip touched down about 9 a.m. on Easter Sunday. Bob Gurney, the pilot of Guinea Airways, was amazed to have seven Europeans greet him.' Rev. W. A. Ross, S.V.D., 'Catholicism in the Western Highlands', in *The History of Melanesia*, Second Waigani Seminar (Canberra, 1967). (*Societas Verbi Divini*)

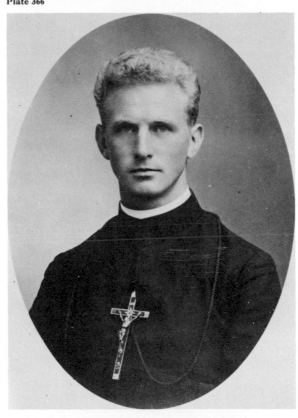

Plate 366. Father Karl Morschheuser, S.V.D. (1904–1934), was assigned to New Guinea in 1932. He was killed on 16 December 1934 when two Kukane clansmen shot him with an arrow in the mouth and another in the throat at Baglmenigl gully in the Chimbu Valley of the New Guinea Highlands. His death resulted from the killing of a Kukane pig by another missionary. (*Societas Verbi Divini*)

Plate 367

Plate 367. Brother Eugene Frank, S.V.D. (1900–1935), right, was assigned to New Guinea in 1929. Not knowing of Father Morschheuser's death, he walked into the same area on 10 or 11 January 1935, and on the Yongamugl Road and at Anganere and the Gianigl River was hit by at least eight arrows. Friendly Barengigl people cared for him until 16 January, when he was taken to the Protestant mission at Kundiawa and the next day by plane to the Salamaua hospital, where he died on 23 January 1935. Photo taken at Alexishafen. (*Societas Verbi Divini*)

Plate 368

Plate 369

Plate 368. Father Richard Nowak, S.V.D., camped at Musak, not far from Sepu on the Ramu River. (*Societas Verbi Divini*)

Plate 369. Father Franz Kirschbaum, S.V.D. (1882–1939), famed explorer of the Sepik River, at left, and Father Georg Holtker, S.V.D. (b. 1895), who conducted a one-man ethnographical expedition in New Guinea from 1936 to 1939 for the Anthropos Institute of St Augustin, Siegburg, West Germany. Father Kirschbaum was assigned to New Guinea in 1907. He died in a plane crash at Alexishafen on 6 August 1939. (*Societas Verbi Divini*)

Plate 370. Marienberg on the Sepik River. This station was first established by Father Franz Kirschbaum in 1913 and was developed as the headquarters station for a number of substations on the lower Sepik. In 1939 there were eight stations in the Marienberg district. (Hallstrom Pacific Library)

Plate 370

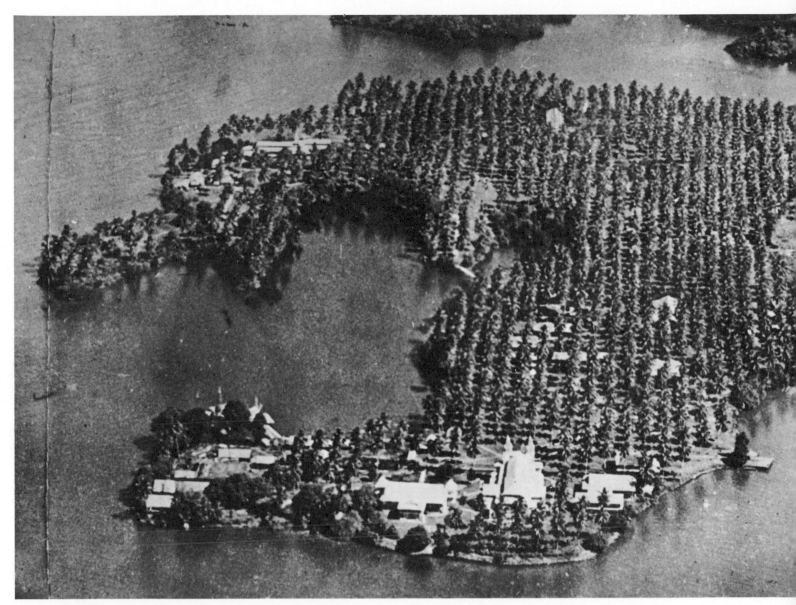

Plate 371

Plate 371. Alexishafen mission of the Divine Word completely planted with coconut palms. Cathedral at lower centre with a large residence to the left. Buildings for the Holy Spirit missionary sisters at upper left. The wharf at lower right was built in 1913 and could take vessels from 300 to 400 tonnes. Photograph taken around 1940. (*Societas Verbi Divini*)

18 The Australian Military Occupation of German New Guinea, 1914-21

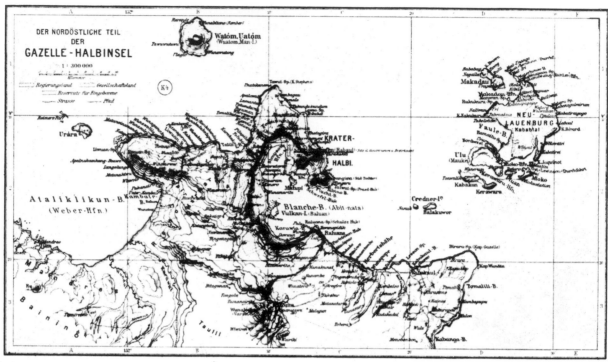

Plate 372

Plate 372. The north-east area of the Gazelle Peninsula in New Britain, the site of hostilities between German and Australian troops during World War I. At the outbreak of war in 1914 this area was of considerable importance in the naval strategy of the Pacific Ocean. Germany had a powerful naval force deployed in the Pacific, and Rabaul was a coaling station close to important Allied sea lanes. Also, the Germans had almost completed the erection of a wireless-telegraph station at Bitapaka, a few kilometres inland from Kabakaul on Blanche Bay. This station was part of a communications network that linked German Pacific naval headquarters at Tsingtao in China with Samoa, Nauru and the Caroline Islands.

The capture and occupation of this area by British troops was accorded a high priority by military authorities in Britain and Australia. On 12 August 1914 an Australian naval force entered Blanche Bay and naval landing parties destroyed the telephone services at Rabaul and at Herbertshöhe. At the same time recruiting began in Sydney for a combined military and naval force of approximately 2000 men, to be named the Australian Naval and Military Expeditionary Force (A.N. & M.E.F.). This force was to be sent to New Britain for the capture of the Blanche Bay area and the military occupation of the whole of German New Guinea.

The A.N. & M.E.F., under the command of Colonel (later Major General) William Holmes of Sydney, arrived in Blanche Bay on 11 September 1914. Herbertshöhe and Rabaul were occupied at once, without resistance. Armed detachments were landed at Kabakaul to advance inland to the Bitapaka wireless station. Some fighting took place along the line of advance and six Australian soldiers were killed. The German defenders lost one European soldier and thirty New Guinean soldiers. Bitapaka was captured late on 11 September.

Before the arrival of the A.N. & M.E.F., the German government had removed to Toma; it negotiated from there with the invaders until terms of capitulation were signed on 17 September. On 21 September a surrender of the German armed forces took place at Herbertshöhe and on that day the executive and administrative authority in the Protectorate passed into British hands. (S. S. Mackenzie, *The Australians at Rabaul* [Sydney, 1938], p. 82.) Subsequently, various centres in German New Guinea were occupied by detachments of the A.N. & M.E.F. Madang was occupied on 24 September, Kavieng on 17 October, the Admiralty Islands on 19 November and Kieta on 9 December. German New Guinea was placed under military occupation in terms of the Hague Convention. Colonel Holmes had been instructed by his superiors to make arrangements for the temporary administration of the territory but not to proclaim any formal annexation. '. . . The sovereignty of the legitimate owner of the territory is not destroyed or transferred, but is merely in abeyance during the period for which military occupation lasts.' (S. S. Mackenzie, ibid., p. 92.)

The military occupation by Australia of German New Guinea lasted until 9 May 1921. On that day the mandate for New Guinea received by the Commonwealth of Australia from the League of Nations came into force and the territory passed into another phase of its administration.

Administrators of German New Guinea during the Military Occupation, 1914–21

Col. W. Holmes—21 Sept. 1914–8 Jan. 1915

Col. S. Pethebridge—8 Jan. 1915–21 Oct. 1917

Lt Col. S. S. Mackenzie (acting administrator)—21 Oct. 1917–21 April 1918

Brig. Gen. G. J. Johnston—21 April 1918– 1 May 1920

Brig. Gen. T. Griffiths—1 May 1920– 9 May 1921

('Der Nordöstliche Teil der Gazelle-Halbinsel', inset to sheet map 'Deutsch-Neuguinea (Ostliches-Blatt)', Abgeschlossen, February 1909, in the possession of Hans Mannsfeld)

Plate 373

Plate 374

Plate 373. A platoon of German soldiers in Rabaul in 1914. By a proclamation of 6 August 1914, all reservists of the German army in New Guinea were called up for active service. After mobilization, the force consisted of 2 regular officers, 7 Landwehr officers and 52 non-commissioned officers and men, besides 240 New Guinean soldiers. This force was placed under the command of one of the two regular officers, von Klewitz, captain of cavalry. The other regular officer, Eisen, is here seen leading the platoon. (Mitchell Library)

Plate 374. Major General William Holmes (1862–1917), who commanded the Australian Naval and Military Expeditionary Force, which captured and occupied German New Guinea in September 1914. Holmes was relieved as military administrator of German New Guinea by Brigadier General S. Pethebridge in January 1915. Subsequently Holmes served in the A.I.F. in France, where he was killed in 1917. (Reproduced by permission of the Commonwealth Archives Office)

Plate 375. Members of the Australian Naval and Military Expeditionary Force embark at Kabakaul on Blanche Bay after the action along the Bitapaka Road, September 1914. (Australian War Memorial)

Plate 375

Plate 376

Plate 376. Dr Haber, acting governor of German New Guinea, and Captain von Klewitz arriving at Herbertshöhe on 17 September 1914 to confer with Colonel Holmes about terms of surrender. In accordance with their plan to meet possible enemy action, the German government in Rabaul moved from Herbertshöhe to Toma in the face of the Australian occupation of the former place. On 14 September 1914 a ridge near Toma was shelled by the guns of a naval vessel, and a detachment of the A.N. & M.E.F. advanced towards it. Dr Haber under a flag of truce conferred with the Australian officer commanding the detachment. It was arranged that Haber would come to Herbertshöhe to negotiate with Colonel Holmes. Meetings took place at Herbertshöhe over the next two days, and the photograph shows the German party coming to the final conference on 17 September at which the terms of capitulation for German New Guinea were signed by Holmes and Haber. (Mitchell Library)

Plate 377

Plate 377. The raising of the Union Jack in Rabaul, 13 September 1914, marking the beginning of the Australian military occupation of German New Guinea. The official history of the occupation describes the scene: '. . . All available troops, including a newly-enrolled native police force under British officers, were formed up on three sides of a square, facing the flagstaff, with the band of the *Australia* in the centre. The fourth side of the square was occupied by Rear-Admiral Patey, the officers of the Royal Australian Navy, and residents of Rabaul. Punctually at 3 o'clock the flag was broken by Lieutenant Basil Holmes and saluted by the troops, the warships at the same time firing a salute of twenty-one guns. The national anthem was sung; three cheers were given for the King; the military occupation of the Territory was formally proclaimed by the brigade-major, and the naval and military officers and troops, followed by the native police force, marched past in column of route and saluted the flag.' S. S. Mackenzie, *The Australians at Rabaul* (Sydney, 1938), pp. 75–6. (Mitchell Library)

Plate 378

Plate 378. A detachment of the Naval Reserve leading the march of the Australian Naval and Military Expeditionary Force through Rabaul on 13 September 1914, following the reading of the proclamation establishing the military occupation of New Britain. (Australian News and Information Bureau)

Plate 379. Garrison Headquarters in Rabaul, 1916. The Australian military occupation of German New Guinea began on 12 September 1914, when Colonel William Holmes, officer commanding the Australian Naval and Military Expeditionary Force, proclaimed, '. . . From and after the date of these presents, the Island of New Britain and its dependencies are held by me in military occupation in the name of His Majesty the King.' The military occupation came to an end by proclamation on 9 May 1921, during the military administration of Brigadier General T. Griffiths. (Information and Extension Services, Administration of Papua New Guinea)

Plate 379

Plate 380. The German native constabulary of New Guinea on parade in Rabaul in November 1914. At the time of the German capitulation, 17 September 1914, the force numbered about a thousand men and these were a trained military force; as such it was taken over by the Australian Naval and Military Expeditionary Force and used throughout the territory for the period of occupation. (Australian War Memorial)

Plate 380

Plate 381. A detachment of the New Guinea police in Rabaul in 1915. The police were distributed among the districts in detachments of about 100. A force of 250 highly trained men was kept at Rabaul for service in any part of the territory. Article 7 of the Terms of Capitulation for German New Guinea of 17 September 1914 said, 'As it is understood that the safety of the white population depends to an extent on the existence of a Native Constabulary which now forms part of the German Forces in the field, if found satisfactory, it will be transferred to the Military Administration.' The detachment pictured is in the charge of an Australian sergeant and a private. (Australian War Memorial)

Plate 381

Plate 382

Plate 382. The capture and occupation of Madang (Friedrich-Wilhelmshafen) on 24 September 1914, by a detachment of the Australian Naval and Military Expeditionary Force from Rabaul. (Australian War Memorial)

185

Plate 383

Plate 383. A squad of police, formerly under German command, at Kieta on Bougainville Island, December 1914. On 7 December 1914, Colonel Holmes, officer commanding the Australian Naval and Military Expeditionary Force, dispatched an expedition from Rabaul for the capture and occupation of the German Solomon Islands. This force arrived at Kieta on 9 December. There was no opposition from the Germans and the terms of capitulation were accepted. (Australian War Memorial)

Plate 384

Plate 384. The Rev. W. H. Cox, Methodist missionary, who at Namatanai on New Ireland on 26 October 1914 was assaulted by a group of German officials led by the resident medical officer. The Germans who assaulted Cox believed him to be a spy. Cox reported the affair to Colonel Holmes in Rabaul. (Mitchell Library)

186

Plate 385

Plate 385. Pay-back, European style—Rabaul, 30 November 1914. Following the assault on the Rev. W. H. Cox at Namatanai in October 1914, Colonel Holmes instructed his judicial officer, Major C. E. Manning, to carry out an investigation and to report to him on the affair. On 28 November 1914, Holmes issued an order in the following terms:

'This report fully bears out the complaint made to me by the Reverend Mr Cox, that a gross and unprovoked assault had been perpetrated upon him. . . .

'In view of the indignity and humiliation inflicted upon the Reverend Mr Cox, a British subject, whose calling as a minister of religion should have protected him from such an attack, I consider it necessary that a short, sharp, and exemplary punishment should be meted out to all concerned. . . .

'I therefore direct that a parade of all available troops of the Rabaul and Herbertshöhe garrison be held on Monday next, 30 November in Proclamation square at 10 a.m.'

The order prescribed that the German doctor should receive thirty strokes with the cane, and the others twenty-five strokes each, with the exception of the German doctor's young assistant, who was to receive ten strokes. (Information and Extension Services, Administration of Papua New Guinea.)

Plate 386. Brigadier General Sir Samuel Pethebridge, military administrator of German New Guinea 1915–18, with members of his personal staff in Rabaul in 1916. (Information and Extension Services, Administration of Papua New Guinea)

Plate 386

187

Plate 387

Plate 387. Men of a village in the Baining Mountains of the Gazelle Peninsula in New Britain meet their new masters. Two members of an expedition of the Australian Naval and Military Expeditionary Force, Colonel L. F. Hore and Sergeant Gouday, halt in the course of a journey; probable date 1915. (Australian War Memorial)

Plate 388

Plate 388. Confidence in a change of loyalty from Germans to Australians by the local people is stressed in the caption to this drawing published in the *Sydney Mail* of December 1914. Entitled 'The Black-Birds in the Tree-Tops of New Guinea', it was explained that, 'When the Australians were taking possession of New Guinea they were sniped from the tree-tops by natives who had been persuaded by the Germans that the enemy would inflict great cruelties upon them if he were not repelled. The poor natives did their best, but one of their former masters said that they were worthless, and had no stomach for fighting. Now—as our artist-contributor points out— the natives are proud of being "Inglis".' (Mitchell Library)

Plate 389. The district station at Namatanai, New Ireland, in 1916. In the 1905 report of German New Guinea, it was stated, 'In the newly opened Namatanai Station district in Middle New Mecklenburg, the promulgation of a government order for the restoration of public peace and for the amalgamation of the natives into public unions founded on local homogeneousness was, in places, associated with bloody conflicts fought out with the troops at Namatanai. The opposition in the northerly part of the terrain by the residents of the Mesi district and in the south by the mountain residents around Maliama was particularly violent.' (Australian War Memorial)

Plate 389

Plate 390. The sergeants' mess, Rabaul, about 1920, when German New Guinea was administered by the Australian military administration. (B. B. Perriman Collection)

Plate 391. The Regimental Institute, Mango Avenue, Rabaul, about 1919. (B. B. Perriman Collection)

Plate 392. The Native Affairs Staff at Rabaul in 1916. Seated at centre, Captain H. Ogilvy, officer in charge of native affairs and previously district officer at Kieta on Bougainville Island. (Information and Extension Services, Administration of Papua New Guinea)

Plate 393

Plate 393. Brigadier General G. J. Johnston and staff officers, Rabaul, 1918. Appointed administrator on 21 April 1918, after service in France, Johnston held office until 1 May 1920. During his term, administrative out- stations were established on Buka Strait, at Gasmata on the south coast of New Britain and at Vanimo adjoining the border with Dutch New Guinea. (Australian War Memorial)

Plate 394

Plate 394. 'Staining the Australian flag: the natives of ex-German New Guinea are still flogged by the Hun, the law of the former German possession remaining paramount until peace terms have been decided.' This *Bulletin* cartoon by Norman Lindsay was published on 27 February 1919, and led to public comment in Australia on the corporal punishment of New Guinea people. This in turn led to a Cabinet decision of the Federal govern- ment on 10 March 1919, which instructed the Australian military administration in Rabaul to impose 'absolute prohibition of flogging'. (Mitchell Library)

Plate 395. Prisoners undergoing No. 1 Field Punishment at Rabaul gaol in 1919. With the abolition of flogging as a form of punishment in March 1919, No. 1 Field Punishment was instituted by the administrator, Briga- dier General G. J. Johnston. This form of punishment was hitherto inflicted on soldiers under military law, but by amendment to the Native Labour Ordinance of 1 January 1919 it was imposed for 'serious' offences by indigenes and was practised until 1922. (Mitchell Library)

Plate 395

Plate 396

Plate 396. Field Punishment No. 1 being administered to labourers in New Britain, *c.* 1920, during the term of office of Brigadier General G. J. Johnston as military administrator of German New Guinea.

Under military law British soldiers on active service could be sentenced to Field Punishment No. 1 by a court martial or by a commanding officer for a period of three months or twenty-eight days respectively. It was laid down that a soldier could 'be kept in irons, i.e. in fetters or handcuffs, and secured so as to prevent his escape'. When in irons a soldier could 'be attached for a period or periods not exceeding 2 hours in any one day to a fixed object' but he was 'not to be so attached during more than 3 out of 4 consecutive days, nor during more than 21 days in all'. Straps or ropes could be used in lieu of irons. It was laid down also that 'every portion of a field punishment shall be inflicted in such a manner as is calculated not to cause injury or to leave any permanent mark on the offender.' Extracts from Rules for Field Punishment under Section 44 of the Army Act. (M. von Hein Collection)

Plate 397. The administering of corporal punishment at Lae, *c.* 1920. The question of corporal punishment throughout the period of the Australian military administration of New Guinea was a contentious one. The right of the employer of indigenous labour to inflict corporal punishment on his workers was withdrawn in August 1915. Corporal punishment, employing a variety of safeguards, was still administered and the Native Labour Ordinance (1919) laid down that corporal punishment could only be inflicted on conviction by a court. The photograph depicts corporal punishment imposed presumably by a court conviction and administered by members of the constabulary. (E. E. Jones Collection)

Plate 397

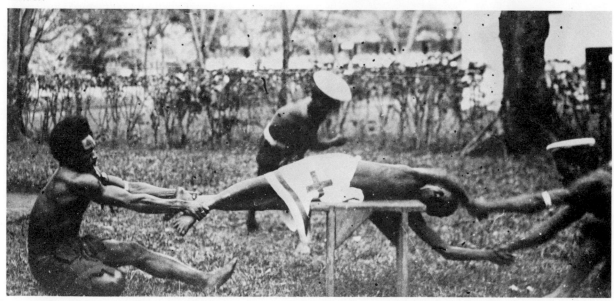

Plate 398

Plate 399

Plate 400

Plate 398. Government House on top of Namanula Hill overlooking Rabaul, 1921. Formerly the centre of German administration of New Guinea, it was at this time occupied by Brigadier General E. A. Wisdom who was the first administrator of the Mandated Territory, being appointed to the office on 9 May 1921. (Information and Extension Services, Administration of Papua New Guinea)

Plate 399. Brigadier General E. A. Wisdom. On 9 May 1921 civil government was established in the Mandated Territory of New Guinea and Brigadier General Wisdom was appointed administrator by the Australian government. (Reproduced by permission of the Commonwealth Archives Office)

Plate 400. The Royal Commission on Late German New Guinea at Government House, Rabaul, 1920. Seated, left to right, W. H. Lucas (member), Islands manager for Burns, Philp and Company; the administrator, Brigadier General T. Griffiths; Judge J. H. P. Murray (chairman of the Royal Commission), lieutenant governor of Papua; Atlee Hunt (member), secretary of the Department of Home and Territories.

Brigadier General Griffiths was appointed administrator on 1 May 1920 and was the last administrator of the military government, being succeeded on 9 May 1921 by the first head of the civil government of the Mandated Territory, Brigadier General E. A. Wisdom (see plate 399). Griffiths had another term as administrator in 1932–34.

Standing, left to right, Leonard Murray, aide to his uncle, Judge Murray; J. E. Streeter, Papuan medical officer; unidentified aide of the administrator.

Leonard Murray succeeded his uncle as administrator of Papua on Sir Hubert Murray's death in 1940, and continued in office until the dissolution of civil government in Papua in February 1942. (Department of Territories)

Plate 401

Plate 402

Plate 401. Members of the Royal Commission on Late German New Guinea visiting a village near Kieta on Bougainville Island in 1920. Left to right, H. Farrands (secretary); Atlee Hunt (secretary, Department of Home and Territories); Captain Cardew (district officer); Judge Murray (lieutenant governor of Papua and chairman of the Royal Commission); and W. H. Lucas (Islands manager for Burns, Philp and Company).. The Royal Commission was appointed in August 1919 and was asked to report on the future of the Mandated Territory in respect to administration, revenue, trade and its relationship with Papua. Murray's report (the minority report) differed from that of Atlee Hunt and Lucas (the majority report) in several aspects, and the latter became the basis for the New Guinea Act of 1920. Murray's recommendation that Papua and the Mandate should be administered as one was rejected. The majority recommendation on the expropriation of German property was adopted and Lucas was appointed chairman of the Expropriation Board, which carried out the virtual liquidation of the German presence in the Mandated Territory. (Australian War Memorial)

Plate 403

Plate 402. Colonial administrators and some of the administered at Government House, Rabaul, in 1920, during the visit of the Royal Commission on Late German New Guinea. The Royal Commissioners are in the group (see plate 401). The administrator of New Guinea, Brigadier General T. Griffiths, is standing on the steps at the extreme right. At the time this photograph was taken, the status of New Guinea was changing from that of a German territory occupied by the Australian military to that of a mandated territory under the provisions of Article 22 of the Covenant of the League of Nations. In September 1920, the Commonwealth Parliament passed the New Guinea Act of 1920 in anticipation of the acceptance of the mandate; *inter alia* it stated that '. . . the Territories and Islands formerly constituting German New Guinea as specified in the Preamble to this Act are hereby declared to be a Territory under the authority of the Commonwealth by the name of the Territory of New Guinea.'

On 17 December 1920, the mandate for New Guinea was conferred upon Australia as mandatory for the League of Nations. On 6 April 1921, a certified copy of the instrument was received by the Commonwealth government. On 7 April 1921, the New Guinea Act of 1920 was promulgated to come into force on 9 May 1921, and on that date the military occupation of New Guinea was succeeded by a civil administration. (Department of Territories)

Plate 403. Captain Hermann Detzner, German army officer, who refused to surrender himself in New Guinea during World War I. Detzner was leader of a survey team near the border of Kaiser-Wilhelmsland and Papua when war broke out. Unaware of the war, Detzner and his companion, Sergeant Konradt, moved into Papua near Lakekamu gold field. George Chisholm, patrol officer at Nepa station, sent him a message requesting his surrender, but Detzner refused. He went to Morobe. Konradt was captured and Detzner took a party of loyal New Guinea police and carriers with him into the mountains behind Sattelberg, a Neuendettelsau mission station. Dr Christian Keysser and his wife supplied him with food, and for the duration of the war Detzner remained in hiding around Sattelberg and later on the coast near Deaf-adder Bay. At the end of the war he went to Finschhafen, from where he was sent first to Morobe and then to Sydney. There he was interned briefly before being repatriated to Germany. (Landeshauptstadt und Universitätsstadt, Mainz, Stadtbibliothek)

Plate 404

Plate 404. 'Jack Tars' of S.S. *Berrima* carrying supplies in Rabaul harbour, 1920. The *Berrima* transported the A.N. & M.E.F. from Sydney to Rabaul. (B. B. Perriman Collection)

Plate 405. Peterhafen, Witu Island, near New Britain. The harbour, a volcanic crater, was reputed to have been a lurking place for pirates and privateers. A coral reef protected the narrow entrance, which could not be detected easily from the ocean. In 1914 the *Komet*, the German administration's new 997 tonne yacht, took refuge here, but she was captured when she moved on to Talasea. In this photograph taken in 1922, the Burns Philp steamer *Mataram* can be seen alongside the wharf, taking on a cargo of copra. (B. Backus Collection)

Plate 405

Plate 406

Plate 406. Kieta on Bougainville Island in 1915. The government residence is in the centre, the government office on the left and the police office and quarters on the right. Kieta was established by the German New Guinea administration as a government station in 1906. On 9 December 1914, a detachment of the Australian Naval and Military Expeditionary Force from Rabaul received the capitulation of the German officials at Kieta and it was occupied by an Australian garrison. (Australian War Memorial)

Plate 407. Rabaul social life, 1916. A cricket match between military and civilian teams, presumably all Australian. (Australian War Memorial)

Plate 407

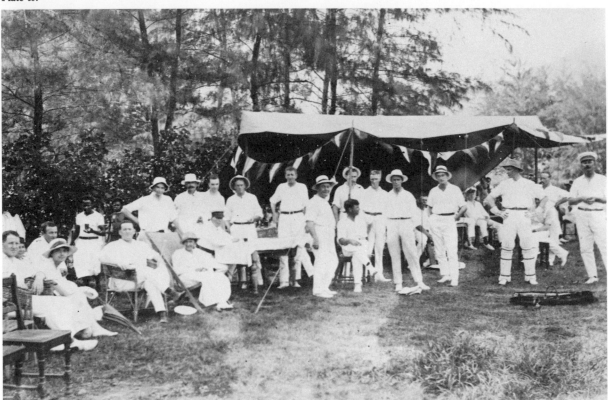

195

19 The Developing Towns

Plate 408

Plate 408. A general view of Port Moresby from Touaguba Hill, *c.* 1909. (Mitchell Library)

Plate 409. Kieta as a government station on Bougainville Island in 1916. (Mitchell Library)

Plate 409

Plate 410. The waterfront at Port Moresby, *c.* 1913, looking towards Paga Point. (R. Speedie Collection)

Plate 411. Port Moresby, *c.* 1914, looking towards Paga Hill with the Burns Philp store (with tower) as the most prominent building. (Department of Territories)

Plate 411

Plate 410

Plate 412

Plate 412. The main wharf at Port Moresby, *c.* 1919. (S. Stephenson Collection)

Plate 413

Plate 413. The wharf at Samarai, 1919, with Miss Sommerhoff, an Australian governess, at the end of the wharf. At this time Samarai had a population of 293 Europeans, a European and a New Guinean hospital, a post office, a district magistrate, an armed constabulary, and a jail. It was also a port of entry, and a centre for the large copra trade in the eastern part of the Territory. (S. Stephenson Collection)

Plate 414. The residential section of Samarai in 1920. (S. Stephenson Collection)

Plate 414

Plate 415. Samarai waterfront in 1920. (S. Stephenson Collection)

Plate 415

Plate 416. Copra warehouses on the Samarai waterfront, 1919. Samarai was the commercial centre of the eastern part of the Territory for the export of copra. (S. Stephenson Collection)

Plate 416

Plate 417. A street in Madang in 1920. (S. Stephenson Collection)

Plate 417

Plate 418. A view of Port Moresby in 1922 with the tower of the Burns Philp store prominent. (Mitchell Library)

Plate 418

Plate 419. The second store of W. R. Carpenter and Company Ltd being erected in Rabaul in 1924. This store proved inadequate to handle the increase in business so a third, larger store was acquired and this store became Palms Restaurant. (B. B. Perriman Collection)

Plate 419

Plate 420. Rabaul from the north-west about 1912. Near the wharf can be seen the large stores of the Neuguinea-Kompagnie and Hasag; behind the town a road wound up to Namanula Hill where Government House, the hospital and various officials' residences stood. (Hallstrom Pacific Library)

Plate 420

Plate 421. A street in Rabaul lined with casuarina trees planted in German times. (S. M. Matthews Collection)

Plate 421

Plate 422. General view of Kokopo Hotel, Kokopo, built by the German administration when Kokopo (Herbertshöhe) was the centre of administration. Photograph taken in 1920. (S. Stephenson Collection)

Plate 422

Plate 423

Plate 423

Plate 423. Employees of Hernsheim and Company at work in the company's offices at Rabaul, *c.* 1916. (M. von Hein Collection)

Plate 424. Track along the foreshores of Blanche Bay from Rabaul to Kokopo, 1919. (S. Stephenson Collection)

Plate 424

Plate 425. The Hernsheim and Company station at Matupi, 1916. (M. von Hein Collection)

Plate 425

Plate 426. The Hernsheim and Company store at Rabaul, 1915. (M. von Hein Collection)

Plate 426

Plate 427. Offices of Hernsheim and Company, Rabaul, 1915. (M. von Hein Collection)

Plate 427

Plate 428

Plate 429

Plate 428. Ratavul Pass, the tunnel linking Rabaul to the north coast of New Britain. Constructed by the German administration. (M. von Hein Collection)

Plate 430. The Neuguinea-Kompagnie pier at Rabaul, 1916. (M. von Hein Collection)

Plate 430

Plate 429. The Norddeutsche Lloyd pier at Rabaul, with S.S. *Prinz Sigismund* and S.S. *Sumatra* at berth, 1914. (M. von Hein Collection)

Plate 431. A section of the botanical gardens at Rabaul established during the German administration, *c.* 1905. The gardens contained a great variety of tropical plants and provided a plant nursery service to residents. (M. von Hein Collection)

Plate 431

Plate 432. The Rabaul headquarters of Burns, Philp and Company, *c.* 1916. This firm had previously operated in the Bismarck Archipelago in competition with the Norddeutsche Lloyd line, but in 1909 it withdrew. With the advent of the Australian military administration in September 1914, Burns Philp reentered the area and as early as October 1914 was operating to Rabaul with a Commonwealth government subsidy. In 1916 the firm secured the agency of the Hamburg South Sea Company and Hernsheim and Company. Its prospects were further enhanced by the majority report of the Royal Commission of 1919, one of whose members was W. H. Lucas (see plate 400), the Islands manager for Burns, Philp and Company until 1920, and technical adviser to the Commonwealth government for New Guinea and chairman of the Expropriation Board, 1920–25. (Information and Extension Services, Administration of Papua New Guinea)

Plate 432

Plate 433

Plate 434

Plate 435

Plate 433. Ah Chee's hotel, 'Tuck Wah', Rabaul, 1916. (M. von Hein Collection)

Plate 434. Lauri's cinema, Rabaul. The cinema was across the road from Ah Chee's hotel, and ex-residents recall how on many occasions Ah Chee's customers would 'take around the hat' and with the generous proceeds persuade the owner of the cinema to run a film; then they would all adjourn to Lauri's, where not even the most melodramatic film had the power to dampen the high spirits of the audience. In 1915 when the Australian Naval and Military Expeditionary Force occupied German New Guinea, German nationals were interned in Lauri's cinema behind barbed wire. (M. von Hein Collection)

Plate 435. The Cosmopolitan Hotel, Rabaul, once famous as Ah Chee's. (R. Clark Collection)

Plate 436. The Pacific Hotel, Rabaul, once known to the locals as Ching Hing's Pub. (R. Clark Collection)

Plate 437. A communications system in Rabaul in 1914. This photograph from the *Sydney Mail* had the caption, 'Conveying mails to the post office at Rabaul', and the comment, 'It is a curious fact that each residence in the settlement has a line like this connecting it with the wharf, so that goods can be conveyed direct from the boat side.' (Mitchell Library)
Pages 306-309

Plate 436

Plate 437

Plate 438

Plate 439

Plate 440

Plate 438. The Customs House, Rabaul, 1923. Some of the staff in this year were E. Featherstone Phibbs, chief collector of customs; 'Joe' Provan, chief clerk; Captain 'Jimmy' Duncan, harbourmaster; Baden Backhouse, cashier and customs clerk. (B. Backus Collection)

Plate 439. Street scene in Chinatown, Rabaul, in 1916. In April 1907, the German governor granted a Chinese businessman, Ah Tam, seven hectares of land in Rabaul on a thirty-year lease. Under the terms of this lease Chinese had to live in Chinatown (Ah Tam's lease). In 1907 there were about 250 Chinese in the Bismarck Archipelago, made up of skilled tradesmen, labourers, domestic servants, engineers, planters, gardeners and traders. (Information and Extension Services, Administration of Papua New Guinea)

Plate 440. Chinatown, Rabaul, 1920. A visitor in 1920 described the district as '. . . the commercial centre . . . very quaint and orderly. Numerous shops sell rubbish of all kinds at prices far beyond the wildest dreams of profiteers down South. The shopkeepers are letting their stocks run low, for the Mandate has not come through yet, and their tenure is uncertain.' Lilian Overell, *A Woman's Impressions of German New Guinea* (London, 1923), p. 8. (B. B. Perriman Collection)

Plate 441

Plate 441. The main avenue from Bagail Wharf to the township of Kavieng, New Ireland, in 1923. The road was made of coastal coral. It continued for about 160 kilometres along the coast and was considered one of the finest motor runs in the north-west Pacific. The German district officer, Boluminski, directed the construction of the road and it was maintained by labour from adjacent villages. (B. Backus Collection)

Plate 442

Plate 442. The hotel at Kavieng Harbour, New Ireland, in 1915, built by the German administration. (M. von Hein Collection)

Plate 443. The hospital for indigenes at Kavieng, 1917, built and maintained by the German administration. The hospital was noted for its modern equipment. (M. von Hein Collection)

Plate 443

Plate 444

Plate 444. The Hernsheim and Company mess at Kavieng, New Ireland, 1917. (M. von Hein Collection)

Plate 445. The residence of Rudolph Richter, a clerk of Hernsheim and Company, Kavieng, New Ireland, 1915. (M. von Hein Collection)

Plate 446. Part of the coral road skirting the east coast of New Ireland for thirty-two kilometres and built by local labourers under the direction of Franz Boluminski, district officer at Kavieng 1910–13. (M. von Hein Collection)

Plate 445

Plate 446

Plate 447

Plate 447. A New Irelander sweeps the coast road free of even small obstacles—see plates 441 and 446. (M. von Hein Collection)

20 The Expropriated: German New Guinea

Plate 448

Plate 448. A group at the home of Mrs Kaumann on Kurakakaul plantation, nine kilometres from Rabaul on the north coast, in 1921. Left to right, Mr Sparrow; Mrs Eileen Hertz; Mrs Emma Kapel; Mrs E. Kaumann; Louise Miller; Mr King; [unidentified]; Mrs Carolina Schultze. Lilian Overell visited Kurakakaul with Phoebe Parkinson in 1920, and described the house and its owner: 'It was furnished rather after German ideas with heavy chairs and sofas and solid-looking cabinets and bookcases. The dining room was very inviting with its snowy cloth, and its silver and glass gleaming in the lamplight. . . . Mrs Kaumann's husband was in Germany. He had made himself very obnoxious to the Australian Government and there was no likelihood of his ever being allowed to return. The conversation soon turned to the Mandate and the Expropriation Board. Mrs Kaumann was trying to divorce her husband, and claimed half of the property as her own. His half would certainly be taken over by the Board, but she hoped to retain hers. . . . "I made this plantation", she said, "and I may lose it all. The German Government would never refund the value of our lands to us Samoans. And how would we, a dark race, live in Germany?"' (Lilian Overell, *A Woman's Impressions of German New Guinea* [London, 1923], pp. 80–83.) Mrs Kaumann died in the Japanese prison camp, Ramale, near Vunapope, Kokopo. (B. B. Perriman Collection)

Plate 449

Plate 450

Plate 449. German nationals awaiting the outcome of World War I take the air in their carriages along the coast road, Kavieng, New Ireland, 1917. (M. von Hein Collection)

Plate 450. Matanatar plantation, New Britain, in 1914. The text accompanying this photograph in the *Sydney Mail* of 23 September 1914 read, 'A recent German publication points out, with reference to New Guinea and the neighbouring islands, that cocoanut planting offers a wide and profitable field for capital but cannot be recommended to those who must look for a quick return for their money unless carried on in conjunction with other pursuits such as trading and growing of minor products for the Australian market. The cost of planting an area of 500 hektars [1236 acres] with cocoanuts and its upkeep for 6 years is given at from £3500 to £4500. A hundred trees are planted to the acre and each tree carries on an average 80 nuts with normal rainfall. After 14 years at the latest the plantation is in full bearing. From 7000 to 8000 nuts make a ton of marketable copra.' Matanatar was originally a part of Ralum plantation belonging to Emma Kolbe, and was sold by her to a German firm; as a German owned property, it was expropriated by the Australian government in the early 1920s. (Library of New South Wales)

Plate 451

Plate 451. Frau Furter (left), Herr Kirchner, Frau Kirchner, and Miss Sommerhoff, an Australian governess, on the veranda of Haus Kirchner plantation, Kavieng, New Ireland, in October 1919. Herren Furter and Kirchner were managers for the German firm Hasag. Under the Australian military occupation of German New Guinea, German businessmen were invited to retain their positions. This was necessary in order not to dislocate the New Guinea economy. When the Australian government set up the Expropriation Board, the large firms like Hasag were the first to be expropriated. (S. Stephenson Collection)

Plate 452

Plate 453

Plate 454

Plate 452. This photograph of the labour force on a plantation in the Kavieng district of New Ireland, taken over by the Expropriation Board in 1923, shows a high percentage of small boys among the recruits. (Hallstrom Pacific Library)

Plate 453. Front, Herr and Frau Kirchner; back, with Herr Furter, their son Georg, and the son's governess, Miss Sommerhoff, in New Ireland, 1920. Herr Kirchner was manager of the Kavieng branch of Hasag. (S. Stephenson Collection)

Plate 454. Kurakakaul plantation bungalow in 1925. The coconut plantation was about nine kilometres from Rabaul on the north coast of New Britain, and had an area of 400 hectares, of which 300 hectares were planted with palms. It was of wood, with cement floors and an iron roof; kitchen and wash houses were annexes on the same floor level as the main building. The plantation, owned by Mrs Kaumann, was listed for expropriation (see plate 448). (Hallstrom Pacific Library)

Plate 455. The bungalow of Raulawat coconut plantation on the north coast of New Britain, 38 kilometres from Rabaul, in 1925 when it was owned by Mrs Mabel Jolley. Mr Jolley was British consul in German New Guinea before World War I. After the war he became liaison officer between the German population and the Australian administration. Raulawat was one of the older plantations, covering 650 hectares, of which 225 were planted with coconut palms. Of the 28 000 palms, 12 500 were at least ten years old. The Tabaule River flowed through the property, which employed sixty-three labourers. (Hallstrom Pacific Library)

Plate 456. The bungalow of Wunawutung plantation, 1925. This plantation was part of Wunabugbug plantation, on the north coast 11 kilometres from Rabaul. It produced about eight tonnes of copra monthly and employed forty labourers. Small bungalows housed Asiatic overseers. The plantation was expropriated by the Australian government and sold. Its new owners turned the bungalow into a hotel. (Hallstrom Pacific Library)

Plate 457. Herr Ehrmann, manager for the German firm Hasag at Kokopo in 1921. (S. Stephenson Collection)

Plate 455

Plate 456

Plate 457

Plate 458. House servants at Gunantambu plantation, Kokopo, 1920. Left to right, Peter, Moka, Baby, (unidentified]. (S. Stephenson Collection)

Plate 459. The Round House near Toma, 1921. This building was erected by the German administration on the heights of Varzin. In World War I the German administration retreated from Simpsonhafen (Rabaul) to Toma. In 1921 the house was run as an inn by a German, whose compatriots frequented it while awaiting a decision by the Australian government as to their future. It was rumoured that German nationals buried their gold somewhere near this spot. The building was later bought by W. R. Carpenter and Co. Ltd from the Expropriation Board, as a recreation place for the firm's staff. (B. B. Perriman Collection)

Plate 460. *Sing-sing* at Gunantambu plantation, 1920. (S. Stephenson Collection)

Plate 458

Plate 459

Plate 460

211

Plate 461

Plate 461. Herr Kirchner (right), Frau Kirchner and Mrs Mister at Kavieng, 1919. (S. Stephenson Collection)

Plate 462. The treasury building, Rabaul, 1925, known by the people of Rabaul as *haus money gammon*. (S. M. Matthews Collection)

Plate 462

Plate 463

Plate 463. Kokopo Hotel, side view, 1925. The hotel was the chief feature of Kokopo. The main hotel building was constructed of hardwood with a galvanized iron roof. A 3-metre veranda ran along the front and one side. The dining room of 15 x 8 metres was built on a solid concrete floor and had latticed walls; the bar was 6 x 3·5 metres, the same size as the office. A 2-metre-wide covered passage connected this main building to the guest house. 'It stood on top of the cliff and faced the Pacific. Its verandahs were ornamented with quaint green carvings that reminded the planters of many a familiar *Gasthaus* in the far-away Fatherland. . . . The spacious dining-room, with the bar at one end, opened into a huge Trinkhalle, where there were very merry gatherings in the old German days.' Lilian Overell, *A Woman's Impressions of German New Guinea* (London, 1923), pp. 27–8. (Hallstrom Pacific Library)

21 Administration Between the Wars: Papua and the New Guinea Mandate

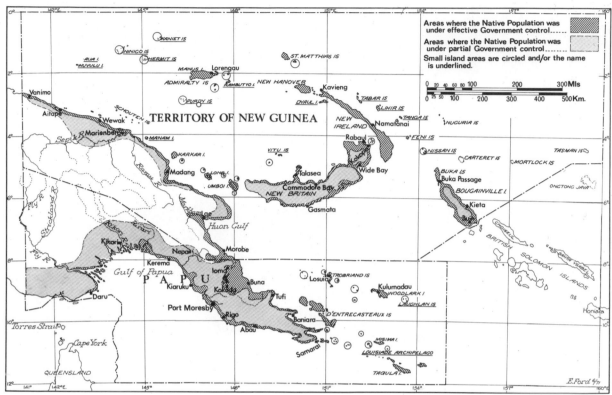

Plate 464

Plate 464. Map of the Territories showing the areas under effective or partial government control by 1921. It can be seen that almost all the coastal fringe was a controlled area, but only in a few places was there effective control more than a few kilometres from the coast. The incursions inland from Morobe and Buna were the result of gold strikes. In the early 1920s the Australian administration was forced to extend control over the middle Sepik to deal with the Tugeri headhunters. By this time only the Western District between the Kikori and Strickland Rivers awaited exploration and the Highlands were completely unknown. Most Europeans thought that the centre was thinly populated because of the rough, mountainous nature of the country. (Map drawn by Edgar Ford)

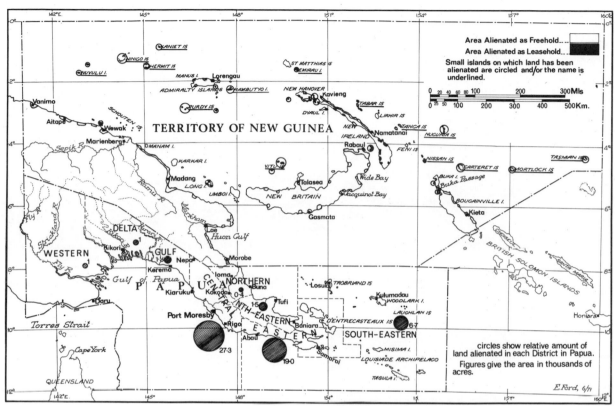

Plate 465

Plate 465. Map of the Territories in 1921, showing the degree of land alienation. In German New Guinea, which at this time was under Australian military rule, all land alienation was confined to the coasts and to islands. The areas marked illustrate the German policy of consolidating rule at coastal points before spreading inland. Most alienation to this time occurred in New Britain, New Ireland, the Madang coast and the main island groups. In Papua, the exact areas of alienation at this date are unavailable. Alienation has been shown proportionally for each division. Most alienation occurred in the Central Division, but the amount alienated was only 27·3 per cent. Apart from the Eastern Division, the amount alienated in other divisions was so low as to be insignificant. (Map drawn by Edgar Ford)

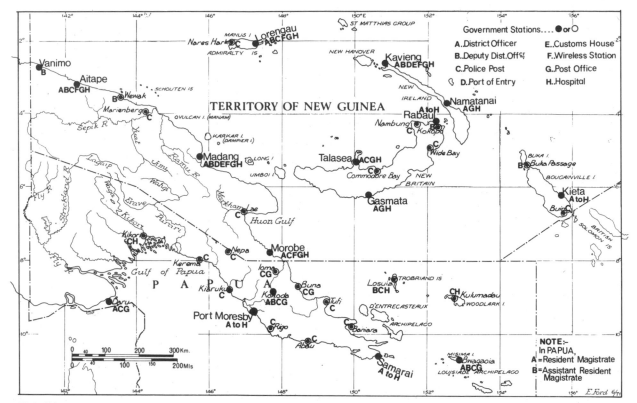

Plate 466

Plate 467

Plate 466. Map of the Territories showing the various facilities available at the main European population centres. In 1921 facilities were more widespread in New Guinea than in Papua. Centres with a full range of services were Port Moresby (non-indigenous population 488); Samarai (non-indigenous population 293); Rabaul (non-indigenous population 1350); Kavieng (non-indigenous population 356); Kieta (non-indigenous population 148). In New Guinea, Administration officials in charge of districts were known as district officers and deputy district officers, whereas in Papua they were known as resident magistrates and assistant resident magistrates. (Map drawn by Edgar Ford)

Plate 467. Sir Hubert Murray (1861–1940), lieutenant governor of Papua, 1908 to 1940. Murray was appointed chief judicial officer for British New Guinea in 1904 (see plate 126) and acting administrator in 1907. In November 1908 he was appointed lieutenant governor of Papua by the Australian government and he held this post until his death at Samarai in February 1940.

Murray was chairman of the Royal Commission on Late German New Guinea (see plates 400 and 401). During his term as lieutenant governor of Papua, he built up a reputation as one of the great colonial administrators. He formulated a policy of protection for the Papuan people, with controlled European economic activity and a careful application of law and administration. (Mitchell Library)

THE POLICE BOY: Yes; of course you lads wish to help each other. But the Law says that you belong to different countries, and that you must not cross that border. And you must not say such things about the Law. He is a big fella sorcerer, and lives in Canberra, or Geneva, or somewhere.

Plate 468

Plate 468. The difficulties of a divided administration are the subject of this cartoon in the *Pacific Islands Monthly* of 17 April 1935. (Mitchell Library)

Plate 470. Members of the Papuan constabulary at Ononé in 1928. (Father Coltré Collection)

Plate 470

Plate 469

Plate 469. Papuan police at Buna, 1920. (E. E. Jones Collection)

Plate 471

Plate 471. The governor general, Lord Forster, visiting the European hospital in Rabaul, 1923. From left to right, Mrs Wisdom, wife of the administrator; Lord Forster; the matron and a sister; W. E. Grose, secretary toe the administrator; a sister; [unidentified]; Dr Phyllis Cilento; Mrs Drake-Brockman; and Dr Raphael Cilento. (B. B. Perriman Collection)

Plate 472

Plate 472. The Australian governor general, Lord Forster, with the New Guinea administrator, General Wisdom, and a party reviewing a *sing-sing* at Rabaul in honour of the governor general's visit, 1923. (B. Backus Collection)

Plate 473. The Legislative Council of New Guinea at its inaugural meeting on 9 May 1933. Standing, left to right, V. A. Pratt (non-official member); Dr C. T. Brennan (director of public health); W. E. Grose (non-official member); G. G. Hogan (crown law officer); H. H. Page (government secretary); A. N. McLennan (non-official member); E. W. P. Chinnery (director of district services and native affairs); B. B. Perriman (non-official member). Sitting, left to right, N. P. H. Neal (non-official member); J. C. Mullaby (non-official member); E. P. Holmes (secretary for lands); Brigadier General T. Griffiths (acting administrator); R. L. Clark (non-official member); G. H. Murray (director of agriculture); H. O. Townsend (Treasury). The Legislative Council was created by Act No. 51 of 1932 of the Commonwealth Parliament (An Act to Amend the New Guinea Act 1920-1926, Assented 28 November 1932). The Council was given authority to 'make Ordinances for the peace, order and government of the Territory'. (Department of Information and Extension Services, Administration of Papua New Guinea)

Plate 473

218

Plate 474

Plate 475

Plate 474. Harold E. Woodman supervising construction of a road to the district office at Wewak in 1927. (H. E. Woodman Collection)

Plate 476

Plate 475. The police post at Ambunti on the Sepik River in 1929. Ambunti was at this time the most distant station from the coast of either Territory, being 420 kilometres from the mouth of the Sepik. Three Europeans were stationed there. (Hallstrom Pacific Library)

Plate 476. A *tul-tul* directs the way, Lae, 1933. The appointment of *tul-tuls* was part of the German system of administration through village officials. The *tul-tul* stood next in authority to the *luluai* (see plate 144). Most *tul-tuls* were messengers who could speak Pidgin and could therefore pass information between government officials and the *luluai*. Medical orderlies were called *heiltultuls*. Under the Mandate the village-official system was maintained. (E. E. Jones Collection)

Plate 477

Plate 479

Plate 477. The visit of Lord Gowrie, the governor general of Australia, to Bulolo in August 1937. Left to right, the dredge master; Sir Walter McNicoll (1877–1947), administrator of the Mandated Territory of New Guinea; Lady Gowrie; Lord Gowrie; L. V. Waterhouse; Lord Ranfurly; Commander Dowling; L. Joubert. Sir Walter McNicoll was appointed administrator in 1934 and held the post until 23 January 1942, when in the face of the Japanese invasion of New Guinea he handed over control to the Australian army and retired to Australia. (Mitchell Library)

Plate 478. The governor general of Australia, Lord Gowrie, inspecting a guard of honour of the constabulary at Salamaua in August 1937. Lord Gowrie is attended by District Officer E. Taylor. (Mitchell Library)

Plate 479. Lae in 1933. The town and port developed in the 1930s as a service and supply centre for the Bulolo Valley goldfields. Following the Rabaul volcanic eruptions in May 1937, consideration was given to removing the administrative capital to another town in the Mandated Territory. In 1938 a committee headed by General Griffiths recommended Lae as the site for the capital. It was not until the end of 1941, however, that the administration was moved to Lae. The administrator, Sir Walter McNicoll, took this step following the continued activity of Tavurvur volcano in Rabaul. The Commonwealth government approved the move on 5 September 1941. R. R. McNicoll, 'Sir Walter McNicoll as Administrator of the Mandated Territory', in *The History of Melanesia*, Second Waigani Seminar (Canberra, 1969), pp. 123–4. (Mitchell Library)

Plate 480

Plate 480. H. Leonard Murray (standing to the left of the wheel) and party on board a Sacred Heart mission vessel off the Papuan coast, *c.* 1935. Bishop de Boismenu is on the extreme left, Father Dryserat at the wheel, and Brother Paul on the right. Murray, nephew of Sir Hubert Murray, joined his uncle as assistant private secretary in 1909 and became official secretary in 1915. In 1940 he was appointed administrator of Papua following the death of Sir Hubert Murray. He held this post until February 1942, when civil government was replaced by military government for the duration of the war. (Father Coltré Collection)

Plate 481

Plate 481. Rabaul from the summit of North Daughter volcano, 1923, overlooking Namanula, the harbour and the racecourse (centre). A visitor to Rabaul in 1920 wrote: 'Rabaul is a beautiful little town built on low-lying land with the steep ridge of hills for a background. The well-laid-out streets are lined with rows of trees and frequently there are also rows down the middle. . . . The wooden bungalows, standing on high piles, usually have only two or three rooms, but these are large and airy with many windows and doors. They are surrounded by wide verandas, opening here and there into spacious porches which are furnished as sitting-rooms and adorned with plants, creepers and flowers; and here one chiefly lives.' Lilian Overell, *A Woman's Impressions of German New Guinea* (London, 1923), pp. 7–8. (B. Backus Collection)

Plate 482. A section of the township at Port Moresby on Paga Point as seen from the wharf in 1933. (L. C. Roebuck Collection)

Plate 482

Plate 483. Salamaua in 1933. At this time Salamaua was the principal shipping port for the goldfields. The airstrip can be located by noting the dark line of vegetation in the background, top left. (L. C. Roebuck Collection)

Plate 483

Plate 484

Plate 484. Lae township in 1932. The airstrip in the middle distance is in the same position as today's airstrip. The aerodromes at Lae and Wau were put down at the same time to receive the first aeroplane flown in by 'Pard' Mustar in April 1927. The township grew around the airstrip, which was in full operation by 1929. A broad-gauge railroad ran from the aerodrome to the wharf, a distance of 1·2 kilometres. 'Youthful as it is, Lae already assumes an air of importance. As the head-quarters in New Guinea of Guinea Airways Ltd, with its splendidly equipped workshops, with stores and supplies either coming and going or awaiting transport, it has taken on something of the atmosphere of commerce and industry.' L. Rhys, *High Lights and Flights in New Guinea* (London, 1942), p. 162. (*Commonwealth Records* CRS A24, reproduced by permission of the Commonwealth Archives Office)

Plate 485. Bulolo township, 1934, showing well-laid-out streets and attractive bungalows. The airstrip can be seen in the middle distance. The building at right centre is the mess hut; the large building at left is the recreation centre. Les Roebuck recalls, 'We had a dance in the recreation centre in 1933. There were fifty gentlemen and two ladies. One was Mrs Jean Bowring from Edie Creek.' (L. C. Roebuck Collection)

Plate 485

Plate 486

Plate 486. The government wharf at Rabaul on fire on the night of 3 January 1923. The wharf was owned originally by the Norddeutsche Lloyd company. After its partial destruction by fire it was always referred to as 'burnt wharf'. (B. B. Perriman Collection)

Plate 487. The 'fire brigade' trying to extinguish the fire that was destroying the copra shed at Ah Tam's owned by W. R. Carpenter and Co. Ltd, 3 January 1923. (B. B. Perriman Collection)

Plate 487

Plate 488. The main wharf, Rabaul, partially destroyed by fire in January 1923 with great loss of property. It appears from reports of people who landed here that the wharf was none too safe and had to be approached with caution even before the fire. (B. Backus Collection)

Plate 488

Plate 489

Plate 489. Rabaul racecourse, showing the members' stand and enclosure, about 1928. (B. B. Perriman Collection)

Plate 490. Australian expatriates in Rabaul in the mid-1920s. The photograph was taken the morning after a party. Visitors to the Mandated Territory at this time described the evening social life as invariably a sumptuous dinner followed by dancing to gramophone records on the open verandas until the early hours. (S. M. Matthews Collection)

Plate 491. The Port Moresby cricket team, 1929. This team met each Saturday during the cricket season to compete with the Poreporena Cricket Club and the East Cricket Club. (S. M. Matthews Collection)

Plate 490

Plate 491

Plate 492

Plate 493

Plate 492. A tennis party at Wewak in the early 1930s.
(H. E. Woodman Collection)

Plate 493. European wedding in tropical dress, Rabaul,
1920s. The bridegroom was Mr Justice Karl Drake-
Brockman of Rabaul and previously of Western Australia.
(Library of New South Wales)

Plate 494. The old New Guinea Club, Rabaul, founded
by R. L. (Nobby) Clark, and destroyed in World War II.
(R. Clark Collection)

Plate 494

Plate 495. The Hon. R. L. (Nobby) Clark. Clark was responsible for the evacuation of Rabaul citizens when the Japanese invasion was imminent. He was taken prisoner by the Japanese and lost his life when the *Montevideo Maru* was torpedoed. (R. Clark Collection)

Plate 495

Plate 496

Plate 496. Floats forming part of a procession through Rabaul streets in the late 1920s. (B. B. Perriman Collection)

Plate 497. The Madang Hotel, Madang, about 1928. (B. B. Perriman Collection)

Plate 497

Plate 498

Plate 498. The main road at Salamaua, about 1925. (B. B. Perriman Collection)

Plate 499. The business centre of Salamaua about 1934, showing the Hotel Salamaua and Guinea Airways. (*Commonwealth Records* CRS A24, reproduced by permission of the Commonwealth Archives Office)

Plate 499

Plate 500. The post office at Lae during World War I. (Information and Extension Services, Administration of Papua New Guinea)

Plate 501. Port Moresby post office before World War II. Opened in March 1925, it served first as the treasury and post office but, with reconstruction after the war, the Department of Posts and Telegraphs occupied all the building. (Mitchell Library)

Plate 500

Plate 501

Plate 502

Plate 502. Musgrave Street, Port Moresby, in 1939. (Mitchell Library)

Plate 503

Plate 503. The Hotel Moresby soon after its opening in February 1939. (Mitchell Library)

Plate 504

Plate 504. The original telegraph office in Madang. (Information and Extension Services, Administration of Papua New Guinea)

Plate 505

Plate 505. Rabaul post office, about 1916. During World War I, Burns, Philp and Co. Ltd maintained its shipping service from Australia to New Guinea. Nearly every month a vessel left Sydney for Port Moresby and continued on to Samarai, Rabaul and other points in the Bismarck Sea before calling again at Rabaul and undertaking the return to Sydney. (Information and Extension Services, Administration of Papua New Guinea)

Plate 507

Plate 506

Plate 506. The path along the harbour foreshore between Rabaul and Malaguna, 1923. The path led to the doctor's bungalow and the hospital. Two of the hospital staff in that year were Dr George Heydon, government biologist, and Dr Clive Backhouse, medical officer, who succeeded Heydon as government biologist. (B. Backus Collection)

Plate 507. H. O. Newport, director of agriculture, with friends outside his residence in Rabaul, about 1920. (Information and Extension Services, Administration of Papua New Guinea)

229

Plate 508

Plate 508. A procession of Chinese children, Rabaul, 1920. A visitor to Chinatown in that year gave her impressions of the Chinese community: 'The better-class Chinese women and children are very attractive. They have soft round faces and very gentle self-possessed manners. Some are dressed in dull blue silk trousers and long coats, others are all in black.' Lilian Overell, *A Woman's Impressions of German New Guinea* (London, 1923), p. 8. (Department of Territories)

Plate 509

Plate 509. The European Hospital on Namanula Hill, Rabaul, 1923. Some of the hospital staff in that year were Dr Henman, Dr Carlov, Sister Curtain and Sister Richards. (B. Backus Collection)

Plate 510. The schooner *Lulu*, the first vessel used by W. R. Carpenter and Co. Ltd for the copra trade. The *Lulu*, with a capacity of 75 bags (14 bags to the tonne), brought in copra from plantations to the depot. It was wrecked on a reef shortly after its purchase in 1919. Over the next few years the company bought vessels including the schooner *Camohe* (capacity 240 bags); *Meklong* (capacity 5100 bags); *Vella* (capacity 600 bags); and *France* (capacity 650 bags). (B. B. Perriman Collection)

Plate 511. M.V. *Balangot*, a vessel purchased before World War II by W. R. Carpenter and Co. Ltd for the copra trade. It had a capacity of seventy-five bags of copra. (B. B. Perriman Collection)

Plate 510

Plate 511

Plate 512. The crew and some Rabaul visitors on the deck of the *Queen of Scots*, the first vessel chartered to load copra from New Guinea after the end of World War I for markets in Europe, 1921. The vessel was chartered by W. R. Carpenter and Co. Ltd. Another vessel, the *Sylfid*, was chartered about the same time. (B. B. Perriman Collection)

Plate 512

Plate 513. The M.V. *Columbia*, a vessel chartered by W. R. Carpenter and Co. Ltd to carry copra from New Guinea to Europe, 1926. The success of this venture led to the purchase of the M.V. *Glen Tara*, renamed the *Salamaua*, M.V. *George Washington*, renamed *Rabaul*, and the building of S.S. *Suva*, for the export trade. Each of these vessels carried approximately 6700 tonnes of copra. (B. B. Perriman Collection)

Plate 513

Plate 514

Plate 515

Plate 514. The M.V. *Rabaul*, purchased by W. R. Carpenter and Co. Ltd for the New Guinea–Europe copra trade, following the commercial success of the chartered vessels M.V. *Columbia*, *Queen of Scots* and *Sylfid*. The *Rabaul* carried 6700 tonnes of copra. She was sunk by the Japanese in 1943. (B. B. Perriman Collection)

Plate 515. William Dupain, Mrs Dupain and their daughters Diane and Lucille, leaving Raulauat on the north coast of New Britain, 1919. Dupain was the first manager for Burns Philp at Rabaul. He had been previously a purser for the firm in the Gilbert Islands and later in the Solomons, and was transferred to Rabaul as the Australian occupation was nearing its end. (Information and Extension Services, Administration of Papua New Guinea)

Plate 516

Plate 517

Plate 516. The wharf at Pondo, north coast of New Britain, showing boxes of desiccated coconut being loaded for the Australian market. (B. B. Perriman Collection)

Plate 517. Malaguna coaling wharf, Rabaul harbour, 1923. After the partial destruction by fire of the main wharf (see plate 486) in January 1923, this wharf was used temporarily for discharging and loading general cargo. (B. Backus Collection)

Plate 518. The storage shed and wharf built by W. R. Carpenter and Co. Ltd in Rabaul. A lease was obtained of a portion of Ah Tam's land on the waterfront. The shed had a capacity of 1750 tonnes of copra and also stored marine products. A small wharf was built to enable schooners to discharge copra and shell, and lighters to load produce for transfer to ships for Australia and Europe. The store was destroyed by fire in January 1923 (see plate 487). (B. B. Perriman Collection)

Plate 518

Plate 519

Plate 519. Sulphur Creek, Rabaul, looking down to Blanche Bay in the middle distance; the aerodrome site is to the left of the picture and on the right is the Norddeutsche Lloyd line bungalow, later Jolley's House and still later Coote's House (manager for Burns Philp, Rabaul). The probable date is in the 1920s. (Reproduced by permission of the Commonwealth Archives Office)

Plate 520. W. R. Carpenter's copra sheds at Toboi, 1928. When the company's copra store at Ah Tam's was destroyed by fire in the mid-1920s (see plate 487), the hulk *Loch Katrine* was towed to Rabaul and used for copra storage and coal storage. This proved unsatisfactory so the company purchased 6·7 hectares of land at Toboi, Rabaul harbour. Each shed had a capacity of 3500 tonnes. The trucks on the wharf are loaded with copra. From 800 to 900 tonnes of copra per day could be loaded from this wharf. The area has since been used for a coconut-oil mill, including tanks for coconut oil and fuel oil, and as a depot for copra and cocoa, coconut meal and meal pellets. The oil mill and paint and liquid gas plants have all been erected here since World War II. The water is deep enough to take 25 000 tonne oil tankers. (B. B. Perriman Collection)

Plate 521. S.S. *Duranbah* was the first vessel to be slipped on W. R. Carpenter's new Keravia slipway, completed in 1933. The photograph shows the M.V. *Southern Cross*. Until 1937 the slip was used by vessels operating in New Guinea and the Solomon Islands. In May 1937 the volcanic eruption at Vulcan Island caused the mainland of New Britain and Vulcan Island to become one, and the slipway and the *Durour* (see plates 524, 546), which was on the slip at the time, were covered completely in pumice. Both the slip and the *Durour* had to be abandoned. (B. B. Perriman Collection)

Plate 522. The wharf of W. R. Carpenter's main store block, Mango Avenue, Rabaul, 1928. The trucks on the wharf could carry about one tonne of merchandise or copra. The two-hectare site with this water frontage and wharf was purchased from the Expropriation Board and was originally the property of the German Neuguinea-Kompagnie. (B. B. Perriman Collection)

Plate 520

Plate 521

Plate 522

Plate 523

Plate 524

Plate 525

Plate 526

Plate 523. A desiccated coconut factory at Pondo plantation on the north coast of New Britain, about 145 kilometres from Rabaul, in 1933. The factory was owned by Coconut Products Ltd, a subsidiary firm of W. R. Carpenter and Co. Ltd. A small motor vessel, *Balus*, transported husked coconuts from various plantations on New Britain and New Ireland to Pondo. Production was about a hundred tonnes per month. Vessels called at Pondo to collect the desiccated coconut and ship it to Australia. Coconut fibre and charcoal were also produced. This factory was wiped out by bombs in World War II. In 1948 a second factory was started at Madang on Beliau Island and continued for some years. In 1967 a third factory was erected on Ulaveo plantation, Kokopo, and is still in operation. (B. B. Perriman Collection)

Plate 524. A slipway being erected at Keravia, Rabaul, for W. R. Carpenter and Co. Ltd, to take ships to be overhauled in New Guinea instead of in Sydney. Surplus steel was bought for its erection from the Sydney Harbour bridge construction and shipped to Rabaul. The photograph shows the shore section of the slip ready for the cradle, and the section to go under water buoyed with 44-gallon oil drums to be floated into position to join the shore section. The drums were then to be released. The slip on completion in 1933 took vessels up to 1000 tonnes. (B. B. Perriman Collection)

Plate 525. The official opening of the Keravia (Rabaul) slipway in 1933. Left to right, Dr Hoskings, government medical officer; Herr Fürter (next to pole); Robert Melrose, government secretary; H. A. Gregory, district officer; a bank official; P. Coote, manager of Burns Philp; B. B. Perriman, manager of W. R. Carpenter; George Murray, director of agriculture; Mr Holmes, secretary of lands. (B. B. Perriman Collection)

Plate 526. Burns Philp store, Rabaul, in 1937. (Burns, Philp and Company Ltd)

Plate 527. Burns Philp store, Salamaua, in 1933. (L. C. Roebuck Collection)

Plate 528. Burns Philp store at Port Moresby in 1939. Built in 1912, this building once dominated the town. (Mitchell Library)

Plate 529. Burns Philp store, Samarai, in 1937. (Burns, Philp and Company Ltd)

Plate 530. An Avro Anson plane of the Mandated Airline Company, which was used with Dragon aircraft to freight cargo from Salamaua and Lae to the goldfields. (B. B. Perriman Collection)

Plate 527

Plate 528

Plate 529

Plate 530

Plate 531

Plate 532

Plate 531. An event in Rabaul—the arrival of the weekly plane from the south, 1935. For the Sydney to Rabaul airmail service the Mandated Airline Company purchased three De Havilland 86B twelve-seater bi-planes. Places en route from Sydney to Rabaul were Brisbane, Rockhampton, Townsville, Cairns, Cooktown, Port Moresby, and Lae. Over water (Cooktown to Port Moresby) the planes were permitted eight passengers only to allow for additional fuel to be carried if weather conditions made it necessary to return to point of takeoff. On the outbreak of war in Europe, the government commandeered the three planes for use in the Middle East in the evacuation of sick and wounded troops. The company then purchased two Lockheed 14s, which carried twelve passengers plus two pilots. These operated successfully until the Japanese entered the war and attacked various parts of New Guinea on 21 January 1942. (Z. Mattes Collection)

Plate 533

Plate 532. A vice-regal occasion on the frontier of Australian empire. The ladies of Bulwa talking with Lord and Lady Gowrie on the occasion of their visit to the New Guinea goldfields in August 1937. (Mitchell Library)

Plate 533. Bungalow occupied by the manager of W. R. Carpenter and Co. Ltd in Rabaul in 1920. The manager, Mr B. Perriman, and Mrs Perriman are on the steps. The house, which stood in Casuarina Avenue, was owned originally by Mrs E. Whiteman. The row of trees behind the house divides it from the home of Mr Tom Ellis, Sr. (B. B. Perriman Collection)

Plate 534

Plate 534. The first store of W. R. Carpenter and Co. Ltd, Mango Avenue, Rabaul, opened in June 1924. The principal business at this time was the purchase of island produce and the selling of general merchandise. Transactions were carried out with the German firms who, under the terms of capitulation, were allowed to stay and continue storekeeping and operating coconut and cocoa plantations. Carpenter and Co. supplied finance and goods for various types of ventures undertaken by Europeans, Chinese and Japanese, such as fishing for mother-of-pearl and black lip shell, trochus and green snail shells and bêche-de-mer, timber milling, and plantation development. (B. B. Perriman Collection)

Plate 535. The interior of the W. R. Carpenter and Co. Ltd store in Mango Avenue, Rabaul, 1924. The company obtained agencies for Ford cars, trucks and tractors, Dodge and later Chrysler cars and trucks. (B. B. Perriman Collection)

Plate 536. The third store purchased from the Expropriation Board by W. R. Carpenter and Co. Ltd, in Mango Avenue, Rabaul. Increased merchandise business warranted a third store. A second store had been built alongside the first store, being 18 x 30 metres with office accommodation of 6 x 18 metres on the first floor. This proved inadequate and so Carpenters purchased this Neuguinea-Kompagnie site, which was put up for tender about 1926–27. The two-hectare block was probably the best business site in Rabaul. It had a water frontage and wharf, a large retail store 35 x 25 metres, a bulk store 24 x 45 metres, a separate hardware store 12 x 45 metres, a boat repair building and a number of smaller buildings. The retail store had heavy wooden supports for the upper floors, each about 25 x 25 cm and 2·5 metres apart. These were replaced by steel girders and channel steel; display windows were also installed. The first store was then converted into a staff club and the second store building was run by the company as Palms Restaurant. (B. B. Perriman Collection)

Plate 535

Plate 536

Plate 537

Plate 538

Plate 537. Part of W. R. Carpenter's main store block, Mango Avenue, Rabaul, showing the iceworks and butcher's shop erected on the site that was formerly owned by the Neuguinea-Kompagnie. The supply of ice and meat to householders had been a service of the administration until Carpenter and Co. opened their stores. (B. B. Perriman Collection)

Plate 538. The style of life for a leading member of the expatriate community in prewar Rabaul is revealed in this photograph of the house of the Burns Philp manager in 1941. (Burns, Philp and Company Ltd)

Plate 539

Plate 539. First wireless installation in New Guinea. The transmitter, whose generator is driven by a pedal arrangement, was evolved by Amalgamated Wireless for use in New Guinea. This photograph shows the operator at Rabaul in conversation with Bulolo, 644 kilometres distant. (Hallstrom Pacific Library)

Plate 540. The powerhouse at Rabaul on the day of its official opening, 7 May 1932. It was erected on the corner of Kamarere Street and Mango Avenue. Power was generated at 2300 volts and supplied to three feeders that ran to Chinatown and Namanula, Rapindik and Malaguna. In his opening address Mr H. G. Carter said: 'The street lighting that you will see tonight is not complete; we have some 26 lights erected in the main avenues of the city. This is only about 30% as there are something like 70 lights to be erected altogether, and the balance will go up as soon as possible. The company has gone to some expense in erecting a better class of fitting in Mango Avenue, and we trust that this little addition will be appreciated by residents.' *Rabaul Times*, 13 May 1932. (B. B. Perriman Collection)

Plate 540

Plate 541

Plate 542

Plate 543

Plate 544

Plate 541. The first general store of W. R. Carpenter and Co. Ltd in Kavieng, New Ireland, in 1924. The store was built on leasehold land and merchandise was imported from Australia. Business was similar in every respect to that transacted in Rabaul. A second store was built before World War II, and a third store after the war. (B. B. Perriman Collection)

Plate 542. The second store opened by W. R. Carpenter and Co. Ltd at Madang, on 1 December 1933. (B. B. Perriman Collection)

Plate 543. Matupi and Vulcan volcanoes in eruption in May 1937. Matupi exploded two days after Vulcan, and hurled pumice across the harbour towards the new 450 metre mountain, Vulcan, that had been born out of the island. 'Rabaul residents were first aware of the eruption at 4.25 p.m. on Saturday. Nearly everyone rushed to the waterfront and beheld there a spectacle so colossal that it left the spectators spell-bound. From Vulcan Island there arose a huge column of white clouds, rolling skywards, in undulating folds, impregnated with rocks and pumice. At frequent intervals loud explosions were heard followed immediately by dark brown volumes of smoke.' *Rabaul Times*, 4 June 1937. (B. B. Perriman Collection)

Plate 544. The evacuation of the European and indigenous population from Rabaul in May 1937 during the volcanic eruption. (R. Clark Collection)

Plate 545

Plate 545. Mango Avenue, Rabaul, after the volcanic eruptions of Vulcan and Matupi in May 1937. First building on the left is the chemist shop of D. S. Davies; the second building is the store of W. R. Carpenter and Co. Ltd. Two Europeans and several hundred New Guineans of Keravia and Tavaun villages were killed. Rabaul was evacuated and closed to the public by police who guarded the road at Tunnel Hill. The work of looking after the residents and restoring the town fell on the administration staff who at this time were under the direction of the acting administrator, Judge Phillips. (B. B. Perriman·Collection)

Plate 546

Plate 546. The S.S. *Durour* on Keravia slipway, Rabaul, after the volcanic eruption in May 1937. This vessel, together with S.S. *Duris*, capacity 7000 bags of copra, had maintained an efficient service for W. R. Carpenter and Co. Ltd to centres at Kavieng, Salamaua, Madang and Wewak. The *Duris* was last seen dragging her anchors and heading for Vulcan volcano. In the eruption the island split into two parts, the centre forming a crater into which it is presumed the *Duris* disappeared. B. B. Perriman, manager of W. R. Carpenter and Co. Ltd at Rabaul, described part of the scene: 'An American vessel, S.S. *Golden Bear*, was also in Rabaul at the time and alongside our Toboi wharf. The eruption caused darkness for several miles from its centre. A wireless operator aboard this vessel was lost and it is presumed

fell through the ropes at the top of the gangway and was not seen again. Another man, a Mr Elsworthy, endeavoured to climb Matupi mountain, which was also in eruption, to take photographs and was not seen again. It is presumed he fell into the crater. . . . On returning to Rabaul, the *Golden Bear* ploughed through pumice 8 to 10 feet deep, the steel hull being polished by the pumice. For some time vessels could not get closer than 10 to 12 feet from the wharf. Slings of bags of copra would fall on the pumice between the ship and the wharf. Natives would stand on the pumice and remake the sling.' 'Perriman Papers', New Guinea Manuscript Collection, Hallstrom Pacific Library. (B. B. Perriman Collection)

23 Inland Exploration, 1890-1939

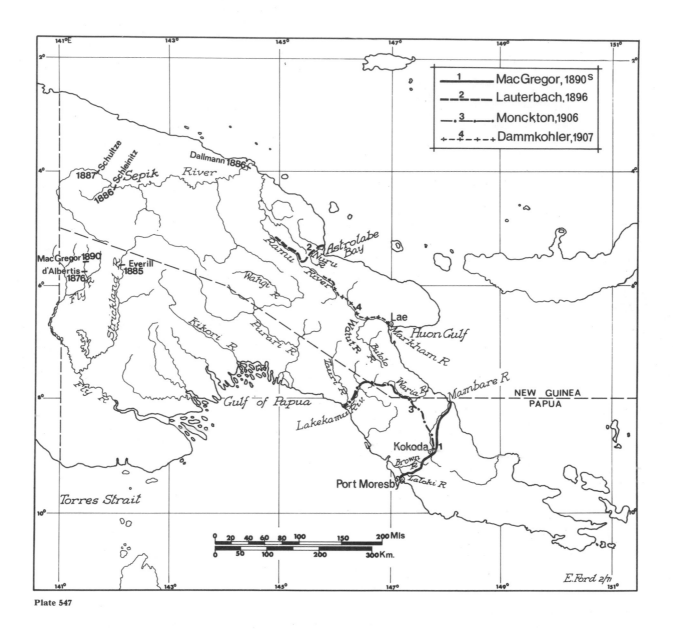

MacGregor, 1890ˢ
Lauterbach,1896
Monckton,1906
Dammkohler,1907

Plate 547

Plate 547. Sir William MacGregor, who was appointed administrator of British New Guinea in 1888, shared with his three predecessors a conviction that the government had to know the territory for which it was responsible before it could govern. He carried on the policy of official exploration started by Sir Peter Scratchley. Private endeavours were frowned upon.

MacGregor twice crossed the isthmus from Port Moresby to the Mambare; he ascended all the rivers to the point that they were navigable; in 1889 he climbed the Owen Stanley Range to reach and name its highest peak, Mount Victoria. Charles Monckton, a New Zealander, was resident magistrate under MacGregor. From his patrol post at Kokoda, Monckton climbed

Mt Albert Edward and later in the same year (1906) attempted to find a route by which miners could reach a gold strike on the Upper Waria without going through German territory. Monckton reached the headwaters of the Upper Waria, crossed the Central Range and reached the south coast by the Lakekamu River. Judge Murray's disapproval of Monckton's journey, on the grounds that it was undertaken solely for adventure, underlines the British policy that was carried on by Murray for thirty-four years.

Official German policy towards exploration differed from that of the British. The Neuguinea-Kompagnie concentrated on consolidating its claims along the coast. Most of the inland explorers were men of science—scholars, rather than government officials. Hugo Zöller was the first to penetrate the interior to the Finisterre Range (plate 550). Dr Carl Lauterbach, a botanist, ascended the Gogol River for 64 kilometres in 1890 and six years later led an expedition that mapped the entire Ramu River system (plate 551). This journey was made only a year after Otto von Ehlers' tragic attempt to cross New Guinea from the Francisco River to the Lakekamu (plate 554). Wilhelm Dammköhler was the most colourful of the German explorers. He ascended the Waria River with Rodatz in 1901 (plate 551), was with Klink and Schlenzig on an expedition to the Ramu in 1902, and in 1907, with a surveyor, Fröhlich, he trekked from the Markham headwaters to the Ramu. Two years later on a trip along the Watut River, Dammköhler and his partner, Rudolph Oldorp, were attacked by New Guineans and Dammköhler died of his wounds. (Map drawn by Edgar Ford)

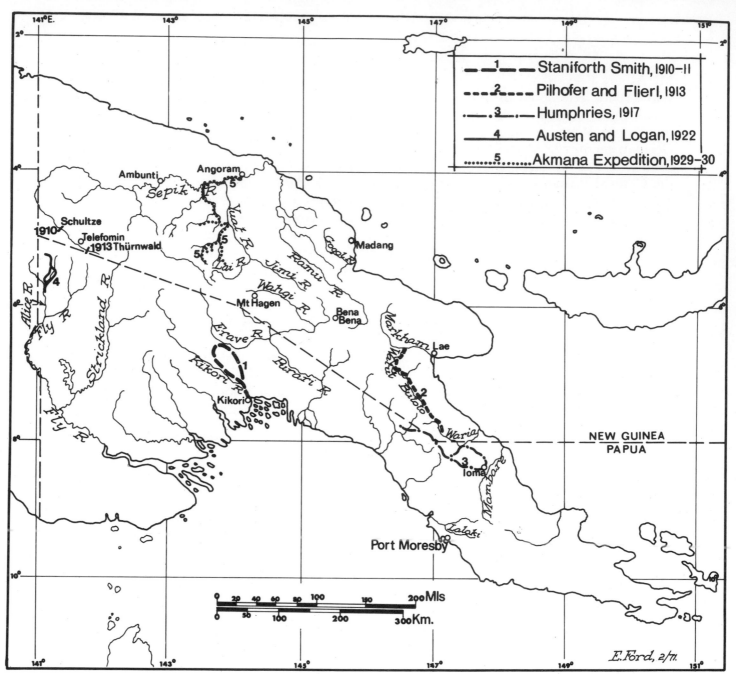

1 —— Staniforth Smith, 1910–11
2 ---- Pilhofer and Flierl, 1913
3 —·—· Humphries, 1917
4 ——— Austen and Logan, 1922
5 ········· Akmana Expedition, 1929–30

E. Ford, 2/71.

Plate 548

Plate 548. By 1910 most of the coast of Papua was under government control. The Australian government now made money available for official penetration of the interior, so that sources of labour might be opened up for the struggling plantations. Staniforth Smith in 1910 led an expedition up the Kikori, lost his way, but reached the coast after a three-month journey during which one-third of his party perished. Henry Ryan had more success the following year on a trip that took him west from the Kikori to a tributary of the Bamu. The most outstanding exploit of the Lutheran missionary-explorers was the journey of Dr Georg Pilhofer and the Rev. Leonhardt Flierl from the Waria to the Markham in 1913 (see plate 555). This year also a survey team led by Dr Walter Behrmann explored the Kaiserin Augusta (Sepik) basin (plate 552). Dr Richard Thurnwald, an ethnologist with Behrmann, returned to the upper Sepik the following year to study the Banaro people and was still there, unaware of the outbreak of war, when the Australian military force occupied German New Guinea. During the war W. R. Humphries opened up a path between the Gulf of Papua and Huon Gulf.

The 1920s saw increased interest in gold prospects, and much of the interior was opened up in this period by prospectors and by Administration officers like R. M. Lyons and patrol officers Austen and Logan, who were often occupied in protecting the prospectors. The decade ended with the first penetration of the Western Highlands by a party of prospectors—Shepherd, Beazley, Seale, MacGregor and Freeman (plates 558–561). (Map drawn by Edgar Ford)

244

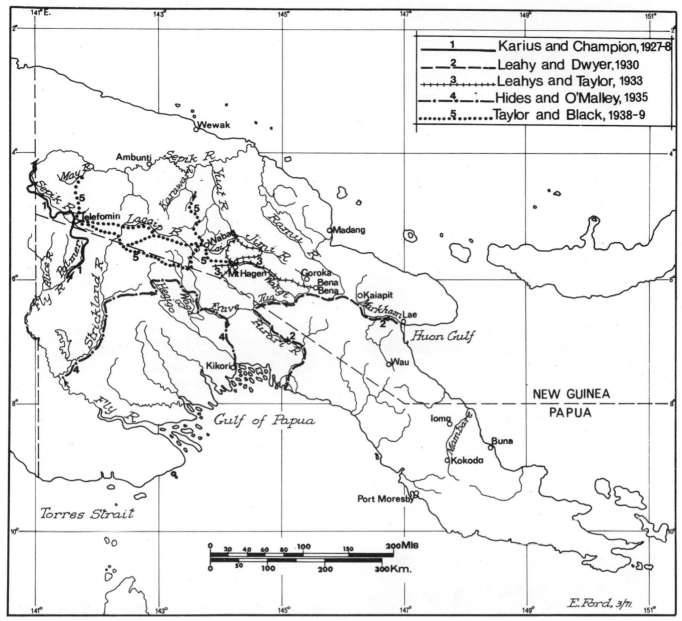

Legend:
- 1 ———— Karius and Champion, 1927-8
- 2 —·—·— Leahy and Dwyer, 1930
- 3 ++++++ Leahys and Taylor, 1933
- 4 —··—··— Hides and O'Malley, 1935
- 5 ·········· Taylor and Black, 1938-9

E. Ford, 3/71.

Plate 549

Plate 549. Until gold was discovered in plentiful quantities, the interior of Australian New Guinea continued to be relatively neglected. Apart from the charting of the river system, the German rule in New Guinea had seen few attempts to extend control very far from the coast. In the early 1920s the Australian contribution was limited to the opening of the Ambunti patrol post in 1924 and the patrolling of the middle Sepik district.

In Papua, exploration continued as a regular feature of Murray's policy of peaceful penetration. Murray was proud of the achievements of his 'outside men' and, when in 1926 he learned of a British team's intention to find the source of the Sepik, he determined that the honour should go to his own men. The Fly–Sepik crossing was achieved by Karius and Champion in 1927–28 (plates 556, 557). At the advent of the 1930s only the Highland region of New Guinea, an area of about 95 kilometres by 325 kilometres, remained a mystery.

The opening up of the rich goldfields at Bulolo and Edie Creek by mining corporations led to searches for new goldfields further west, and to the introduction of air services. Companies were able to finance well-equipped expeditions and sometimes a company joined with the Administration to promote exploration and prospecting. The penetration of the Wahgi Valley by Jim Taylor and Mick and Dan Leahy in 1933 was one expedition shared by the Administration and New Guinea Goldfields Company. From 1933 exploration was aided by aircraft, which carried out reconnaissance work and dropped supplies. Nevertheless, the real exploration could be done only on foot and in some ways the difficulties were greater than those experienced in Papua; the Mandated Territory was more densely populated and patrolling was rendered dangerous in areas where the people had engaged in hostilities with prospectors. (Map drawn by Edgar Ford)

245

Plate 550

Plate 551

Plate 550. Hugo Zöller, the first German to reach the Finisterre Mountains. Zöller was a newspaper correspondent with the *Kölnische Zeitung*. The trip was made in 1888 with three other Europeans from Konstantinhafen. The party journeyed up the Kabenan River and then climbed Neven du Mont-berg (2654 m), which Zöller named after his employer. From the mountain they had a view of the Bismarck Range. Zöller named its four highest peaks after the chancellor and his children: Ottoberg, Herbertberg, Mariaberg and Wilhelmberg. (Mitchell Library)

Plate 551. Members of a German expedition mounted to explore the river system of Kaiser Wilhelmsland. Seated, Dr Carl Lauterbach, botanist; standing, left to right, Hans Klink, a Kompagnie official; Hans Rodatz, formerly an officer in the Prussian army; and Robert Phillip, an Australian gold prospector. Dr Lauterbach led an expedition for the Neuguinea-Kompagnie into the Bismarcks to find the headwaters of the Markham River and to return by it to the Huon Gulf. On 10 July 1896, accompanied by Dr O. Kersting and Ernst Tappenbeck, Lauterbach reached a river that was obviously not the Markham. Shortage of food and attacks on the party forced them to return to Stephansort. In 1898 Ernst Tappenbeck, accompanied by Rodatz, Klink, Phillip and Hans Blum, set out to establish the identity of this river. They identified it as the Ramu (the river that von Schleinitz had named the Ottilie in 1886). The party established a station on the river and mapped the Ramu and its major tributaries. Photograph taken in 1899. (Landeshauptstadt und Universitätsstadt, Mainz, Stadtbibliothek)

Plate 552

Plate 552. Members of a large German expedition mounted to survey the Kaiserin Augusta (Sepik) basin. Back row, left to right, Dr Roesside; Dr Behrmann; Dr Thurnwald; seated, left to right, Lebermann; Etollé; and Dr Bürgers. Of the task before them, Behrmann wrote: 'In a territory 250 miles long and 150 miles wide, only the course of the main river was known. Any work in the jungle is a matter of feeling one's way in the dark. It is mostly a matter of good luck that in the chosen direction there are no impassable thickets, swamps or waterways that hinder progress.' (W. Behrmann, *Im Stromgebeit der Sepik: Eine Deutsche Forschungs-Reise in Neu-Guinea* [Berlin, 1922]. Unpublished translation in the Mitchell Library.) The party examined tributaries of the main river by steamer and pinnace and then penetrated the interior into the Central Range for ten weeks. Dr Richard Thurnwald ascended the main river to a point about thirty-two kilometres upstream from the Dutch-German border. In 1914 he returned there to study the Banaro people, and he was still there when World War I broke out. He was forced to leave New Guinea for Australia in 1915. Later he was permitted to go to America, from where he eventually returned to Germany. (Landeshauptstadt und Universitätsstadt, Mainz, Stadtbibliothek)

Plate 553. Some well-known identities of the Gazelle Peninsula take time for a rest on an excursion into the Varzin Mountains of Neu Pommern (New Britain). Left to right, Richard Parkinson, brother-in-law of 'Queen' Emma; Boolsen, of Hernsheim and Co.; Thiel; Chancellor Schmiele, administrator (1892–95), based at Friedrich-Wilhelmshafen (Madang); Forsayth of Farrell and Co.; Count Joachim Pfeil. Photograph taken about 1894. (Staatsbibliothek, Berlin)

Plate 554. Survivors of Otto Ehlers' expedition in 1896. Crouched in centre front and wearing hats are the two Bukas, Opia and Ranga, who were charged with the murder of Ehlers and Piering, and who, after their escape from jail, were responsible for the death of the administrator of German New Guinea, Kurt von Hagen (plate 138). They were eventually killed by Gaib people and their heads sent to Stephansort. (Mitchell Library)

Plate 555. Dr Georg Pilhofer of the Neuendettelsau Lutheran mission. In 1912 Pilhofer and Keysser reached the Markham River and descended it to the coast. The following year Pilhofer, in company with Dr Leonhardt Flierl, crossed the headwaters of the Waria River and the Biaru River, and then climbed the mountains into the Bulolo-Watut Valley. They continued down the valley to the Markham River. The journey took forty-six days and, although they passed amongst Kukukuku people who were known for their aggression, the two missionaries achieved their goal without hostilities. (Mitchell Library)

Plate 553

Plate 555

Plate 554

Plate 556

Plate 556. Patrol officer Ivan Champion who, with Charles Karius (see plate 557), was chosen by Hubert Murray to make the crossing from the Fly to the Sepik. On their first attempt from Daru on 8 December 1926 they ascended the Fly River and established a base camp over 1100 kilometres from the coast, whereupon they separated to explore. Karius reached a valley that would have led him to the Sepik, before returning to Daru via the Strickland and Fly. Champion discovered the headwaters of the Fly and made friendly contact with the Bolivip villagers. A second attempt was made from Daru on 27 September 1927 with a party of six police, a cook, twenty-six volunteer carriers and ten convict carriers. The party made for Bolivip and then crossed the Victor Emmanuel Range to reach the Sepik. When about 840 kilometres from the mouth of the Sepik the party was suffering greatly from exhaustion and illness. They built rafts to float down the river but had not gone far before they were met by the government yacht *Elevala*. Of this happy end to the first crossing of New Guinea, Champion wrote: 'Karius and I gazed, fascinated, as at a phantom; we could not speak. For there, more than 500 miles up the Sepik, her white sides gleaming in the sun, her blue ensign floating gently from the mizzen, lay the *Elevala*, with her able commander Ritchie frantically waving his white shirt from the forecastle. The silence was broken by the sobs and hysterical laughter of the police and carriers who madly clutched at one another, and who then, with triumphant shouts, reached for the oars.' I. Champion, *Across New Guinea from the Fly to the Sepik* (London, 1932), p. 252. (Mitchell Library)

Plate 557

Plate 557. Charles Karius, who with Ivan Champion made a successful crossing from the Fly to the Sepik (see plate 556). Karius was praised by Sir Hubert Murray for his courageous and wise leadership. Although they were frequently in potentially hostile situations, neither Karius nor Champion entered into hostilities with the inhabitants. (Mitchell Library)

Plate 558

Plate 558. Members of the Akmana expedition with some of the local people at Marienberg on the Sepik in 1929. From left, E. A. Shepherd; Reg. Beazley; H. V. Seale; 'Bert', an engineer on Dick Glasson's schooner; Father F. Kirschbaum (behind); Mrs Walton (Glasson's niece); Dick Glasson; Sam Freeman. Shepherd, Beazley, Seale, Freeman and Bill MacGregor, who took the photograph, made up the field party of the Akmana Gold Prospecting Company. They travelled by the company steamer *Banyandah* from Madang up the Sepik River and reached Marienberg on 19 September 1929, and Yimas, a village on the Arrabundie, a tributary of the Karawari, on 10 October. Leaving the steamer there, the party crossed the range to the upper Yuat. The country yielded interesting but not worthwhile results, and, as Freeman was not well, the party returned to Marienberg and so to the coast. The company decided on a second expedition, and on 19 February 1930, Beazley, Shepherd, Seale and MacGregor moved back into the same area, this time concentrating on the Maramuni area. They reached Jimi junction and a river flowing to the south which was known as the 'Baiyer', but which is not the river rising on the east side of the Hagen Range that bears the name Baiyer today. 'The Baiyer we knew as the Baiyer ended where the Maramuni flows in from the south-west and the Tarua from the south-east, and to that spot we gave our own name—Akmana Junction!' (E. Shepherd, 'Akmana: A New Name in the Continuing History of New Guinea Exploration', *Pacific Islands Monthly*, April 1971, p. 43.) At Akmana Junction they built a palisaded base camp and prospected the Maramuni to its main source at 2135 metres, many of its tributaries, and the Tarua. The party was about forty-eight kilometres north-west of where Wabag stands today. (E. A. Shepherd Collection)

Plate 559. The first people contacted by men of the Akmana expedition in the mountains. 'We referred to them as the Nomads as we did not find any village in the near vicinity, but in our travels prospecting the many small streams we came on a number of small oases where the few Sago Palms had been worked and the trees had been hunted for grubs. They had no steel or any modern material, carried stone axes and bows and arrows and had brought betel nut to trade. At a later date they raided our Arrabundie base camp when we were away on the Maramuni, and stole some plane-blades and knives. They were probably Garramut people, and were of different appearance from any other people we contacted.' 'Recollections of Ernie Shepherd', MS. in the possession of E. A. Shepherd, Sydney. (E. A. Shepherd Collection)

Plate 559

Plate 560

Plate 561

Plate 560. A group of Highland 'wig men' with Beazley and MacGregor. The wig men were typical of the people of Akmana Junction country. 'These people did not know salt and the big pack we carried in was useless for trade. They did not have betel nut and their teeth were ivory white although they smoked tobacco. Small shells were good trade in buying the plentiful good quality sweet potato (Ina) but carpenters' plane blades of 2″ were most sought after as were long knives and toma-hawks, and full size steel axes were revered. The Akmana Junction district people were the "Emigata" on the West side of the river around Akmana Palisade main base and the Poomani tribe on the East side of the Baiyer (today called the Maramuni) and along the Tarua. They all had a similar dialect and apparel.' 'Recollections of Ernie Shepherd', MS. in the possession of E. A. Shepherd, Sydney. (E. A. Shepherd Collection)

Plate 561. Beazley and Shepherd, members of the Akmana expedition, prospecting on the Tarua River in 1930. 'After prospecting the Junction again and the streams nearby we travelled south east from Akmana base and half way up a large mountain through open grass country. It appeared to be an area that had been culti-vated as the thick timber that clothed the top made a straight line that would have done credit to a team of ring-barkers in our country. If this conjecture is right it must have been a very big area of gardens.' ('Recollec-tions of Ernie Shepherd'.) The party travelled south-east to the Tarua and left the river at intervals to prospect likely places. So they came to a well-established native road running east and west and grasslands that extended to the horizon. Prospects did not warrant further effort and the party decided to end the search for gold in the Tarua. (E. A. Shepherd Collection)

Plate 562. Members of the New Guinea expedition which sought disease-resisting sugar cane along the Fly, Strickland and Sepik Rivers in 1929. From left to right, Peck, Champion, Brandes, Pemberton and Bannon. (Photograph by J. Jeswiet, *National Geographic Magazine*, September 1929.)

Plate 562

Plate 563. Michael J. (Mick) Leahy making contact with the people of the upper Purari River during the expedition (April to September 1930) across New Guinea from Salamaua to Port Romilly at the mouth of the Purari River. (Mitchell Library)

Plate 563

Plate 564. Michael Dwyer and Michael Leahy with a carrier line setting off on one of the ten expeditions that they carried out between April 1930 and October 1934, by which an extensive area of the central Highlands of New Guinea was explored and prospected for gold. (Mitchell Library)

Plate 565. Michael Dwyer, who with Michael Leahy linked the Ramu and Purari Rivers in 1930, and over the following four years explored an extensive area of the central Highlands. According to Leahy, Dwyer was 'a good mate, a splendid physical specimen, no fat on him, a non-smoker and non-drinker'. Dwyer claimed that his partner, Mick Leahy, 'could handle the country and the natives better than any man he knew'. Words of M. Leahy and M. Dwyer as cited in Gavin Souter, *New Guinea: The Last Unknown* (Sydney, 1963), p. 177. (Mitchell Library)

Plate 565

Plate 564

Plate 566

Plate 566. Mick, Jim and Dan Leahy with pilot Bob Gurney at Bena Bena airstrip in 1932. The airstrip was built by Mick and Dan Leahy with the help of the local people as a forward base for reconnaissance flights over the country west of Bena Bena. On Christmas Day 1932, the Gypsy Moth, piloted by Bob Gurney, put down on the strip. Mick Leahy and his friend Mick Dwyer (see plate 564) had been prospecting in New Guinea for several years when in 1930 they travelled from Salamaua up the Markham River, across the Ramu, then south to reach eventually the Purari River and the south coast. The following year Mick Leahy and his older brother Pat were hired by the New Guinea Goldfields Company to prospect in Kukukuku country east of the upper Purari. On this trip they were attacked—Mick was clubbed, Pat (Paddy) received arrows in the arm, and five carriers were killed. On 8 March 1933, Mick, Dan and Jim Leahy, with Major G. A. Harrison (New Guinea Goldfields) and pilot Ian Grabowsky, flew from Bena Bena over the Wahgi Valley. The valley was then explored by a joint Administration–New Guinea Goldfields Company expedition, made up of James Taylor (assistant district officer), Mick and Dan Leahy, Ken Spinks (surveyor) and twelve police. From May to July 1933, Mick Leahy and James Taylor explored from Mount Hagen north, down the Baiyer River towards the Yuat River and up the lower Jimi River. In July 1933 Mick and Dan Leahy prospected south from Mount Hagen down the Nebilizer and Gauil Rivers, and in June 1934 they went up the Gai (Lai) River about thirty-two kilometres past the present site of Wabag. (Michael J. Leahy Collection)

Plate 567. Michael Leahy at the head of the Gai River, June 1934, in the course of an expedition west to north-west of Mount Hagen. Leahy recorded: 'Broke camp 49 on the 23rd, 6100 feet above sea-level. Followed the course of the Gai, crossing it twice by native bridges. It is now running very slow and deep, and with its banks lined with Casuarinas and high grass is not unlike the western country streams of Queensland. A big mob of yelling natives accompanied us all day . . . very big population in this valley, it being one of the most thickly populated and most intensely cultivated valleys I have yet seen in New Guinea. Camped at 1 p.m.' (Mitchell Library)

Plate 567

Plate 568

Plate 568. A break in a cricket match at Mount Hagen about 1934. Left to right, Father William Ross, Tom Fox, Brother Eugene Frank, Dan Leahy and Jack Fox. Father Ross, an American Divine Word missionary, early in 1934 led a party of five missionaries of his order from Bundi to form a station near Kundiawa. He later set up a station at Mount Hagen with another American, Brother Eugene Frank. The English brothers Tom and Jack Fox were prospectors who reached Mount Hagen later in 1934, set out for Wabag and then towards the Strickland River. It was rumoured that the brothers were dead, so Mick Leahy and Bob Gurney flew over the area and searched, but in vain. The party returned via the Tari Valley, exhausted but intact, and disappointed that they had found no sign of gold. 'We've been clear to the foot of the rainbow,' Tom Fox told Leahy, 'and there is no pot of gold anywhere about.' M. Leahy and M. Crain, *The Land That Time Forgot* (London, 1937). (Information and Extension Services, Administration of Papua New Guinea)

Plate 569. Jack Gordon Hides, who patrolled the new grassland valley between the Fly and the border of the Mandated Territory. Jack Hides was born in Port Moresby, where he spent his early childhood. Under the patronage of Sir Hubert Murray he joined the Papuan Service as a postal clerk. In 1926 he became a patrol officer. He patrolled in the upper Purari in 1931, and in 1934 with Jim O'Malley (see plate 571) carried out difficult patrol work in the Kunimaipa Valley. On 1 January 1935, Hides and O'Malley left Daru to ascend the Fly and Strickland Rivers, with Police Sergeant Orai, nine constables and twenty-eight Orokolo carriers. Their route took them north-east to the border of the Mandated Territory, then south-east to the Purari. They were attacked by natives in the Tarifuroro Valley and the Waga Furari Valley. On the final leg they took to rafts to reach the Erave River, walked across the Samberigi Valley and along the Kikori River to Ogamobu plantation (see plate 202). Sir Hubert Murray disapproved of the bloodshed they reported but acknowledged the patrol's feat by attempting to have Hides honoured by the Royal Geographical Society. (Mitchell Library)

Plate 569

Plate 570

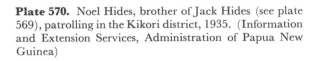

Plate 570. Noel Hides, brother of Jack Hides (see plate 569), patrolling in the Kikori district, 1935. (Information and Extension Services, Administration of Papua New Guinea)

Plate 571

Plate 571. Patrol officer Jim O'Malley with Southern Highlanders in 1935. O'Malley accompanied Jack Hides (see plate 569) on his 1935 expedition from Daru into the Southern Highlands. They ascended the Fly and Strickland Rivers, then travelled in a north-easterly direction into the grasslands of the Highlands across the Hegigo and Waga Rivers. The coast was reached again by crossing and recrossing the Erave River and joining up with the Kikori River, down which they floated to eventually reach Kikori plantation. (Mitchell Library)

Plate 572. Air reconnaissance played a useful role in explorations of the Highlands of New Guinea in the 1930s. Shown here is a party that secured preliminary data on an unexplored area in the Highlands, preparatory to the dispatch of land patrols. Left to right, E. Taylor, district officer; Dr Sinclair, medical officer, Morobe district; E. W. P. Chinnery, director of district services and native affairs; T. O'Dea, pilot. (Mitchell Library)

Plate 572

Plate 573

Plate 573. Assistant district officer James Taylor and patrol officer John Black, who walked from Mount Hagen to Telefomin in 1938–39. The expedition they led was the largest and longest of its kind and was assisted in its work by radio and aircraft. With Taylor and Black went C. B. Walsh, an officer from the Department of Health, twenty police and 230 carriers. The party travelled by way of the Lai Valley into the Lagaip Valley. At Hoiyevia, near the Papuan border, they built an airstrip (see plate 576) and received fresh supplies. Black then took a small section of the party to reach Telefomin while Taylor and the remainder returned to the Lai Valley and built an airstrip. Taylor established a base at Wabag, and Walsh remained there to maintain radio contact while Taylor moved on to Telefomin where Black was waiting. Together they crossed the Thurnwald Range to the May River where they parted again, Black to return to Wabag via Telefomin and Taylor to proceed to the Sepik. Taylor was met on the river by the *Sirius*, which took him to Kopa for a brief rest. On 27 January 1939 he made the eight-week trip back to Wabag. Walsh was there; Black arrived on 16 April. (Mitchell Library)

Plate 574. Carriers of the Hagen-Sepik patrol on the move in the Ambum Valley. The patrol, led by James Taylor, left Wabag on 26 August 1938 and crossed from the Lai to the Ambum. It then proceeded up the Ambum River to Lorndore. 'From Lorndore we crossed the Ambum and ascended over well worn tracks to about 10,000 feet. The people were helping us and we were travelling fast, rising at about 1200 feet an hour. The weather was fine and cool, particularly at night. . . . Leaving the 10,000 feet crest we descended through the timber and came out on to a grass plateau and there found the Chirunki Lake, Ivivor, below us.' J. L. Taylor, 'Hagen-Sepik Patrol 1938–39', pp. 198–9, New Guinea manuscript collection, Hallstrom Pacific Library. (J. L. Taylor Collection)

Plate 574

Plate 575

Plate 576

Plate 577

Plate 575. Shaking hands with men of the Wabag Valley during the Hagen-Sepik patrol led by James Taylor. The patrol was at Wabag from 21 July to 26 August 1938. Of this initial meeting, James Taylor wrote: 'I explained to the people what we were going to do, through Leo, who was now our best interpreter. He made an eloquent speech which impressed the people, or so it appeared to me, for they listened in silence and at its conclusion struck the ground ecstatically with their stone axes and told us to carry on. I think they wanted to see the aeroplane.' J. L. Taylor, 'Hagen-Sepik Patrol 1938–39', p. 184, New Guinea manuscript collection, Hallstrom Pacific Library. (J. L. Taylor Collection)

Plate 576. The camp at Hoiyevia established by James Taylor, the leader of the Hagen-Sepik patrol. The patrol was here from 8 April to 17 June 1938. An airstrip was built to receive fresh supplies and to open up the Highlands. James Taylor described the camp: 'Our houses were on a ridge near a small clump of casuarina, and looked out on to a level field covered with old gardens, that ran down to a wooded creek, beyond which were large green sweet potato patches. . . . Behind us the ground slipped down quickly to a small but pleasant stream with pools deep enough in parts for bathing and swimming. . . . Beyond the stream the cultivated and wooded undulations continued for miles to the south-west, to the base of a noble mountain with two peaks standing wide apart and intensely blue—Hari Lu. We were fortunate to be in such a beautiful country.' J. L. Taylor, 'Hagen-Sepik Patrol 1938–39', pp. 162–3, New Guinea manuscript collection, Hallstrom Pacific Library. (J. L. Taylor Collection)

Plate 577. 'Tommy' O'Dea, pilot, is greeted by James Taylor, leader of the Hagen-Sepik patrol, at Wabag, where the patrol had built an airstrip to receive the plane, a three-engined Ford. The landing was made at 10.25 a.m. on 8 August 1938. Taylor had requested the plane for a three-hour reconnaissance flight. He described the event: 'People flocked to the camp from every direction, there was much dancing and singing. O'Dea was a great success as he always is with inland people. From 1932 he has worked with us in all parts of the plateau, and being a singer of no mean order the people shriek with delight when he sings to them songs from Pagliacci, Cavalleria Rusticana and Tosca. They love to see a white man act as a human being.' J. L. Taylor, 'Hagen-Sepik Patrol 1938–39', New Guinea manuscript collection, Hallstrom Pacific Library. (J. L. Taylor Collection)

Plate 578. The lookout tower built by assistant district officer H. E. Woodman in 1937 at Wosser, after the local people had converted it into a dwelling. 'The fabrication on the ground and erection of the framework of the tower was a matter of intense amazement to the local natives, and, daily, large parties of natives from villages two and three days' walk away came in to view the construction work. And one day when the framework was completed some 200 or so natives, to my great concern, clambered all over the framework and completed all the covering thereto. And when you consider that most of the natives in question had never seen a white man previously it was quite a remarkable achievement, and very friendly relations were established with all the natives in question.' Private Correspondence of Col. H. E. Woodman, New Guinea manuscript collection, Hallstrom Pacific Library. (H. E. Woodman Collection)

Plate 578

Plate 579

Plate 579. Three men of Yikai and one of Malu village, in the Wahgi area, south-west of Ambunti. After friendly contact with this area had been established by assistant district officer Harold Woodman and his patrol, the three men on the left made a return visit to Ambunti to see the patrol post, in company with the villager at right, who had been, until this time, a hereditary enemy. March 1937. (H. E. Woodman Collection)

Plate 580. Colonel H. E. Woodman, assistant district officer at Ambunti, and men of Waratu-Serangwantu-Wosser, in the Sepik District, in front of a house used by Woodman as a temporary camp while establishing contact with the Wosser people in April 1937. In consequence of reported murders and burning of villages along the Sepik, G. W. L. Townsend, district officer at Wewak, instructed Woodman and his cadet, Reading, to investigate. Two men in the foreground hold the skull of a female who was murdered by men of Palgeler-Wosser. Col. Woodman reported: 'About 8.30 that same night whilst Turigo was being further interrogated, the Tul Tul of Bamjin returned to the camp with five natives of Wogiera-Wosser—two of whom were carrying skulls. . . . The Wogiera natives reported that the two skulls were those of Yalm and Pagadowa—two females of Wogiera—whom, they allege, were murdered whilst they were working sac sac.' (H. E. Woodman, Patrol Report No. S.D. 1936/37, MS. in possession of H. E. Woodman, Penrith, N.S.W.) It was alleged that the women were killed because they worked *sac sac* (sago) on land whose ownership was disputed by the murderers. At right, Woodman interrogates two men of Nanela-Wosser about the whereabouts of the Palgeler men. (H. E. Woodman Collection)

Plate 580

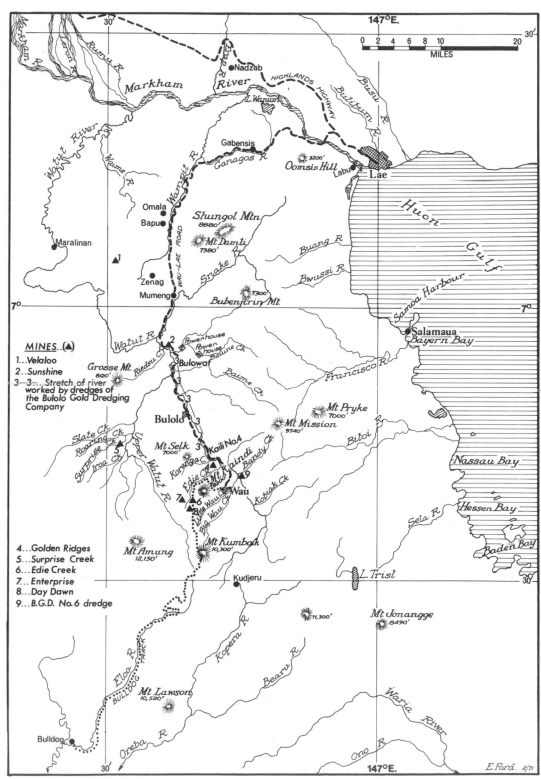

MINES.. (▲)

1...Velaloo
2...Sunshine
3—3...Stretch of river worked by dredges of the Bulolo Gold Dredging Company

4...Golden Ridges
5...Surprise Creek
6...Edie Creek
7...Enterprise
8...Day Dawn
9...B.G.D. No.6 dredge

E.Ford. 2/71

Plate 581

Plate 581. Map showing the Bulolo Valley and the gold-bearing streams flowing into it that drew hundreds of prospectors in the 1920s and 1930s. The richest claims were on upper Edie Creek, where the gold was of a distinctively light colour, and the Bulolo River. The gold industry was the result first of individual efforts and then of companies such as New Guinea Gold, Placer Development and Bulolo Gold Dredging. The townships of Lae, Bulolo and Wau grew up to serve the populations of the goldfields. In the absence of roads into the goldfields, supplies were flown in, Pard Mustar making the first trip into Wau in 1927. It was not until all-metal Junkers planes fitted with three Wright Cyclone motors were employed to fly in the heavy machine parts needed for dredging that more extensive alluvial mining was possible. The first dredge commenced work in 1932. A gold royalty of one per cent imposed in 1927 was raised the following year to five percent. By 1940 the royalty yielded about £440 000. The output of gold reached £3 000 000 in that year. (Map drawn by Edgar Ford)

Plate 582

Plate 582. William ('Shark-eye') Park, a legend in his own lifetime, who prospected for gold in New Guinea as early as 1911, with Crowe, Preston and Auerbach, first between the Ramu and Markham Valleys and then in the Morobe district. Like Arthur Darling (see plate 584), Park found gold in the Watut River. He was given prospecting rights by the German administration. In 1922 he crossed into the Bulolo Valley and camped at the head of Edie Creek. Here he struck gold at Koranga Creek. He formed a partnership with Jack Nettleton. News of the strike reached the coast and a rush started. After making a small fortune, Park sold his property to Cecil Levien (see plate 589) and in 1926 he left New Guinea forever. He died in Vancouver in 1940. (Mitchell Library)

Plate 583

Plate 583. 'Lucky' Joe Sloane, gold prospector, who in 1912 unearthed the largest gold nugget ever found on the Lakekamu field. Two years later Sloane and Jim Preston prospected the Biaru River with no luck. In 1918 Sloane received a government subsidy to prospect the upper Musa River, but the gold he found there was not payable. With two friends in 1920 he panned osmiridium (£30 per ounce) by the Gira River. When the Morobe field was proclaimed, Sloane moved up the Markham Valley where he found Bill Park and his mate Jack Nettleton. Sloane pegged out a claim of six hectares on Namia Creek, north of Park's boundary, and by 'dummying' pegged also the Buwut leases lower down. He formed the Alpha syndicate in opposition to the Park-Levien partnership. In 1925 a new syndicate was formed, consisting of Sloane, Dick Glasson, Bill Money, Frank Chisholm, Bill Royal and his brother Bert. The syndicate was known as the 'Big Six'. The following year Bill Royal and Glasson discovered the Edie Creek gold pocket. During 1926–27, over three tonnes of gold was taken out of the Top Edie. (Mitchell Library)

Plate 584

Plate 584. Arthur Darling, who began gold prospecting in New Guinea in 1901. In 1906, with Matt Crowe, Darling discovered the Waria field. Inspired by rumours of a rich strike by the German W. Dammköhler, he took a party of Orokaiva natives up the Markham Valley into the upper reaches of the Watut, where he found gold, probably near Mt Kaindi. Here he was laid low by blackwater fever and was attacked by Kukukukus. Darling's return trip to Buna with the surviving Orokaivas is a tale of great hardship and endurance. In 1910 he staked a claim at the Lakekamu field, where he became friendly with William ('Shark-eye') Park. Darling returned to Samarai the following year, intending to mount a second expedition to the Waria field, but he collapsed at Samarai and died. (Mitchell Library)

Plate 585. Albert Bethune, who spent many years prospecting alone for gold along the Tauri and Lakekamu Rivers. Jack Hides met him in 1930 when he was on a patrol to investigate a native raid on a miner's camp far up the Lakekamu River. The patrol reached Tiveri landing and then proceeded through dense bush for six or eight kilometres to reach Bethune's camp on Twisty Creek. Hides wrote of Bethune: 'One of the old prospecting type, Mr Bethune spends a good deal of his life in the interior of Papua fighting danger and fever in his pursuit of gold. His tiny camp at Twisty Creek, consisting of four native-built dwellings, stood in the middle of a large garden, which provided him with corn, sweet potatoes, taro and sugar-cane. Twenty-five native labourers, who had accompanied him from the coast, and upon whose loyalty he depended, shared with him the hardships inseparable from such a life.' J. G. Hides, *Through Wildest Papua* (London, 1935), pp. 79–80. (A. A. Speedie Collection)

Plate 585

Plate 586

Plate 586. The mining camps of Jack Hides and W. Garbutt at the Tauri field. On 15 July 1930, Hides left Kerema for the Lakekamu River to arrest Kukukukus who had attacked the camp of prospector Albert Bethune (see plate 585). The search took Hides and his patrol to the watershed of the Tauri River, where he found gold. Hides made a second and then a third trip to Tauri, where he established a base camp from which he hoped to pacify the Tauri people and continue prospecting. His party was attacked. He was joined by a prospector, W. Garbutt, and seven of his Papuan mine workers. On 27 February 1931 they left the base camp and ultimately crossed the border into the Mandated Territory, where they met the German prospector Helmuth Baum. Short of food and exhausted, Hides and Garbutt walked on to Lae, which they reached on 17 March 1931. After a brief recovery period Hides walked back to Kerema. Sir Hubert Murray was annoyed by Hides's entry into the Mandated Territory; however, he appreciated his daring. He wrote, 'Any similar escapade in the future will be regarded as a serious breach of duty. At the same time I think that the Patrol Officer is to be congratulated upon the skill and pluck displayed by him, and thanks largely to his example, by his patrol.' (R. Speedie Collection)

Plate 587

Plate 588

Plate 587. Jim Pryke with Kukukuku friends. Pryke was an Australian gold prospector who, with his brother Frank and Matt Crowe, prospected in the upper Tauri and Lakekamu Rivers about 1909. In 1910 Judge Murray visited the area with Matt Crowe and established a patrol post at Nepa. The prospectors were twice attacked by Kukukukus, and in the second attack Frank Pryke was wounded by an arrow. (Mitchell Library)

Plate 588. Members of the armed constabulary guard the Kukukuku murderers of Helmuth Baum and his carriers. Baum, called 'Master Boom' by his carriers, was a well-known prospector who was taken by a surprise attack while camped on the upper Watut River, and with twelve of his carriers was battered to death. Baum and his friend, a fellow prospector, Soltwedel, had escaped deportation when the Australians occupied German New Guinea. After the war they found payable gold at Surprise Creek, a small tributary of the upper Watut. (Mitchell Library)

Plate 589

Plate 589. Cecil John Levien on his lease in 1925. Levien was a patrol officer at Morobe, where he learned of William ('Shark-eye') Park's strike at Koranga Creek. He took a patrol to Koranga, and although mining regulations had not been issued at that date and he had the power to confiscate the gold panned by Park and Nettleton, he did not. However, he permitted the partners to peg a claim for him at the head of the creek. After the issue of the Mining Ordinance, Levien was made mining warden; when the Mines Department granted the Koranga leases, Levien resigned from the Administration to work this claim and other claims he had pegged on the lower Bulolo. He contacted friends in Australia and the result was the formation of the Guinea Gold No Liability Company. Levien saw the prospect of riches from another source—aerial transport in and out of the goldfields—and the company successfully floated the Guinea Airways Company. Later, Placer Developments Limited secured an option over the Guinea Gold Bulolo leases, and the all-metal Junkers 31 machines were introduced to carry into the valley the heavy dredging equipment needed for more extensive alluvial mining. Levien died on 20 January 1932, just before the official opening of the first dredge at Bulolo. After the opening ceremony his ashes were scattered over the Bulolo Valley from one of the Junkers. (Mitchell Library)

262

Plate 590

Plate 590. Employees of the Day Dawn Company (1928), one of the subsidiary companies of New Guinea Goldfields Limited, founded by the Big Six syndicate. The Day Dawn Company was formed to work a gold reef at Wau. (Mitchell Library)

Plate 591. Miners' huts on Edie Creek, *c.* 1925. The creek rises at 2135 metres and falls into a gully to reach the Bulolo River. It was along this stretch that leases were pegged when news of William Park's and Jack Nettleton's strike brought hundreds of prospectors into the Bulolo Valley. (Mitchell Library)

Plate 591

Plate 592

Plate 593

Plate 592. 'Cliffside', Doris Booth's claim at Edie Creek. The story of Doris Booth's adventures in the New Guinea goldfields is told in her book, *Mountains, Gold and Cannibals*. Charles and Doris Booth arrived at the goldfields in 1924. Doris Booth managed William ('Shark-eye') Park's mining interests at Koranga while he was in Rabaul. Her husband struck it rich in the Bulolo. It is believed that Park pegged the claim for her in recognition of the help she gave him. In September 1926, Doris Booth became a heroine for her work in the valley helping those stricken by an epidemic of dysentery. (Mitchell Library)

Plate 594

Plate 593. Miners at their camp at Edie Creek, 1926. (M. von Hein Collection)

Plate 594. Miners at Edie Creek, 1926. (M. von Hein Collection)

Plate 595. Part of the old track running from Wau to Edie Creek, a distance of 14·5 kilometres. The country rises 900 metres in the first thirteen kilometres, then to 1950 metres at Kaindi. The mountain at the right is part of Mt Kaindi; the slope at left continues sheer to Lower Edie, near its junction with the Bulolo River. The depth of the gorge is about 600 metres and it is within sound of the waterfall. Landslides were frequent and could block the road for several days. Total cost of road construction was in the region of £25 000. All cargo to Edie Creek was carried by New Guineans; freight charges were fourpence per pound. (L. C. Roebuck Collection)

Plate 595

Plate 596

Plate 596. Some of the employees at Edie Creek gold mines in 1933. They wore ex-navy jackets, flannel singlets or jerseys and sou'westers provided by the employer, and worked in gangs of twelve in three shifts: 8 a.m. to 4 p.m.; 4 p.m. to 12 a.m.; 12 a.m. to 8 a.m. European miners worked two shifts of twelve hours each. New Guinea employees received food, clothing, tobacco, soap, etc., and were paid ten shillings per month. Les Roebuck, who worked with these young men in 1933, describes their conditions. 'Contract time for boys was two years, after which they could return to their villages and live in affluence for a long time. Few boys, none at all that I can remember, ever made a second paper to work at Edie Creek. The reasons were the extremely wet climate (over 125 inches a year), the cold at night, and the belief that the place was haunted by malevolent tambarans or devils. None would venture out alone at night.' From left to right, standing, Timgimbunti (Sepik); Ramu (Ramu Valley); [unidentified]; Koi Koi (Sepik); [unidentified]; Bosifen (Madang); Long Long (Sepik). Sitting at the extreme right is Maisim (Sepik). The other four men in the front row were new recruits. (L. C. Roebuck Collection)

Plate 597

Plate 597. Alluvial workings, Edie Creek, 1933. Here the No. 1 (George) Lease is being worked. The yield from this paddock was better than 11·3 kilograms of gold for two weeks' work; this was an average yield for George Lease, although some paddocks turned in 20 kilograms or more. Power was by gravity from races or flumes, some 18 metres up on the side of the hill, thence by pipeline to the elevator. Floods were a constant danger. (L. C. Roebuck Collection)

Plate 598

Plate 598. New Guineans employed in alluvial workings at Edie Creek, 1930. This paddock yielded 12·7 kilograms of gold in five days. As soon as one paddock was worked out the whole elevator was moved to another paddock. (L. C. Roebuck Collection)

Plate 599. Nozzleman Dennis Budden 'blowing in' or washing down a gold-bearing bank at Edie Creek, 1933. (L. C. Roebuck Collection)

Plate 599

Plate 600. Alluvial workings at Edie Creek in 1933. Bosifen from Madang (left) and Timgimbunti from the Sepik District (right) are feeding water, gravel and sand into the suction pipe. The material was raised hydraulically into the sluice box at the top, where the gold was retained and lighter materials were washed off as tailings. (L. C. Roebuck Collection)

Plate 600

Plate 601

Plate 602

Plate 601. View of Edie Creek looking upstream to Hector and Baden Wales's workings at left, and the New Guinea Gold ground with a flume in the background; 10·2 kilograms of gold were taken from this section in one day. The method of working a flowing creek like this one was to divide the creek longitudinally by a natural stone wall, to divert the water into one side of the creek while the other was being worked. Then water was turned into the worked portion and the other side of the creek was worked. Finally, the wall was moved and the middle section worked. This photograph was taken after a flood in which the wall was badly knocked about. (L. C. Roebuck Collection)

Plate 602. On the old track, Wau to Edie Creek, 1933. Vehicles were cut down to have a track of about one metre. Tray bodies were added and chains were used on the wheels. The narrow track of such vehicles was still barely able to take the primitive road. The whole trip uphill was done in first or second gear. The advent of the motor into the gold fields did not reduce freight rates. (L. C. Roebuck Collection)

267

Plate 603

Plate 603. The whole of the hydraulic elevator system on the Royal Lease at Edie Creek in 1933. Standing at the left are Larrie Knightley, Jack Carpenter, Helmuth Baum and Dennis Budden. (L. C. Roebuck Collection)

Plate 604. A general view of the Administration reserve and some of the mining camps at Edie Creek in the 1930s. The gold rush to this spot started in 1922, when 'Shark-eye' Park found gold in Koranga Creek at the head of Edie Creek. 'Into Edie they came, over the mountains and up the creek. Dishevelled, bleeding and bruised, faint from hunger and exhaustion they walked in, some almost naked, with their wet clothes hanging about their shoulders to dry. Already, up and down the creek, miners and natives were shovelling, panning and fixing boxes. Feverishly they worked, and very soon the whole creek was muddy with their stirring. There was not a moment to lose.' (L. Rhys, *High Lights and Flights in New Guinea* [London, 1942], p. 75.) Some of those working for the New Guinea Goldfields Company in the early 1930s were: Major Harrison (general manager); Dela-tour (manager of Edie Creek); Dickson (medical officer); Kingsbury (geologist); Dennis Budden (alluvial fore-man); Bill Pope and John Tamblyn (winding-engine drivers); Bill Edwards (compound master at Upper Edie, responsible for native welfare); Larrie Knightley (later succeeded by Mick Irwin), compound master at Lower Edie, responsible for native welfare. Individuals working claims in this period were Hector and Baden Wales, Tom Skiffington, Cyril Eldrid and Bill Abbey. (*Commonwealth Records* CRS A24, reproduced by permission of the Commonwealth Archives Office)

Plate 604

Plate 605. No. 2 Dredger at Bulolo. The entire structure was transported to Bulolo by Junkers aircraft of Guinea Airways. (Information and Extension Services, Administration of Papua New Guinea)

Plate 605

Plate 606

Plate 606. Some of the men who worked for Placer Development Company Limited in June 1929, when the company was investigating the possibility of taking over the Bulolo option from Guinea Gold No Liability Company. Left to right, Decoto, Arnold, Waterhouse, Bayliss, Franklin. A. M. Healy, 'A History of the Development of the Bulolo Region, New Guinea', *New Guinea Research Bulletin* no. 15, 1967. (Hallstrom Pacific Library)

Plate 607. Part of the workshops at Bulolo, 1933. (L. C. Roebuck Collection)

Plate 607

Plate 608a

Plate 608b

Plate 608. Views of dredging operations on the Bulolo goldfields prior to World War II. From 1926 to 1928 Guinea Gold No Liability Company established an organized system of gold recovery in the valley and ran an air service to and from the coast. By 1928 the company realized the potential for development and the need for machinery and capital. It offered options to companies that could raise capital. Placer Development Limited took over the Bulolo option on 4 January 1930. The value of gold produced in the Territories of Papua and New Guinea reached nearly £1 000 000 in 1933 and a peak of over £3 000 000 in 1940. Of this, production by Bulolo Gold Dredging Limited reached £1 750 000 in 1940. (L. C. Roebuck Collection)

Plate 608c

Plate 609

Plate 610

Plate 609. Aerial view of dredge and workshops of Bulolo Gold Dredging Company, Bulolo, on 21 March 1932 when the dredge was officially opened. 'The Administrator of the Territory was there; all the directors had flown up accompanied by their wives. Pilots, engineers, miners and natives swelled the crowd. After a brief ceremony the machinery was put into operation and the noise of the dredging buckets on their great rolling chain belts drowned the roar of the planes.' (L. Rhys, *High Lights and Flights in New Guinea* [London, 1942], p. 188.) After the opening, a Junkers plane took off and from it the ashes of C. J. Levien (see plate 589) were scattered over the ranges. (Hallstrom Pacific Library)

Plate 610. Burleigh Gorman's store on the beach at Salamaua. The store was built by Bill Money, one of the Big Six syndicate. Gorman, a well-known ex-Rugby Union footballer, managed the store in 1925. (Mitchell Library)

Plate 611. Salamaua in the 1920s. The hut in the foreground was occupied by 'Shark-eye' Park when he visited Salamaua between long periods spent in the interior prospecting for gold. (Mitchell Library)

Plate 611

Plate 612

Plate 613

Plate 612. Clearing Salamaua aerodrome site. The first flight from Port Moresby to Salamaua was made by Ray Parer in 1927. The route took him over 3000-metre mountains of the Owen Stanley Range and almost a full circle around Mount Victoria standing at 3900 metres. The air route pioneered by Parer is almost the same as that flown today. (Mitchell Library)

Plate 613. The aeroplane hangar at Salamaua in the early 1930s owned by W. R. Carpenter and Co. Ltd. After Carpenters started commercial enterprises in Wau, they decided to cut freight costs by operating an airline. A company was then formed and known as Mandated Airlines Ltd. Two Fox Moths (De Havillands) were purchased, each carrying about 225 kilograms. The operation proving successful, another Fox Moth was bought, as were five Dragons, each with capacity of 570 kilograms, and an Avro (A. V. Rowe and Co.) with a capacity of 1135 kilograms. The company later bought out Stephens Aviation Company. (B. B. Perriman Collection)

Plate 614. The first store erected by W. R. Carpenter and Co. Ltd at Salamaua in the early 1930s. It was a 12 m x 6 m steel-frame building with two lean-tos and an office adjoining. A portion of the manager's bungalow can be seen at the left. A new store was later erected opposite, but was destroyed in World War II. (B. B. Perriman Collection)

Plate 614

Plate 615. Unloading a cow at Wau airfield, 1933. This was the first of two cows that were brought into the town to supply fresh milk for the miners. (L. C. Roebuck Collection)

Plate 616. The first store erected in 1930 by W. R. Carpenter and Co. Ltd at Wau, behind the Bulolo Hotel. The company purchased a controlling interest in the Bulolo Hotel, then owned by Mrs Stewart, as well as in the Wau Hotel and the Salamaua Hotel, Salamaua, to enable it to supply beer, wines and spirits as well as merchandise. (B. B. Perriman Collection)

Plate 617. Party leaving by car from Wau to Edie Creek, 1921. Behind the wheel is Mr Deckert, W. R. Carpenter's manager at Salamaua; Mr J. B. Sedgers; and behind him Mr B. Perriman, W. R. Carpenter's manager at Rabaul, and Mrs Perriman. The car, known locally as 'Deckert's bitzer', was made from bits and pieces specially designed to negotiate the hairpin bends on the Wau–Edie Creek road. (B. B. Perriman Collection)

Plate 618. A Junkers tri-motor at Bulolo, *c.* 1933. The G31 Junkers were all-metal planes purchased in Germany. With a full load, the planes could climb to an altitude of 1000 metres on only two engines. The first Junkers went into service in April 1931; by November there were two Junkers operating, lifting over 270 tonnes a month. (L. C. Roebuck Collection)

Plate 615

Plate 616

Plate 617

Plate 618

273

Plate 619. A Junkers aircraft at Lae loads a car destined for Wau in the interior, 1933. (L. C. Roebuck Collection)

Plate 620. A tumbler shaft, the heaviest single unit flown to Bulolo during dredge construction. The tumbler shaft, which provided the main drive for the bucket line, was normally cast in one piece, but for Bulolo parts had to be made separately and fitted together on the field. The piece in this photograph weighed three and a half tonnes and the only aircraft capable of lifting it was the Junkers fitted with three Wright Cyclone motors. (L. C. Roebuck Collection)

Plate 619

Plate 620

Plate 621. Part of Bulolo, the township built by Bulolo Gold Dredging Company, about 1934. Everything for the construction of this township, except timber, had to be air-freighted into the valley over mountains 3000 metres high. 'Gardens and roads were planned with care. Bungalows were built, attractive in design and setting. There is no sign of higgledy-piggledy haphazard growth: no disorder and ugliness as is so common in Australian towns. I had occasion to visit some of its homes, administrative offices, the hospital, the Club, and other buildings. All were built to suit the climate, and all had a pleasant atmosphere of comfort and ease that was not experienced in any other part of New Guinea. The township of Bulolo is certainly a model of its kind.' L. Rhys, *High Lights and Flights in New Guinea* (London, 1942), p. 189. (L. C. Roebuck Collection)

Plate 621

25 World War II and Postwar Reconstruction

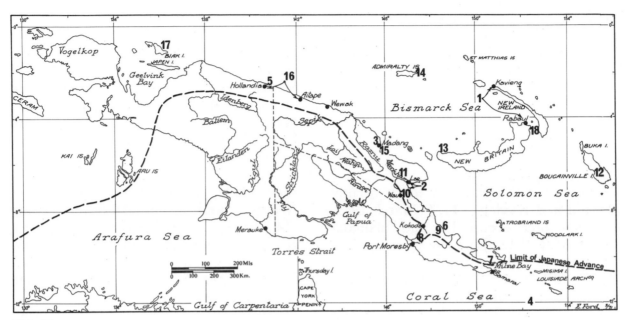

Plate 622

Plate 622. World War II in New Guinea, 1942–45. The war began in Rabaul and ended there. Japanese armed forces committed their first act of war on New Guinea soil with the aerial bombardment of Rabaul on 4 January 1942. Hostilities ceased in New Guinea when, on 6 September 1945 at Rabaul, the commander-in-chief of Japan's South-eastern Army surrendered to the commander, First Australian Army.

The front in New Guinea was the limit of the Japanese advance southwards. Rabaul was developed as the main base to service this front and to support naval and air operations in the South Pacific Ocean generally. During 1942 the Japanese pursued a strategy aimed at creating a perimeter extending from Tulagi (south Solomon Islands) in the east to Port Moresby in the west. The Battle of the Coral Sea, the occupation of Tulagi, the Milne Bay and Kokoda Trail campaigns

were all a part of the Japanese attempt to implement this strategy.

The Allied response was to thwart the Japanese by denying them naval mastery of the Coral Sea and the sea approach to Port Moresby, and to deny them a land base on Milne Bay and the land approach to Port Moresby by way of the Kokoda Trail. The Allies accomplished these aims during 1942.

The next phase of the war was the Allied counterattack and the eviction of Japanese forces from New Guinea, together with the neutralization and isolation of enemy strength in island bases, for example Rabaul. The Allied campaigns against Lae and Salamaua in September 1943, the campaign from the Ramu River towards the north coast, and the recapture of Madang and Aitape in 1944 were a part of the Allied design in this phase.

As the war passed out of eastern New Guinea towards Hollandia and Biak and thence northwards towards the Philippine Islands, the third and final phase of the war in New Guinea was undertaken. The neutralized concentrations of Japanese strength in the Gazelle Peninsula of New Britain and in Bougainville were completely isolated and invested by Allied land campaigns. This phase of the war was continuing when the general surrender of the armed forces of Japan occurred in September 1945.

Chronology of the War in New Guinea, January 1942 to September 1945

23 January 1942, Japanese forces occupy Rabaul and Kavieng (**1**); 8 March 1942, Japanese forces occupy Lae and Salamaua (**2**); 1 May 1942, Japanese forces occupy Madang (**3**); 4–8 May 1942, Battle of the Coral Sea (**4**); 6 May 1942, Japanese forces occupy Hollandia (**5**); 22 July 1942, Japanese forces occupy Buna and Gona (**6**); 25 August to 8 September 1942, Battle for Milne Bay (**7**); 25 September 1942, Japanese forces reach their limit of advance towards Port Moresby at Ioribaiwa and begin retreat towards Kokoda (**8**); 23 January 1943, U.S. and Australian troops complete the conquest of the Buna-Gona-Sanananda area (**9**); 30 January 1943, Japanese forces attack Wau and are repulsed by Australian troops (**10**); 5 September 1943, Allied paratroops land at Nadzab in the Markham River Valley (**11**); 1 November 1943, Allied troops invade Bougainville Island (**12**); 25 December 1943, U.S. troops land at Cape Gloucester in New Britain (**13**); 29 February 1944, Allied troops invade Los Negros Island in the Admiralty group (**14**); 24 April 1944, Australian troops reoccupy Madang (**15**); 27 April 1944, Allied forces capture Aitape and Hollandia (**16**); 27 May 1944, Allied forces capture Biak (**17**); 6 September 1945, surrender of Japanese forces at Rabaul (**18**). (Map drawn by Edgar Ford.)

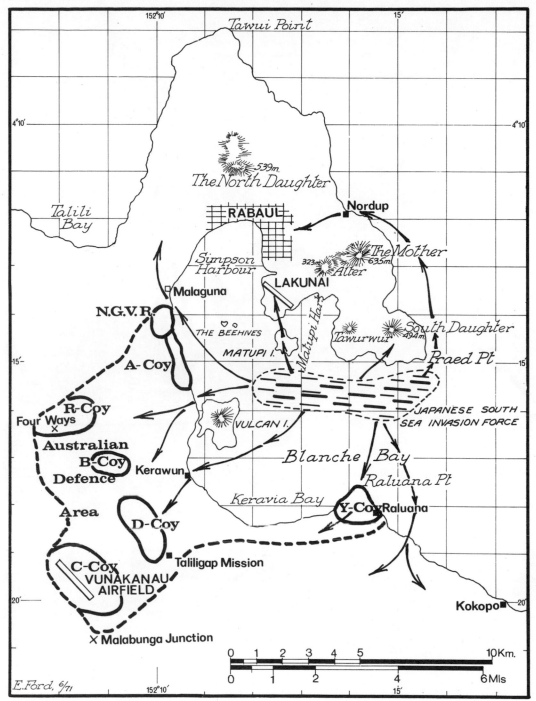

The map shows the following labels:

152°10'
15'
Tawui Point
4°10'
539m.
The North Daughter
Talili Bay
Nordup
RABAUL
The Mother
635m.
323m.
Alter
Simpson Harbour
Malaguna
LAKUNAI
N.G.V.R.
THE BEEHIVES
Tawurwur
South Daughter
494m.
A-Coy
MATUPI I.
Matupi Harb.
Praed Pt
15'
R-Coy
VULCAN I.
JAPANESE SOUTH SEA INVASION FORCE
Four Ways ×
Australian
Blanche Bay
B-Coy
Kerawun
Raluana Pt
Defence
Keravia Bay
Y-Coy Raluana
Area
D-Coy
C-Coy
Taliligap Mission
VUNAKANAU AIRFIELD
Kokopo
× Malabunga Junction

0 1 2 3 4 5   10 Km.
0   1   2   4   6 Mls

E. Ford, 6/71
152°10'
15'

Plate 623

Plate 623. The Japanese attack on Rabaul, January 1942. After heavy Japanese bombing of Rabaul from 4 January onwards, the 1400 Australian troops deployed within and around the town were withdrawn to defensive positions in the Vulcan volcano, Vunakanau airfield and Raluana areas. The Japanese force, the Nankai or South Seas Force, under the command of Major General Horii arrived off Rabaul early on 23 January and troops were landed at Nodup, Praed Point and on Matupi Island. Other Japanese landings took place between Malaguna and Vulcan volcano, Keravia Bay and Raluana.

The Australian garrison opposed these last landings but in the face of determined Japanese attacks their position became untenable. The garrison fell back towards Vunakanau and thence towards Malabunga and Keravat. Of the Australian garrison only about 400 men succeeded in escaping into the Baining Mountains and thence to the north and south coasts of New Britain, where they were rescued by Allied ships. The remainder of the garrison were killed or taken prisoner.

Rabaul was subsequently developed by the Japanese as their main base in the south-west Pacific theatre of operations. It remained in Japanese hands until the surrender of the Japanese to the Allies in September 1945. (Map drawn by Edgar Ford and adapted from that in Lionel Wigmore, *The Japanese Thrust* [Canberra, 1957], p. 401)

277

Plate 624

Plate 625

Plate 624. Japanese soldiers of the Nankai or South Seas Force landing near Rabaul on 23 January 1942. The operation was under the command of Major General Tomitaro Horii. One battalion landed at Praed Point and another at Nodup. These two battalions converged on Lakunai airfield and Rabaul township. (Embassy of Japan, Canberra)

Plate 625. Japanese troops of the Nankai Force at Rabaul watching the town burning. Rabaul suffered severe bombing from the air before the Japanese landings. On 22 January the Praed Point coastal battery was destroyed by aerial bombing and the Lakunai airfield made unserviceable. The officer commanding the garrison thereupon ordered the evacuation of the town and demolitions were carried out as the garrison retired to positions near Vulcan volcano. (Embassy of Japan, Canberra)

Plate 626

Plate 626. Lieutenant General Hitoshi Imamura, general officer commanding 8th Area Army from 16 November 1942 to the surrender of the Japanese in September 1945. General Imamura, with headquarters in Rabaul, had overall command of Japanese land operations in New Guinea, New Britain, New Ireland, and the Solomon Islands. On 6 September 1945, General Imamura surrendered his forces to General Sturdee of the Australian Army on board H.M.S. *Glory*, off Rabaul. (Embassy of Japan, Canberra)

Plate 627

Plate 627. Lieutenant General Hatazo Adachi, officer commanding the 18th Army in New Guinea from November 1942 to 1945. General Adachi had field command of all Japanese military operations in New Guinea in this period. He surrendered to the Australians at Cape Wom near Wewak on 13 September 1945. In 1947 he was tried for war crimes and on 12 July was sentenced to life imprisonment. On 10 September 1947 he killed himself in the Rabaul prisoners' compound. In a last message to his fellow prisoners of the 18th Army he wrote, '. . . During the past three years of operations more than 100,000 youthful and promising officers and men were lost and most of them died of malnutrition. . . . God knows how I felt when I saw them dying, my bosom being filled with pity for them, though it was solely for their country that they dedicated their lives. At that time I made up my mind not to set foot on my country's soil again but to remain as a clod of earth in the Southern Seas with the 100,000 officers and men, even if a time would come when I would be able to return to my country in triumph.' (Embassy of Japan, Canberra)

Plate 628

Plate 628. Japanese troops at the capture of Lae in March 1943. Lae and Salamaua were attacked by about 3000 navy and army troops who came from the Japanese base at Rabaul. (Embassy of Japan, Canberra)

Plate 629. The absolute destruction caused by war to civilian facilities in New Guinea is shown here in a photograph taken at Lae in March 1943 by a Japanese photographer at the time of the landing of Japanese troops. (Mainichi Press, Tokyo)

Plate 629

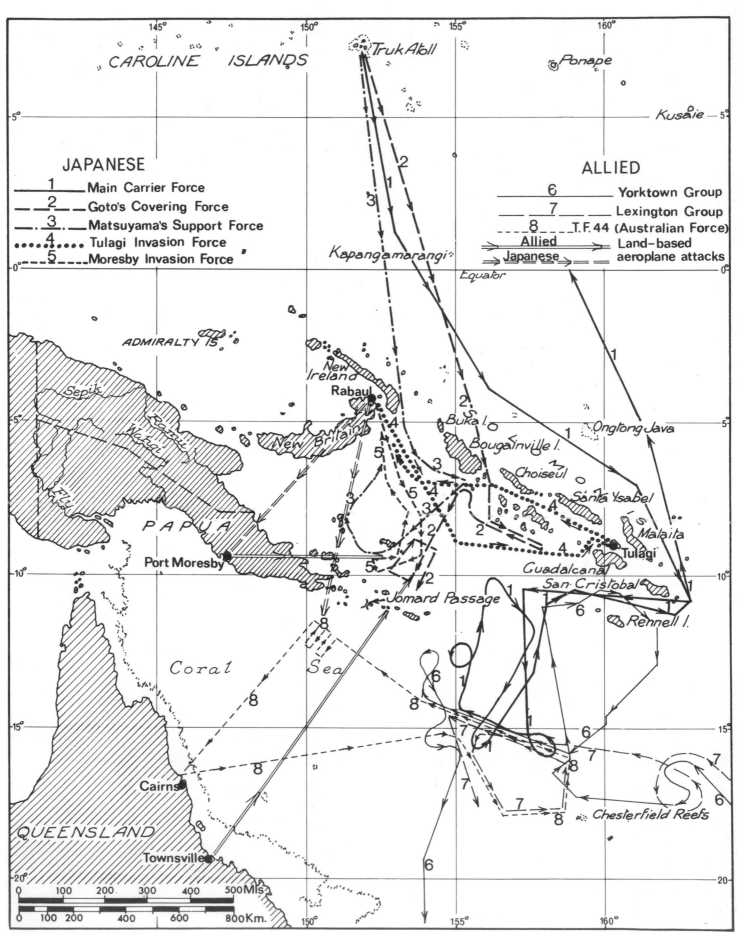

JAPANESE

—— 1 ——	Main Carrier Force
— — 2 — —	Goto's Covering Force
—·— 3 —·—	Matsuyama's Support Force
····4····	Tulagi Invasion Force
— — 5 — —	Moresby Invasion Force

ALLIED

—— 6 ——	Yorktown Group
— 7 —	Lexington Group
——8——	T.F.44 (Australian Force)
Allied ⇒	Land-based
Japanese ⇒	aeroplane attacks

CAROLINE ISLANDS

Truk Atoll

Ponape

Kusaie

Kapangamarangi

Equator

ADMIRALTY IS.

Sepik

New Ireland

Rabaul

New Britain

Buka I.

Onglong Java

Bougainville I.

Choiseul

Santa Ysabel

Malaita

PAPUA

Port Moresby

Tulagi

Guadalcanal

San Cristobal

Jomard Passage

Rennell I.

Coral Sea

Cairns

QUEENSLAND

Chesterfield Reefs

Townsville

0	100	200	300	400	500 Mls.
0	100 200	400	600	800 Km.

Plate 630

282

Plate 630. The Battle of the Coral Sea, 1 May to 8 May 1942. By the end of March 1942 the Japanese invaders had captured Rabaul, Kavieng, Lae and Salamaua. In May 1942 they attempted to create an outer perimeter based on Tulagi in the Solomon Islands to the east and on Port Moresby in the west. Tulagi was secured, but a seaborne invasion force aiming to capture Port Moresby by sailing from Rabaul and entering the Coral Sea by the Jomard Passage was turned back by an Allied naval presence in the Coral Sea.

The Battle of the Coral Sea was a confused encounter fought between carrier and land-based aircraft and ships. There was no direct contact between ships of the opposing fleets. Allied intelligence anticipated the Japanese move south and a naval force of Allied ships was deployed in the Coral Sea when the Japanese thrust towards Tulagi and Port Moresby took place.

The Opposing Forces

Japanese organized in five forces commanded by Vice-Admiral Inouye from Rabaul:

1. *Main Carrier Force* (Vice-Admiral Takagi) made up of carriers *Zuikaku* and *Shokaku*, cruisers *Myoko* and *Haguro* with six destroyers.

2. *Goto's Covering Force* (Rear-Admiral Goto) made up of carriers *Aobo*, *Kinugasa*, *Kako*, *Furutaka*, light carrier *Shoho* and a destroyer.

3. *Matsuyama's Support Force* (Rear-Admiral Matsuyama) made up of cruisers *Tenryu* and *Tatsuta*, seaplane carrier *Kamikawa Maru* and three gunboats.

4. *Tulagi Invasion Force* (Rear-Admiral Shima) made up of two destroyers, two submarine chasers, five minesweepers and one transport.

5. *Moresby Invasion Force* (Rear-Admiral Kajioka) made up of one cruiser *Yubari* and six destroyers, a minelayer and four minesweepers escorting eleven troop transports.

Allied organized in three forces under overall command of Commander-in-Chief, Pacific Fleet, Admiral Chester W. Nimitz, U.S.N., from Pearl Harbour:

6. *Yorktown Group* (Task Force 17, Rear-Admiral Fletcher, U.S.N.) made up of the carrier *Yorktown*, cruisers *Astoria*, *Chester* and *Portland* with destroyers and oiler.

7. *Lexington Group* (Task Force 11, Rear-Admiral Aubrey W. Fitch, U.S.N.) made up of carrier *Lexington*, cruisers *Minneapolis*, *New Orleans*, *Chicago* and *Perkins* with escorting destroyers and oiler.

8. *Task Force 44* (Australian Force, Rear-Admiral Crace, R.N.) made up of cruisers H.M.A.S. *Australia* and H.M.A.S. *Hobart* and destroyer escort.

The Main Movements of the Battle

29 April, *Tulagi Invasion Force* (4) leaves Rabaul; *Matsuyama's Support Force* (3) leaves Truk.

30 April, *Goto's Covering Force* (2) leaves Truk.

1 May, *Main Carrier Force* (1) leaves Truk; *Task Force 44* (*Australian Force*) leaves Sydney for Coral Sea via North Queensland. *Yorktown Group* (6) and *Lexington Group* (7) rendezvous 483 kilometres south of San Christobal Island.

2 May, *Yorktown Group* (6) sails west at slow speed into Coral Sea and makes aircraft search for Japanese ships; *Lexington Group* (7) continues refuelling. *Tulagi Invasion Force* (4) 740 kilometres north-north-west of *Yorktown Group* (6) and turning north-east for Tulagi; air attacks

on Tulagi and Port Moresby; Allied detachment evacuates Tulagi.

3 May, *Tulagi Invasion Force* (4) occupies and secures Tulagi; *Goto's Covering Force* (2) and *Matsuyama's Support Force* (3) manoeuvre to north-west of Tulagi; Tulagi being secured, they sail west. *Yorktown Group* (6) sails north to strike at Japanese on Tulagi; *Lexington Group* (7) completes refuelling and sails to rendezvous with *Yorktown Group* (6).

4 May, *Yorktown Group* (6), 160 kilometres south-west of Guadalcanal, at 6.30 a.m. launches aircraft to attack Japanese ships at Tulagi; one Japanese destroyer and three minesweepers bombed and sunk. *Moresby Invasion Force* (5) sets sail from Rabaul and is covered in the Solomon Sea by *Goto's Covering Force* (2) and *Matsuyama's Support Force* (3).

4 May, *Yorktown Group* (6), 160 kilometres south-west of *Force 44* (*Australian Force*) rendezvous 515 kilometres south of Guadalcanal, and fuel from oiler *Neosho*. *Main Carrier Force* (1) 650 kilometres to north-north-east of Allied force and steaming south-east to east of Malaita to enter Coral Sea between San Christobal and Rennell Islands. *Goto's Covering Force* (2) 800 kilometres north-west, south of Bougainville Island and fuelling. *Matsuyama's Support Force* (3) steering south-west near Woodlark Island. *Tulagi Invasion Force* (4) sailing westward to meet *Moresby Invasion Force* (5) sailing south-south-east in the latitude of New Britain's southern extremity.

6 May, *Yorktown Group* (6), *Lexington Group* (7) and *Task Force 44* (*Australian Force*), now combined as Task Force 17, complete refuelling. Oiler *Neosho* and destroyer escort *Sims* detached to go to next refuelling rendezvous. *Task Force 17* (6, 7, 8) sails north-west so as to be within striking distance of *Moresby Invasion Force* (5) by 7 May. *Main Carrier Force* (1) 110 kilometres due north of Allied force and fuelling, its position not known to Allies and Allies' position not known to it.

7 May, *Neosho* and *Sims* attacked by planes from *Main Carrier Force* (1). *Sims* sunk and *Neosho* crippled. *Goto's Covering Force* (2) north of Misima Island and providing cover for *Moresby Invasion Force* (5) 50 kilometres to the south-west and heading for Jomard Passage shepherded by *Matsuyama's Support Force* (3). *Task Force 44* (*Australian Force*) (8) detached from *Yorktown Group* (6) and *Lexington Group* (7) and ordered to sail north-west to intercept and destroy enemy ships passing through Jomard Passage; attacked by Japanese aircraft, it retires south to a position about 350 kilometres south-east of Port Moresby and continues patrolling for enemy ships. Aircraft from *Yorktown Group* (6) and *Lexington Group* (7) locate *Matsuyama's Support Force* (3) 360 kilometres north-west. Aircraft despatched to attack this force but actually attack *Goto's Covering Force* (2) north of Misima Island; light carrier *Shoho* sunk. Admiral Inouye orders *Moresby Invasion Force* (5) to turn back before entering Jomard Passage.

8 May, mutual location of each other's force by aircraft from *Main Carrier Force* (1) and *Yorktown and Lexington Group* (6, 7); aircraft attacks launched by each side; Japanese carrier *Shokaku* bombed and left crippled. *Lexington* bombed and crippled, and scuttled after internal explosions; *Yorktown* bombed, and disengaging heads south. *Task Force 44* (*Australian Force*) (8) retains position south of China Strait. *Main Carrier Force* (1) ordered by

Admiral Inouye to retire to Truk base. *Yorktown Group* (6) ordered by Admiral Nimitz to retire from Coral Sea area. **9 May,** *Main Carrier Force* (1) has order to retire countermanded by Commander-in-Chief Admiral Yamamoto, and turns south again.

10 May, *Main Carrier Force* (1) sails to position in Coral Sea 160 kilometres south of position where *Lexington* was sunk and then leaves area by a route south and east of the Solomons. *Task Force 44 (Australian Force)* (8) holds position south of China Strait and then retires south-west.

The Battle of the Coral Sea is considered to have been 'a tactical victory for the Japanese but a strategic victory for the Allies'. (G. Hermon Gill, *Royal Australian Navy, 1942–1945* [Canberra, 1968], p. 53.) The Japanese expedition that had planned to capture Port Moresby had to turn back. Never again would Japanese surface forces attempt to enter the Coral Sea in strength. Having failed in their objective to capture Port Moresby by sea, the Japanese were forced to attempt its capture by land and the costly Milne Bay and Kokoda Trail campaigns resulted. (Map by Edgar Ford)

Plate 631. The attack on the Japanese light carrier *Shoho* of *Goto's Covering Force* (2) by bombers and torpedo-carrying aircraft of the *Yorktown and Lexington Group* (6, 7) on 7 May 1942. This action took place just north of Misima Island in the Louisiade Archipelago. The *Shoho*, a Ryukaku class carrier of 26 520 tonnes, was sunk. The loss of the *Shoho* deprived the *Moresby Invasion Force* (5) of its seaborne air cover and was a probable factor in Admiral Inouye's recall of this force to Rabaul. (National Archives, General Services Administration, Washington, D.C.)

Plate 631

284

Plate 632

Plate 633

Plate 632. The U.S. carrier *Lexington* as it was being abandoned by its crew on 8 May 1942. In an earlier action on the same day, aircraft of the *Main Carrier Force* (1) attacked the *Yorktown and Lexington Group* (6, 7) about 560 kilometres north-west of the Chesterfield Reefs. The *Lexington* of 33 660 tonnes was hit by two bombs and two torpedoes and after recovering its aircraft began to retire southwards. Internal explosions finally crippled the ship and it was abandoned. Shortly after this photograph was taken the *Lexington* was sunk by torpedoes fired by U.S. destroyer *Phelps* about 400 kilometres west of Chesterfield Reefs. (National Archives, General Services Administration, Washington, D.C.)

Plate 633. Colonel Yosuke Yokoyama (left), who led the advance force of Japanese which landed at Gona on 22 July 1942, with another Japanese officer and some local men. Yokoyama had been ordered by Major General Horii, general officer commanding South Seas Force, to advance as far as Kokoda and reconnoitre the track leading to Port Moresby, prepare the coastal section for motor traffic, and hold the area between the coast and Kokoda. Yokoyama made the landing with a force of about 2000 troops and had with him about 1200 men from the Rabaul area who had been conscripted as carriers and labourers. (Embassy of Japan, Canberra)

Plate 634

Plate 635. The road between Lilihoa and Gili Gili along which the main action of the Milne Bay campaign was fought between Australian and Japanese troops. (Australian War Memorial)

Plate 635

Plate 634. The north-west corner of Milne Bay in south-east Papua, the site of the Battle for Milne Bay in World War II.

Following the Battle of the Coral Sea early in May 1942, the Allies sought to reinforce their forward defences in New Guinea. Accordingly Milne Bay was selected as a site for the building of airstrips from which air attacks could be made on Rabaul, Lae and Salamaua. In June 1942 American and Australian troops were sent to the area to construct and to defend the airstrips, the first of which (No. 1 Gurney) was sited near Gili Gili. By the end of August about 9000 troops were deployed in this area. Of these about half were infantrymen.

At the same time the Japanese revised their plan to attack Port Moresby by a seaborne invasion. Their aim now was to take Port Moresby from the rear, via the Kokoda Trail, and to establish a base at Milne Bay from which a combined land, sea and air assault could be launched towards Port Moresby.

The American invasion of Guadalcanal in the British Solomon Islands caused the Japanese to revise their original plans for the occupation of Milne Bay, but commencing on 25 August about 2000 troops were landed. The Allies lacked naval forces in the region at this time and Japanese ships were able to enter the bay under cover of darkness. In the daytime, however, the Japanese were harassed from the air as No. 1 Strip was by this time operational.

The Japanese established a base area along the shore of the bay in the Goroni, Lilihoa, Ahioma area and from here attacks were launched towards the partly con-structed No. 3 (Turnbull) Strip along the road that ran from Ahioma to Gili Gili. The Japanese succeeded at their furthest extent in reaching No. 3 Strip but were beaten back by determined Australian resistance and counterattack. On 6 September Australian troops penetrated the Japanese base area and early on the following day the Japanese evacuated the remnants of their invasion force. In the course of the battle the Australians lost 373 men, the Japanese about 700.

The defeat of the Japanese at Milne Bay removed the threat to Port Moresby from this flank. The Japanese had perforce to attempt to gain their objective by the Kokoda Trail campaign alone and this proved an impossible task. (Royal Australian Air Force)

Plate 636

Plate 636. An aerial photograph of Port Moresby taken in November 1942; at this time Port Moresby was an important forward base for the campaign along the Kokoda Trail. On 6 November, General MacArthur came to Port Moresby with an advanced echelon of general headquarters and before that, in September 1942, General Blamey had set up his headquarters in the Port Moresby area at the behest of the Australian government in order to exercise overall control in the field. (Australian School of Pacific Administration)

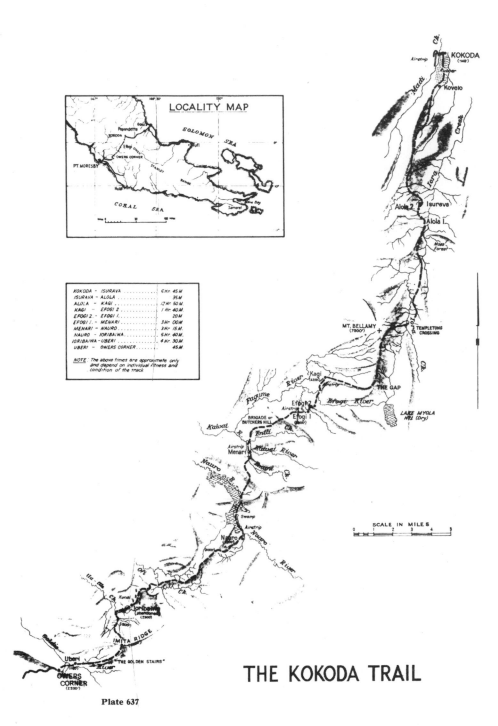

LOCALITY MAP

KOKODA - ISURAVA	5Hr. 45 M.
ISURAVA - ALOLA	35 M.
ALOLA - KAGI	2 Hr. 50 M.
KAGI - EFOGI 2	1 Hr. 40 M.
EFOGI 2 - EFOGI 1	20 M.
EFOGI 1 - MENARI	3 Hr. 00 M.
MENARI - NAURO	3 Hr. 15 M.
NAURO - IORIBAIWA	5 Hr. 40 M.
IORIBAIWA - UBERI	4 Hr. 30 M.
UBERI - OWERS CORNER	45 M.

NOTE: The above times are approximate only and depend on individual fitness and condition of the track

SCALE IN MILES

THE KOKODA TRAIL

Plate 637

Plate 637. The Kokoda Trail, 1942. Following the Japanese landings at Gona and Buna in July 1942, Australian and Papuan troops were sent to secure the area around Kokoda and to prevent any Japanese movement towards Port Moresby. In the face of an energetic Japanese advance the Australians retreated from Kokoda, which the Japanese captured on 29 July. During August the Japanese landed about 13 500 troops at Gona–Buna with the intention of advancing on Port Moresby by way of the Kokoda Trail. The final assault was to be coordinated with a force from Milne Bay, which the Japanese planned to secure as a base during August. The Japanese vigorously pursued their aims during August, and in the face of a determined enemy the Australians fought a stubborn rearguard action as they fell back towards Port Moresby.

The Japanese advanced as far as Ioribaiwa, 48 kilometres from Port Moresby, which they reached on 20 September. The Australians had established a strong defensive position on Imita Ridge between Ioribaiwa and Uberi. The Japanese now faced the formidable difficulty of supply from their Gona–Buna base along an extended line of communication through extremely difficult country. This, combined with their defeat at Milne Bay in August and the diversion of forces to Guadalcanal to meet the American attack there, meant that the Japanese had reached the limit of their effort. They thereupon retreated from Ioribaiwa back across the Owen Stanley Range with the Australians in close pursuit. *Insets:* top, locality map; bottom, walking times for carriers over sections of the trail. (Map by the Information and Extension Services, Administration of Papua New Guinea)

Plate 638. Allied leaders in Port Moresby, 2 October 1942. Left to right, F. M. Forde (minister for the army, Australia); General Douglas MacArthur (supreme commander, south-west Pacific area, United States); General Sir Thomas Blamey (commander of Allied land forces, south-west Pacific area, Australia); and Lieutenant General George C. Kenney (commander Fifth Air Force, United States). (Australian War Memorial)

Plate 638

Plate 639

Plate 640

Plate 639. A company of the first Australian troops to cross the Owen Stanley Range to meet the Japanese invaders: men of the 39th Battalion (militia) moving up past McDonald's Corner on 29 June 1942. This company reached Kokoda by 15 July and made first contact with the Japanese at Gorari on 25 July. Subsequently they fought a stubborn rearguard action in the face of the Japanese advance over the Owen Stanleys. It was not until 5 September that this battalion was relieved at Efogi on the southern side of the crest. By then it had lost 117 men in battle casualties. Their average age was approximately eighteen and a half years. (Department of Information and Extension Services, Administration of Papua New Guinea)

Plate 640. Men of the 39th Battalion (militia) at Menari, 6 September 1942, on their way back to Port Moresby after being relieved following contact with the enemy, 25 July to 5 September 1942. (Australian War Memorial)

Plate 641

Plate 642

Plate 641. The recapture of Kokoda by Australian troops on 2 November 1942. (Australian War Memorial)

Plate 642. The 'Fuzzy Wuzzy Angels' in action on the Kokoda Trail, as depicted in a popular Sydney publication. With this the journal printed the poem 'Fuzzy Wuzzy Angels', which concluded:

May the mothers of Australia
When they offer up a prayer,
Mention those impromptu angels,
With the fuzzy wuzzy hair.

An editorial in the same edition said: '. . . We know that wise and kind administration in Papua in the past helped to produce in the natives a willingness to serve the white soldiers with such devotion. We feel too that the heroism and friendliness of our troops have helped to change that willingness to eagerness. But still a debt remains. Many an Australian soldier will come home from the war because a black-skinned brother carried him over the Owen Stanley Range. And in any plans for a better way of life when the war is over the New Guinea native must have a place.' Editorial, *Australian Women's Weekly*, 9 January 1943. (Library of New South Wales)

Plate 643

Plate 643. A section of the Kokoda Trail: the 'Golden Stairs' ascending to the 825 metres of Imita Ridge in the Owen Stanley foothills about 48 kilometres from Port Moresby. An officer of an Australian Imperial Force unit which fought over the Kokoda Trail recorded what happened when his unit made the ascent: 'Gradually men dropped out utterly exhausted—just couldn't go on. You'd come to a group of men and say "Come on! We must go on." But it was physically impossible to move. Many were lying down and had been sick . . . many made several trips up the last slope helping others. We began to see some of the tremendous efforts the troops were going to make to help the lesser ones in.' (Australian War Memorial)

Plate 644

Plate 645

Plate 644. Wounded Australian soldiers being carried to an advanced dressing station at Buna in 1942. Scenes like this published in Australia created an extraordinary sentiment in the Australian public for the people of New Guinea. (Australian War Memorial)

Plate 645. A scene at the village of Simemi, Papua, in November 1942, during the drive of the American 32nd Division on Buna. A member of the constabulary illustrates Japanese troop dispositions for U.S. intelligence officers. (U.S. Army)

Plate 646. A group in Port Moresby in 1943 and a typical scene in New Guinea between 1942 and 1946 wherever Australian troops were stationed in base areas. The war brought large numbers of ordinary Australians into New Guinea, who worked side by side with local men. The indigenes saw white men doing hard manual labour and being submitted to discipline similar to that exerted over them by European expatriates in the colonial situation. The presence in New Guinea of large numbers of American Negroes was also a part of the wartime education of New Guineans. In addition to these experiences many New Guinea men travelled widely and visited urban centres in Australia, with notable effect in some cases on their postwar attitudes to the re-imposition of Australian civilian rule. (A. E. Ross Collection)

Plate 647. An American army engineer supervises labourers in road building after the capture of Buna in January 1943. By June 1943 approximately 25 500 New Guineans had been recruited into the Native Labour Service of the Australian New Guinea Administrative Unit. (Australian War Memorial)

Plate 646

Plate 647

Plate 648. Carriers under the control of members of the Australian New Guinea Administrative Unit (ANGAU) taking supplies to a forward area. On 15 June 1942, Major General Morris, commanding-officer New Guinea Force, invoked the National Security (Emergency Control) Regulations and thereby conscripted labour required for military purposes. Service was for three years and it was laid down that no labourer should:
1. Neglect to enter into a contract of employment.
2. After he had entered into such contract
   (a) desert from such employment;
   (b) absent himself without leave;
   (c) refuse or neglect to perform levy work which it was his duty to perform;
   (d) perform any work in a careless or negligent manner.

(Australian War Memorial)

Plate 648

Plate 649

Plate 649. Wau township and airfield in 1933. The most important town of the Bulolo Valley, Wau served as an important transit and supply point for the goldfields in the 1930s. In early 1942 following the occupation of Lae and Salamaua by Japanese military forces, Wau was the evacuation centre for civilians. The town was damaged by Japanese aerial bombardment in March 1942, and in August 1942 its buildings and installations were destroyed by Australian troops as part of a plan to 'scorch' the Bulolo Valley in the face of a threatened advance by Japanese troops from Salamaua via Mubo. This advance did not take place until January 1943, and its limit was reached at Wau. Fierce fighting occurred between Australian troops and the Japanese around the airfield. On 29 January 1943 Australian troop reinforcements were landed on Wau airfield and went into action immediately in its defence. (Mitchell Library)

Plate 650. Men of the Papuan Constabulary and of the Native Labour Service of ANGAU being thanked by Major General G. A. Vasey, G.O.C., 7th Division A.I.F., for their part in the Allied success in the Papuan campaigns of 1942. (Australian War Memorial)

Plate 650

293

Plate 651. Japanese marine corps troops in action somewhere in New Guinea in July 1943. (Mainichi Press,
Tokyo)

Plate 652. The investment of Lae, September 1943.
American and Australian troops being parachuted into
Nadzab in the Markham Valley on 5 September 1943.
Three hundred and two aircraft from Port Moresby and
Dobodura were used in the operation and a mixed force
of paratroops, pioneers, artillerymen, engineers and
Papuans were soon in occupation of the Nadzab area,
where airfields were constructed for the reception of
airborne troops to be used to advance down river towards
Japanese-held Lae. (Mitchell Library)

Plate 651

Plate 652

Plate 653

Plate 653. Military equipment being unloaded from a
D.C.3 transport plane by members of the Native Labour
Service of ANGAU at Nadzab, Markham Valley, September 1943, during the course of the Australian advance
on Lae. (Australian War Memorial)

Plate 654

Plate 655

Plate 654. The recapture of Salamaua, 15 September 1943. Members of the constabulary driven out of Salamaua by the Japanese occupation returned on its recapture by Australian troops and took part in the flag-raising ceremony. (U.S. Army)

Plate 656. Dumpu on the upper Ramu River from the air on 22 September 1943. Dumpu was captured by Australian troops of the 7th Division on 4 October 1943, as the occupying Japanese troops retreated towards the Finisterre Range. Dumpu subsequently became the base for operations against the Japanese in the Finisterre Range towards the coast at Astrolabe Bay. By November 1943 two landing strips had been built and were operating in all weathers. (Australian School of Pacific Administration)

Plate 655. The changing fortunes of war called New Guineans to different loyalties. Here men of Kaiapit in the Upper Markham Valley, formerly in the Japanese labour service, are addressed by officers of the Native Labour Service of ANGAU, Kaiapit was captured by Australian troops on 19 September 1943. (Australian War Memorial)

Plate 656

Plate 657

Plate 657. Shaggy Ridge in the Finisterre Range, which Australian troops captured from entrenched Japanese defenders in December 1943. An Australian unit involved in the fighting on this ridge recorded: ' "Shaggy Ridge" was a narrow razorback with an altitude of 5000 feet. A thick rain forest covered the crest of the ridge. Heavy mists frequently obscured the position for days at a time. Their observation was limited to less than 100 yards. Such was the vantage point of the eminence that on clear days observation was possible as far as the sea near Madang. The ridge was at no part wider than a few yards, narrowing at the foremost section position. The most forward position, a foxhole, was occupied by a lone Bren gunner. For the first time in its history the battalion held ground with a one-man front. Ahead of him was the enemy who had had weeks to prepare his defences.' M. Uren, *A Thousand Men at War: The Story of the 2/16th Battalion A.I.F.*, quoted in D. Dexter, *The New Guinea Offensives* (Canberra, 1961), p. 688. (Australian War Memorial)

Plate 658. The destruction of war is seen here at Alexishafen after its recapture by Australian troops on 26 April 1943. (Australian War Memorial)

Plate 659. An officer of the Australian New Guinea Administrative Unit recruiting at Wideru village on the Huon Gulf in October 1943. (Australian War Memorial)

Plate 660. Japanese naval construction corps workers building an airfield somewhere in New Guinea in July 1943. Both sides constructed bases, airfields and port facilities exceeding in scale all previous European engineering works, which had been almost totally destroyed by military action. (Mainichi Press, Tokyo)

Plate 658

Plate 659

Plate 660

297

Plate 661

Plate 661. An officer of the Australian New Guinea Administrative Unit addressing village leaders on Karkar Island on 4 June 1944, following its capture by Australian troops after a Japanese military occupation of approximately two years. (Australian War Memorial)

Plate 662

Plate 663

Plate 662. Men of the Papuan Infantry Battalion with their Australian officer at a forward post. The Papuan Infantry Battalion fought in all the main campaigns from Kokoda in 1942 to the Madang–Sepik in 1944. (Australian War Memorial)

Plate 663. Labourers of the Native Labour Service of ANGAU engaged in malaria control drainage work. The value of this and other control work is shown by the fact that the incidence of malaria among Australian troops fell from 8·9 per cent in December 1942 to 0·8 per cent in February 1943. (Australian War Memorial)

Plate 664. The effect of war on New Guinea's economy is shown here; Boram airstrip near Wewak was built by the Japanese within the Boram coconut plantation. It was heavily attacked by Allied aircraft throughout the war, in particular on 17 August 1943, by the U.S. Fourth Air Army, and on 26 August 1944, by the R.A.A.F. This photograph was taken on 25 May 1944. (Australian School of Pacific Administration)

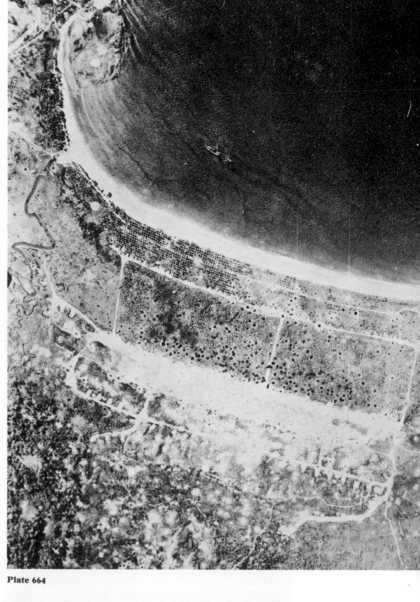

Plate 665. The extent of the Allied military presence in New Guinea is shown in this photograph of the American base near Cape Sud Est on the north coast of Papua, probably taken in 1944. Together with the airfield complex at Dobodura this was one of the big Allied bases in New Guinea. At the end of May 1943, Allied strength in New Guinea was made up of about 63 000 Australian and about 56 500 American servicemen. An estimated 34 200 Japanese troops were deployed in Australian New Guinea at the same time. (Australian School of Pacific Administration)

Plate 664

Plate 665

Plate 666

Plate 667

Plate 666. American troops and armour advancing on Aitape airfield on 22 April 1944. The attack on Aitape was made at the same time as another on Hollandia in Dutch New Guinea. About 80 000 American troops were employed in an amphibious operation against the two Japanese strongpoints. The nearest New Guinea territory held by the Allies was at Bogadjim on Astrolabe Bay. The attack on Aitape represented the beginning of General MacArthur's 'island hopping' strategy. The Japanese in Aitape, about 1000 in number, offered little opposition. Two Americans were killed and thirteen wounded. (U.S. Army)

Plate 667. Japanese soldiers of the 18th Army captured at Ulebilum in the Maprik area in June 1945. It has been estimated that about 300 000 Japanese (including about 20 000 civilian workers) were deployed in New Guinea and the Solomons from 1942 onwards. About 60 000 died in battle and 110 000 died of illness. About 127 000 were alive at the surrender of Japanese forces in New Guinea in 1945. (Australian War Memorial)

Plate 668

Plate 668. During the Japanese army's occupation of Rabaul, extensive tunnelling took place in the pumice bluffs along the waterfront of Blanche Bay. Here the Japanese sheltered war equipment including landing barges, as shown, from the heavy Allied bombing of 1943, 1944 and 1945. Rabaul was built up by the Japanese as the main base for their south-west Pacific military and naval operations. Japanese strength in the Rabaul region at the time of the surrender on 6 September 1945 was 57 368 army personnel, including 4156 civilian workers, and 31 923 naval personnel, including 15 705 civilian workers. (Information and Extension Services, Administration of Papua New Guinea)

Plate 669. The site of prewar Rabaul soon after the reoccupation of the area by Australian troops in October 1945. Rabaul was obliterated by Allied bombardment. Altogether 20 959 tonnes of bombs were dropped on Rabaul from Allied aircraft and 388 tonnes of projectiles were fired at it from naval vessels. (G. Odgers, *Air War Against Japan 1943–1945* [Canberra, 1957], p. 334.) The decision to rebuild Rabaul as the centre of administration was not arrived at until 1951. Between 1945 and 1951 buildings of a temporary type were erected on the site. In 1951 a town planning committee was set up in Rabaul and, in collaboration with a committee of the Administration headed by Acting Administrator D. M. Cleland, the pattern for present-day Rabaul was laid down, (Australian School of Pacific Administration)

Plate 669

Plate 670

Plate 670. The main store block of W. R. Carpenter and Co. Ltd in Mango Avenue, Rabaul, being rebuilt after World War II. Just before the war, on 3 September 1939, a fire destroyed the original store. In the rebuilding, quonset huts were bought from disposals. The units were raised off the ground, and extra ventilation allowed into the roof sections. A new retail and separate bulk store were erected, as well as a freezer products department, a new hardware store, timber rack, wharf shipping offices and other smaller buildings. The new retail store was also destroyed by fire in the early 1960s. The present store premises were then erected. (B. B. Perriman Collection)

Plate 671. Buildings bought by W. R. Carpenter and Co. Ltd at Madang after World War II. The large building was used as a bulk store; the smaller was demolished. (B. B. Perriman Collection)

Plate 672. Mr E. J. Ward speaking to a child at Papa village during his 1945 tour of the Territory. In the background are, from left to right, Mr Donovan, private secretary to the minister; Major General B. M. Morris, ANGAU, Kabua; Lieutenant Colonel A. A. Conlon. (Mitchell Library)

Plate 671

Plate 672

Plate 673

Plate 674

Plate 673. The visit of E. J. Ward, minister for external territories, in 1945, was important because it led to the formulation of government policy as civil government was restored in the Territory. The direction of government policy was given by Mr Ward when he introduced the Papua New Guinea Provisional Administration Bill in the Federal Parliament on 4 July 1945: 'This Government is not satisfied that sufficient interest had been taken in the Territories prior to the Japanese invasion or that adequate funds had been provided for their development and the advancement of the native inhabitants. . . . Advancement can be achieved only by providing facilities for better health, better education and for a greater participation by the natives in the wealth of their country and eventually in the government.'

The photograph shows Mr Ward (fourth from the left) with a party at the headquarters of the Naval Officer in Charge at Milne Bay. Left to right, Colonel R. J. Wright, scientific consultant, Directorate of Research; Brigadier D. M. Cleland, D.A., Q.M.G., ANGAU, chairman of Australian New Guinea Production Control Board; Lieutenant Colonel Wolfenden, commander Milne Bay Base Sub-area; Mr Ward; Mr Donovan, private secretary to the minister; Commander Bowen, N.O.I.C.; Lieutenant V. W. Maxwell, ANGAU; Captain B. Brewer, acting district officer, Milne Bay; [unidentified]. (Mitchell Library)

Plate 674. Colonel J. K. Murray, administrator of Papua New Guinea 1945–1952, formerly professor of agriculture at the University of Queensland. Murray was chief instructor at the army's School of Civil Affairs at the time of his appointment, 30 October 1945. In 1952 Murray's appointment was terminated by the Menzies government and he was replaced by D. M. Cleland (see plate 673). (*Commonwealth Records* CRS A24, reproduced by permission of the Commonwealth Archives Office)

303

Plate 675

Plate 676

Plate 675. Delegates of a visiting United Nations mission meet the people at a *kivung* at Vunakalkalulu village in the Teimber area of Rabaul in March 1950. Paramount *luluai* Topoi is addressing the delegation. Left to right, Mr V. Carpio (Philippines); M. Jacques Tallec (France); Mr Chang (China); Sir Alan Burns (U.K.); and an officer of the New Guinea Administration, Mr D. Fienberg.

In December 1946 the former Mandated Territory of New Guinea became a Trusteeship Territory of the United Nations. The United Nations Organization approved of Australia as the administering authority and approved of the Trusteeship Territory entering 'a customs, fiscal or administrative union' with other dependent territories, i.e. Papua. This union was effected by the Papua and New Guinea Act of 1949. J. D. Legge, *Australian Colonial Policy* (Sydney, 1955), pp. 189–90. (*Commonwealth Records* CRS A24, reproduced by permission of the Commonwealth Archives Office)

Plate 676. A group of Rabaul dignitaries with the governor general, Mr William McKell, as he speaks to some of the schoolchildren of Rabaul, 1949. Left to right, Mr Sansom, district officer, New Britain; the administrator, Colonel J. K. Murray; B. B. Perriman, manager of W. R. Carpenter and Co. Ltd; Malcolm Inglish, district officer; Mr William McKell. (B. B. Perriman Collection)

Plate 677. Victims of the Mount Lamington eruption on 21 January 1951, lying on the road to Higatura. Although the more active phase began four days before the eruption, none of the Orokaiva people left their villages. Mr Cowley, district commissioner at Higatura, and other Europeans such as Mr Phillips, who had witnessed the Vulcan eruption at Rabaul in 1937, expected a far less destructive type of explosion from the volcano and quelled panic by playing down the expected effects of the explosion. Sangara contained the Martyr's School and the main mission centre. Both were destroyed by the blast and everyone in Sangara was killed, for it lay just inside the border of complete devastation. The headquarters of the Northern District government administration at Higatura was also destroyed. Eric Schwimmer spoke to several of the survivors of the eruption: 'All spoke of the cloud of fire that descended after the explosion. One man described how he saw it killing people ahead of him and how, with his brother, he ran past the burnt bodies. Another man told that the wind hit him and threw him down; for hours he remained unconscious and the people who were with him had all gone.' (Eric G. Schwimmer, *Cultural Consequences of a Volcanic Eruption Experienced by the Mount Lamington Orokaiva* [Oregon, 1969], Report No. 9, p. 11.) Sangara plantation became a rallying point for survivors and the centre for the rescue and resettlement work carried out by the Administration. (Information and Extension Services, Administration of Papua New Guinea)

Plate 677

Plate 678

Plate 678. Approaching a crater through Avalanche Valley, Mount Lamington, after the eruption on 21 January 1951. The vent on the left of the dome shows destructive activity. G. A. M. Taylor described the eruption: 'At 1040 hours on Sunday 21 January 1951, a paroxysmal explosion burst from the crater and produced a *nuée ardente* which completely devastated a surrounding area of 68 square miles.' (G. A. M. Taylor, *The 1951 Eruption of Mount Lamington, Papua* [1958].) This explosion, unlike that of Vulcan, Rabaul, in 1937, was a 'Pelean' type of explosion, having a destructive force like an atomic bomb. Destruction of the inner zone was complete, even the earth being swept bare. At Higatura, ten kilometres away from the crater, only one house remained intact. (Information and Extension Services, Administration of Papua New Guinea)

Plate 679

Plate 679. Delegates from the Territory of Papua and New Guinea to the South Pacific Conference held in Suva in 1950. The photograph was taken at Sogeri on the eve of departure of the delegation. Several of those in the group rose to prominent positions in the P.N.G. administration. The men in the photograph are, seated, left to right, [unidentified]; Damona Walo; Miria Gavera; Aisoli Salim. Standing, left to right, George Kassi; Willie Gavera; Aia Ngu and Bondai Pita.

Plate 680

Plate 680. The opening of the Legislative Council for the Territory of Papua and New Guinea at Port Moresby in November 1951. The Papua and New Guinea Act of 1949 made provision for a Legislative Council of twenty-nine members, with election of some nonofficial members, and for representation of the indigenous people. The Council was made up of sixteen official members, three nonofficial elected members, three nonofficial members nominated by the Christian missions, three nonofficial indigenous members and three other nominated nonofficial members. The members in this photograph are, left to right, front row, Mrs Doris Booth, O.B.E.; E. A. Jones; J. T. Gunther; C. Champion; W. Watkins; D. M. Cleland. Second row, left to right, T. P. Byrne; Rev. F. G. Lewis; J. B. McAdam; J. R. Foldi; E. P. Holmes; B. Fairfax-Ross. Third row, left to right, H. H. Reeve; D. Barrett; Rev. J. Dwyer; Aisoli Salin; W. C. Groves. Fourth row, left to right, Merari Dickson; Rev. D. E. Ure; J. H. Jones; H. R. Niall. Back row, left to right, C. M. Jacobsen; C. Marr; S. Elliott-Smith and J. B. Sedgers. (*Commonwealth Records* CRS A24, reproduced by permission of the Commonwealth Archives Office)

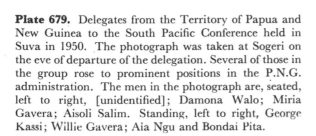

Sources

To locate a photograph the reader should note the broad location given at the end of each caption, e.g. (Mitchell Library). The subject matter of the photograph should then suggest in which particular Mitchell Library collection or other collection it is located. The precise title of the collection and its catalogue number are given below, and this is where the photograph will be found.

LIBRARIES AND ARCHIVES

Australian War Memorial, Canberra, Photographic Collection; Bibliotheek der Rijksuniversiteit Te Leiden; Bibliothèque Nationale, Paris; Burns, Philp and Company Ltd, Sydney, Company Records; Commonwealth Archives Office, Canberra, *Commonwealth Records*, Series CRS A24; Department of Information and Extension Services, Administration of Papua New Guinea, Port Moresby; Department of Territories, Photographic Collection, Canberra; Embassy of Japan, Canberra; Hallstrom Pacific Library, Australian School of Pacific Administration (*Papua and New Guinea Extracts from Newspapers, 1930–35; Aerial Photographs of New Guinea*); Landeshauptstadt und Universitätsstadt, Stadtbibliothek, Mainz; London Missionary Society, London (*Papuan Pictures*); Mainichi Press, Pictorial File, Tokyo, Japan; Mitchell Library, Sydney (*Australia: Department of the Army: Visit of E. J. Ward to New Guinea, 1945*, F988.4/A; *George Brown Photographs*: catalogued with Published Books; *Thomas J. Denham's New Guinea Note Book 1915–1916*, B/695; *Lawrence Hargrave Papers*, MS. FM4/1060; *The Investment of Lae*, 6 Photographs, L/WOR 2/1; *Rev. W. G. Lawes: Photographs of New Guinea*, 998.4/L; *Album, Robert Weinburne Lawry, R.N., 1883–84*, PXA44; *Methodist Church of Australasia:* *Department of Overseas Missions*, Uncat. MSS., Meth. Ch. O.M. 125, Glass Slides; *Methodist Church of Australasia: Department of Overseas Missions: Album, Rev. S. B. Fellows*, Uncat. MSS., Meth. Ch. O.M. 264; *New Guinea and South Sea Islands Album; Newspaper Cuttings*, Q279.8/B; *Photographs of Papua*, F988.4/P; *Picture File*, DG 366; *Ships' Picture Catalogue: The 'Blanche'*, V/Ship/Blan/; *Small Picture File—New Guinea; Uncat. MSS.*, Set 488, Item Ih.; *Waterhouse Photographs*, Q988.4/W); National Archives, General Services Administration, Washington, D.C.; National Library of Australia, Canberra (*The Nixon-westwood Collection*, MD 2153; *The Leahy Collection*); Nederlandsch Historisch Scheepvaart Museum, Amsterdam; Rijksmuseum voor Volkenkunde, Leiden; Royal Australian Air Force, Aerial Photographic Department, Canberra; Royal Geographical Society, London (*The Log and Private Journal of Dr D. Parker Wilson of the South Sea Whaler 'Gypsy' on a Voyage from 23 October 1839 to 19 March 1843*); Staatsbibliothek, Preussischer Kulturbesitz, Bildarchiv, Berlin; Staats-und Universitätsbibliothek, Hamburg; Tropeninstitut, Hamburg; University of Papua New Guinea Library and Department of Anthropology.

PRIVATE COLLECTIONS

B. Backus Collection, Mittagong, N.S.W.; R. Clark Collection, Sydney; Fr Coltré Collection, Papua New Guinea; M. Dick Collection, Port Macquarie, N.S.W.; E. E. Jones Collection, Castle Hill, N.S.W.; Michael J. Leahy Collection, Papua New Guinea; Z. Mattes Collection, Sydney; S. M. Matthews Collection, Papua New Guinea; D. Mercer Collection, East Ballina, N.S.W.; E. Miller Collection, Ballina, N.S.W.; A. V. Noall Collection, Sydney;

B. B. Perriman Collection, Canberra; G. Pilhofer Collection, Neuendettelsau, Bavaria; N. Rickard Collection, Sydney; A. E. Ross Collection, Wollongong, N.S.W.; L. C. Roebuck Collection, Port Macquarie, N.S.W.; H. L. Schultze Collection, Sydney; E. A. Shepherd Collection, Sydney; A. A. Speedie Collection, Melbourne; R. Speedie Collection, Sydney; S. Stephenson Collection, Castle Hill, N.S.W.; J. L. Taylor Collection, Papua New Guinea; M. von Hein Collection, Sydney; H. E. Woodman Collection, Penrith, N.S.W

PERIODICALS AND NEWSPAPERS

Annales de la Propagation de la Foi, 1884, 1885, 1888, 1890, 1891, 1892, 1893; *Australasian Sketcher*, 1875, 1883, 1884, 1885; *Australian Women's Weekly* (Sydney), 1943; *Bulletin* (Sydney), 1883, 1884, 1885, 1886, 1888, 1919; *Illustrated Australian News*, 1884, 1871; *Illustrated London News*, 1848; *Illustrated Missionary News* (London), 1874; *Illustrated Monthly Herald* (Melbourne), 1872; *Illustrated Sydney News*, 1875; *Missionary Review*, 1921–25; *National Geographic Magazine*, September 1929; *New Guinea Research Bulletin* no. 15, 1967; *Pacific Islands Monthly*, 1932, 1935, 1937; *Rabaul Times*, 1932, 1937; *Sydney Mail*, 1884, 1914.

PUBLISHED WORKS

Arago, J. *Voyage Autour du Monde*. Paris, 1843; Baudouin, A. *L'Aventure de Port-Breton et la Colonie Libre dite Nouvelle France*. Paris, 1883; Belloc, M. *Histoires d'Amérique et d'Océanie depuis l'Epoque de la Découverte jusqu'en 1839*. Paris, 1839; Bonaparte, R. *La Nouvelle-Guinée*, book 3, *Le Fleuve Augusta*. Paris, 1887; Brown, R. *Countries of the World*. London, 1892 (?); Cayley-Webster, H. *Through New Guinea and the Cannibal Countries*. London, 1898; Chignell, A. K. *An Outpost in Papua*. London, 1911; Clune, F. *Somewhere in New Guinea*. London, 1951; Commonwealth of Australia. *Handbook of the Territory of Papua*, 3rd ed., compiled by Staniforth Smith, Melbourne, 1912, and 2nd ed., Melbourne, 1909; Commonwealth of Australia. *Catalogue of New Guinea Properties*. Melbourne, 1925; d'Albertis, L. M. *New Guinea: What I Did and What I Saw*. London, 1880; Masefield, J., ed. *Dampier's Voyages*. London, 1906; Danks, B. *A Brief History of the New Britain Mission*. Sydney, 1901; Dauncey, H. M. *Papuan Pictures*. London, 1913; de Groote, P. *Nouvelle-France, Colonie Libre de Port-Breton (Océanie)*. Paris, 1880; de Villiers, J. A. J., ed. *The East and West Indian Mirror*. London, 1906; Domeny de Rienzi, M. G. L. *L'Univers Histoire et Description de Tous les Peuples Océanie*. Paris, 1837; Dupeyrat, A. *Papouasie: Histoire de la Mission, 1885–1935*. Paris, 1935; Dumont d'Urville, J. *Voyage de la Corvette 'L'Astrolabe' Exécuté par Ordre du Roi Pendant les Années 1826, 1827, 1828, 1829*. Paris, 1832; Finsch, O. *Samoafahrten: Reisen in Kaiser Wilhelmsland und Englisch-Neu-Guinea in den Jahren 1884, 1885, an Bord des Deutschen Dampfers, 'Samoa'*. Leipzig, 1888; Fischer, D. *Unter Südsee Insulanern: das Leben des Forschers Miklouho-Maclay*. Leipzig, 1956; Flierl, J. *Forty-Five Years in New Guinea*. Columbus, Ohio, 1931; Flierl, J. *Gottes Wort in den Urwäldern von Neuguinea*. Neuendettelsau, 1906; Heeres, J. E. *The Part Borne by the Dutch in the Discovery of Australia, 1606–1765*. London, 1899; Hides, J. G. *Savages in Serge*. London, 1938; Hides, J. G. *Through Wildest Papua*. London, 1935; Hides, J. G. *Papuan Wonderland*. London, 1936; Huxley, Julian, ed. *T. H. Huxley's Diary of the Voyage of H.M.S. Rattlesnake*. London, 1935; Idriess, I. L. *Gold Dust and Ashes*. Sydney, 1933; Jukes, J. B. *Narrative of the Surveying Voyage of H.M.S. Fly Commanded by Captain F. P. Blackwood R.N. in Torres Strait, New Guinea and Other Islands of the Eastern Archipelago, During the Years 1842–1846*. London, 1847; Kleintitschen, P. A. *Die Küstenbewohner der Gazellehalbinsel (Neupommern-deutsche Südsee)*. Munster, 1906; Leidecker, C. *Im Lande des Paradiesvogels*. Leipzig, 1916; Lyng, J. *Our New Possession*. Melbourne, 1919;

Macgillivray, J. *Narrative of the Voyage of H.M.S. 'Rattlesnake' Commanded by the Late Captain Owen Stanley, During the Years 1846–50, Including Discoveries and Surveys in New Guinea, the Louisiade Archipelago, etc.* London, 1852; Mackay, K. *Across Papua.* London, 1909; Mackenzie, S. S. *The Australians at Rabaul.* Sydney, 1938; Meyer, H. *Das Deutsche Kolonialreich.* Leipzig, 1910; Modera, J. *Verhaal van eene Reize naar en langs de Zuid-Westkust van Nieuw-Guinea Gedaan in 1828, etc.* Haarlem, 1830; Monckton, C. A. W. *Some Experiences of a New Guinea Resident Magistrate.* London, 1921; Moresby, J. *Discoveries in New Guinea.* London, 1876; [New South Wales Government Printer.] *Narrative of the Expedition of the Australian Squadron to the South-East Coast of New Guinea, October to December, 1884.* Sydney, 1885; Niau, J. H. *The Phantom Paradise: The Story of the Expedition of the Marquis de Rays.* Sydney, 1936; Overell, L. *A Woman's Impressions of German New Guinea.* London, 1923; Parkinson, R. *Dreissig Jahre in der Südsee.* Ed. A. Eichhorn. Stuttgart, 1926; Rhys, L. *High Lights and Flights in New Guinea.* London, 1942; Rascher, M. *Aus der Deutschen Südsee.* Munster, 1909; Stevens, H. N., ed. *Relación Sumaria de Captain Don Diego de Prado y Tovar, etc.* Hakluyt Society, ser. 2, vol. 64. London, 1930; Romilly, H. H. *Letters from the Western Pacific and Mashonaland 1878–1891.* London, 1893; Schnee, H. *Bilder aus der Südsee.* Berlin, 1904; Spry, W. J. *The Cruise of Her Majesty's Ship 'Challenger'.* London, 1877; Stone, O. C. *A Few Months in New Guinea.* London, 1880; Strachan, J. *Explorations and Adventures in New Guinea.* London, 1888; *The Voyage of Governor Phillip to Botany Bay* [The Journal of Lieutenant Shortland]. London, 1789; Wieder, F. C., ed. *Monumenta Cartographica.* Vol. 5. The Hague, 1925–33; Wilda, J. *Reise auf S.M.S. 'Möive'.* Berlin, 1903; Wytfliet, C., and others. *Histoire Universelle des Indes Orientales et Occidentales.* Douay, 1605; Zoller, H. *Deutsch-Neuguinea.* Berlin, 1891.

Index

310